A Vindication
of Politics

American Political Thought

Wilson Carey McWilliams and Lance Banning
Founding Editors

A Vindication of Politics

ON THE COMMON GOOD AND HUMAN FLOURISHING

Matthew D. Wright

 UNIVERSITY PRESS OF KANSAS

Published by the University Press of Kansas (Lawrence, Kansas 66045), which was organized by the Kansas Board of Regents and is operated and funded by Emporia State University, Fort Hays State University, Kansas State University, Pittsburg State University, the University of Kansas, and Wichita State University

Library of Congress Cataloging-in-Publication Data

Names: Wright, Matthew D., author.
Title: A vindication of politics : on the common good and human flourishing / Matthew D. Wright.
Description: Lawrence : University Press of Kansas, 2019. Series: American political thought
Identifiers: LCCN 2018046930
ISBN 978-0-7006-2755-4 (cloth)
ISBN 978-0-7006-2756-1 (ebook)
Subjects: LCSH: Common good. | Natural law. | Political participation—Social aspects. | Political science—Philosophy. | BISAC: POLITICAL SCIENCE / Constitutions. | PHILOSOPHY / Political. | POLITICAL SCIENCE / Government / General.
Classification: LCC JC330.15 .W75 2019 | DDC 320.01—dc23
LC record available at https://lccn.loc.gov/2018046930.

British Library Cataloguing-in-Publication Data is available.

Printed in the United States of America

10 9 8 7 6 5 4 3 2 1

The paper used in this publication is recycled and contains 50 percent postconsumer waste. It is acid free and meets the minimum requirements of the American National Standard for Permanence of Paper for Printed Library Materials z39.48-1992.

For Ruthie

". . . but you are the music
While the music lasts."

CONTENTS

ACKNOWLEDGMENTS

I am delighted to acknowledge the many people and institutions upon whom I have relied during the course of writing this book. The University of Texas at Austin was an ideal place to pursue graduate studies, and I am thankful for the many ways the Department of Government supported my work there. Additionally, my research has been generously supported over the years by a number of organizations: the Earhart Foundation, the Intercollegiate Studies Institute, and the Charles Koch Foundation. I am truly grateful for the investment these institutions were willing to make in a young scholar's career.

In the earliest stages of this project, I had the privilege of studying for a year with Robert P. George in the Politics Department at Princeton University. Like so many, I find Professor George's work and scholarly example simply indispensable. I am deeply appreciative of the guidance and friendship he has extended to me over the years.

I owe a great debt to my dissertation committee members at the University of Texas—J. Budziszewski, Rob Koons, Thomas Pangle, Lorraine Pangle, Gary Jacobsohn, and Devin Stauffer—all of whom were persistently helpful. Rob Koons and Tom Pangle deserve special thanks for their extensive and insightful comments on my dissertation (of which this book is a significant revision and expansion). Above all, I am indebted to J. Budziszewski, who possesses a wise and generous heart along with a penetrating and precise intellect. I have benefited incalculably from his mentorship—academic, intellectual, and spiritual—and am profoundly grateful to count him still as a trusted adviser and friend. Beside the work of all these scholars, I am aware of the deficiencies of my own and, of course, am solely responsible for them.

The University of Texas also introduced me to a group of fellow travelers whose enthusiasm and intellectual friendship continue to impact me greatly: Kevin Stuart, Matt O'Brien, Kody Cooper, Paul DeHart, Justin Dyer, and Bill McCormick chief among them. I would have been very lucky to come out of graduate school with one such friend. My professional home, the Torrey Honors Institute at Biola University, is also a community of rich intellectual and spiritual vitality. In so many ways, it has been an ideal place to bring this work to completion. I am daily thankful to be surrounded by colleagues and students seriously committed to the increasingly rare joys of liberal education. Outside of Torrey, I am especially indebted to my Biola colleagues Scott Waller and Darren Guerra, on whose acumen and good humor I continually rely.

My debts to family are even more numerous and profound. My wife, Ruthie, and I are faithfully graced by the friendship, wisdom, and generosity of our extended families. Their love and encouragement sustain us. Whatever there is of value in Chapter 2 was first learned experientially from my parents, Bill and Sarah Wright, and in my own practice of fatherhood. Any attempt to thank my children, Jackson, Harry, and Mary Clement, for the beauty and joy with which they daily infuse my life would be, as T. S. Eliot said, "a raid on the inarticulate." So, I will simply thank them for taking a genuine and benevolent interest in the progress of my writing—and for sharing the fun of the finish line. Finally, there is no way to thank Ruthie adequately. Her labor for our common good has been unstinting and free. Her love, companionship, vision, and creativity animate our life together and profoundly inform all that I am and do. This work is dedicated to her.

INTRODUCTION

James Madison famously described a political faction as "a number of citizens . . . who are united and actuated by some common impulse of passion, or of interest, adverse to the rights of other citizens, or to the permanent and aggregate interests of the community."[1] Since citizens could not be relied upon to "co-operate for their common good,"[2] he argued, the scope of passion and interest should be extended in order to diffuse factious majorities by bringing them into conflict with a wider array of competing interests. This raises the question, did Madison reject the notion of a common good altogether in favor of a public good defined by the fortuitous concurrence or practical compromise of aggregated individual interests? Or did he simply wish to change expectations concerning who could be relied upon to discern and promote a true common good? He does, after all, appeal to the wisdom of statesmen required to discern the "true interest of their country."[3] But is this "true interest" best understood in light of a "common good" central to the classical republican tradition, or in terms of the aggregated, overlapping interests of individuals characteristic of modern thought? This is, of course, a deep dilemma of the American constitutional identity that lies at the core of any attempt to understand and articulate the constitutional aspirations of "We the People."

This, in turn, draws attention to the fact that to a large degree the common constitutional identity of the American people has been defined precisely by protecting individual freedoms—all those "implicit in the concept of ordered liberty," as Justice Benjamin Cardozo famously put it.[4] Still, defining and protecting such rights cannot entirely operate on the notion of simply extending and coordinating individual rights, and constitutional jurisprudence has endeavored to understand and articulate the state's interests vis-à-vis individual rights claims. This requires some notion of what the public good or public interest is.[5] The Court has tended to replace substantive analysis of such questions with juridical tests and levels of review that serve the repetitive applications of stare decisis. Notwithstanding, defining what a "compelling state interest" is requires some knowledge of what interests the state serves, or what the common interest is in relation to which individual rights claims may be considered. Do public health and safety exhaust the possibilities of a compelling public good? How might we conceive of a public or common interest relative to those of individuals? To what degree does our concern with the public interest, if it is to be adequately descriptive and normatively compelling, have to give an account of truly common goods, that is, purposes or aims held in common within a community and at least partially realized in the community itself? Thus, answering fundamental questions of American constitutional identity, principles, and aspirations inescapably involves us in deep theoretical questions about the nature of the common good and human sociability.

Generally speaking, these concerns with understanding the communal nature of human personality, meaning, and practice have motivated communitarian criticisms of John Rawls's contemporary reworking of liberal political theory.[6] Moreover, the pathologies of contemporary liberalism brought to light in this debate have precipitated a diverse exploration of the concept and substance of citizenship (e.g., civic republicanism, civil society theory, liberal virtue theory).[7] A theme of these efforts, seemingly in reaction to liberalism's substantial instrumentalization of political community to an autonomous individual, has been a marked (sometimes aggressive) subordination of the institutions of civil society to the state's interest in promoting democratic virtues and institutions.[8] Yet even while advancing the primacy of state interests these efforts are informed by a pluralistic understanding of basic social institutions. Institutions like the family have an important, if ambiguous, role to play.[9] Thus the current need, as liberal theorists such as William Galston have argued, is for an articulation of the unique goods intrinsic to those associations that engender conflicts of allegiance in the course of political debate.[10] Only when this kind of investigation is undertaken can we have the resources to assess, relate, and order the variegated goods that come within the purview of political authority.[11]

Thus, it is with a view to furthering these general tasks of American constitutionalism and political theory that this work has been undertaken. Moreover, the natural law tradition that broadly informs this investigation has always been much concerned to account for the plural nature of basic human associations.[12] Without cultivating an understanding of the human good and those basic associations that humans naturally form, we cannot hope to have a real grasp of the inherent purposes of political society or the just authority and limitations of government. The central thrust of my argument addresses recent revisionist accounts within natural law theory concerning the character of the political common good. However, I seek to construct a compelling account of the content, value, and uniqueness of the political good by building from the ground up, as it were. This involves an extended treatment of key social goods intrinsic to the family, as well as an account of the formal relationships between subpolitical common goods and the overarching political common good. Let me begin by establishing my basic question and limning its theoretical contours. Then I will give further explanation why, within the context of contemporary natural law theory, this is a timely and important question. Finally, I will give a brief explanation of how I go about answering it.

Establishing the Basic Question

The constellation of questions and difficulties this investigation will seek to address is dictated by one basic concern that may be stated as follows: Is a society's political common good a constituent of full human flourishing— not merely a means to this end? It will be helpful to give at least a brief explanation of what is meant by the question's several terms.

First, then, *full human flourishing* refers to that notion of "happiness" that is the first principle and justifying end of Aristotelian, and subsequently Thomistic, ethics. In this tradition, *eudemonia* (or *beatitudo* for Aquinas) is realized through the virtuous, or excellent, exercise of human capacities, directing them toward those goods to which they are inherently (i.e., naturally) inclined. In addition, the notion of *full* human flourishing indicates recognition of several things. In the first place, human flourishing should primarily be conceived of in terms of those virtues that perfect what is highest or best in human nature.[13] On the other hand, "full" flourishing also denotes the existence of many human capacities, rational, appetitive, and otherwise. Happiness, therefore, cannot be conceived of as the perfection of a single faculty—even the highest—to the neglect of all the others. Rather, flourishing is realized in the balanced pursuit of a range of human goods, rationally ordering and prioritizing according to those goods that most fully instantiate what is best in human nature. Finally, the idea of "full" flourishing necessitates a caveat. For both Aristotle and Aquinas, the human flourishing to which political life may perhaps essentially relate can only be full or complete in a relative sense. For Aristotle, the significance of political life must always be qualified by the possibility of a fully philosophical life. Political interaction may well constitute the highest end of the active life, but the contemplative life by comparison presents itself as the most "divine" of human pursuits.[14] The philosopher participates in what is truly best and highest in human existence, and the single-minded devotion necessary to such pursuits precludes political involvement. Likewise, for Aquinas, political life necessarily diminishes in significance when viewed in relation to the spiritual life, most fully realized in the vision of God. The "full human flourishing" achieved in virtuous action at best provides man a *beatitudo imperfecta*—an imperfect happiness that will only be fulfilled in the perfection of heaven.[15] This is not to derogate the importance of cultivating excellence in moral and political virtue for either theorist, but rather to keep in mind that these pursuits are not the highest human perfections. The central question, then, is whether a society's political common good is a constituent part of the cluster of goods and virtues the possession of which constitutes true human happiness.

Second, what is meant by asking whether the political common good is a *constituent* of human flourishing and not merely a means to this end? I mean this: I want to know whether the political common good in part defines the essence of what it means to be fully human. This goes beyond asking whether the political common good is *necessary* to human goodness, for something can be conditionally necessary to the possession of a good without being part of the essence of what is sought. One thinks, for example, of the way that oxygen sustains human life. Respiration is a function necessary to life, but it is simply a means to being alive. We do not inhale and exhale for the sake of breathing; this process does not serve as its own end. It tells us nothing about what is fundamentally good about human existence or what further aims in human action invest life with the greatest significance. "Breathing" does not show up on anyone's list of those activities that comprise a well-lived life. Similarly, Aristotle points to those external goods that serve as conditional means to happiness, such as friendships of utility, wealth, political power, and so on, but are not themselves the ultimate goods we seek. Rather, these things are sought for their usefulness. Whereas without them one is unable to attain supreme happiness, one is not yet happy merely by possessing them.[16] So, the question is not whether the political common good is conditionally requisite to a well-lived life but whether it actually partially comprises what it means for humans to live well. That is, is it—at least in part—the end that humans seek when they seek to live well? And is it sought for its own sake, not solely as a means of getting at something else that is more desirable? In order to get at what this might mean, a further complication must be introduced.

The contemplative life has already been indicated in which conceiving of the political common good as constitutive of human flourishing must be qualified. There is another way in which any human association that we might deem essential to our understanding of what it means to be human must be classified as, in a sense, an intermediate end—not rightly the final goal of human activity. For both Aristotle and Aquinas, any relationship or association counted as an essential component of human flourishing must ultimately refer to the good of individual humans, for human goodness is precisely that—human—and as such it fundamentally obtains at the level of the human soul, that is, the individual level. Any personification of partnership, corporation, or state is necessarily analogous to the real human person, and to the degree that the welfare of such entities is developed apart from the well-being of the human individuals that comprise them, the bedrock of Thomistic-Aristotelian ethics has been abandoned. Therefore, the possibility that the political common good exists as a constituent part of human flourishing does not leave open the possibility that the family, the state, or any other human organization exists as its own self-referential final end. The existence, maintenance, and perpetuation of the state, for example, are never justified without reference to the ultimate welfare of human persons who comprise it.[17] Notwithstanding their own importance as ordered wholes of which the individual functions in crucial ways as a part, associational entities never attain this status of *human* wholeness.

This qualification, however, must be clarified further. I specified earlier that to say that an associational good such as the political common good is partly constitutive of human flourishing means that it *defines*, in part, what it is that we mean by this ideal. So even as the good of any human association cannot be justly abstracted from the good of its individual members, the individual human goodness that an association ultimately serves is itself informed, enhanced, and at times limited by the unique requirements and ends of the association qua association. Consider, for example, the case of family life, assuming *arguendo* that the family is a constituent element of human flourishing. The basic point being made here about human good entails that a family could never rightly operate as a self-referential, independently justifying entity, "the family," to which the goods of its individual members are instrumentalized, that is, treated merely as a means to the end of the family's prosperous existence. (This is certainly a fundamental commitment of all contemporary western ethics and political theory, but it follows necessarily, if at times more obscurely, from classical and medieval theory. Quoting Aquinas again, "The person is that which is most perfect in all of nature.")[18] The further point being made, however, is that if the good of the family is really of essence to the human good, *its* existence and success is itself partly what we must mean by an appeal to "human flourishing." Therefore, the individual family member's complete good depends upon the individual welfare of its other members *and* upon the complex of relationships, mutually deferential interactions, spiritual and material conditions, and so on that comprise healthy family life.

Another way to say this is that the *subject* of human good is always the individual. Therefore, goods instantiated in whatever context must always ultimately inure to the benefit of individual persons. On the other hand, human goods are very frequently realized in *objects* beyond the individual, and pursuit of these goods necessarily involves an understanding of the context in which the individual interacts, and that informs the makeup of the very good the individual seeks. Further specifying what the relationship is between the individual as subject and basic human associations as constitutively informative of the human person's good is a theme that runs throughout this work (particularly in Chapters 2 and 3).

Finally, we turn to what is meant by a society's *political common good*. The idea of the common good is a notoriously ambiguous one. One may, for example, differentiate goods that are shared in common from goods that are distributed commonly from goods that may be commonly predicated. These various ways of speaking of commonness will be explored in greater detail in Chapter 3. Here it should be noted that the primary intent (and challenge) in specifying the *political* common good is to distinguish goods pursued and realized via political activities, processes, and institutions from those goods characteristic of other forms of human sociability. Friends, families, and civic groups all enjoy common goods, that is, the desired results of their shared activity, and it is relatively easy to make differentiations among common goods based upon the kinds of groups that pursue them. On the other hand, it is not always clear that the common goods actually instantiated in these various groups differ substantially from one another, particularly with respect to the human capacities they develop. For instance, it is possible that civic friendship is little more than the dilution and attenuation of a good more meaningfully pursued between individual friends. Aquinas argued that a king should promote a kind of civic friendship (understanding political "peace" in the fullest sense) in which the life of virtue is shared among the multitude.[19] But as Aristotle argued (and Aquinas would not object to), the highest form of friendship, a shared pursuit of the virtuous life, is possible to enjoy with only a few people throughout one's lifetime.[20] Wouldn't it necessarily be the case, then, that civic friendship is not an expansion or enrichment of the central case but an ersatz expedient, a weak "friendship" several times removed from the real thing? Or again, it might be argued that the kind of concerted redress of common crises or ongoing social problems that governments regularly attempt to organize is often (and frequently with greater effect) addressed by private groups, independently and voluntarily organized to achieve the same ends by nonpolitical means. Moreover, in cases where political, governmental means are clearly more effective in addressing particular community needs, such as national defense or disaster relief, isn't it equally clear that the good sought is purely instrumental, remedial, and not anything that would be considered of essence to human sociability?

These two examples illustrate a critical dilemma encountered in exploring the relationship of the political to human flourishing. Might it not be the case that humankind is more aptly described as a *social* animal than a *political* animal? As the case of friendship indicates, to the degree that the political common good is characterized by civic friendship or a partnership in some form of the virtuous life among citizens, is not political life, then, weakly derivative of humankind's social nature? This raises the possibility that political life itself realizes nothing unique or perfective in human nature but simply provides the conditional means whereby human goods—both individual and social—are pursued. The operation of civil society, moreover, extends the goods of human sociability to great numbers of people, seemingly apart from political or governmental processes. This raises further suspicions that whereas government might be necessary to handle a few (albeit vital) organizational and security matters, political life simply enables the real business of human social flourishing that *already* takes place in the private sector.

At the same time, it is not at all clear that at the level of civil society just described a helpful differentiation can be made between the "social" and the "political." Such an isolation of the social life seems to assume that it is not integrally related to a wider system of customs, laws, political habits, and orientation to the good of the whole community that is most aptly described as political. If this is the case, the appropriate distinction would not seem to be between civil society and political society, but between political society and the state. On the other hand, when the whole spectrum of human sociability is considered, it seems clear that a helpful distinction can be drawn between the social and political. Although Aristotle describes man simply as a "political animal" (*zoon politikon*), the polis arises as a qualitatively distinct kind of association from other social forms.[21] Aquinas appears consciously to emphasize this distinction, making use of distinctions between the social and political in Latin vocabulary and thereby (arguably) assigning greater primacy to the family vis-à-vis the political community.[22] So notwithstanding the substantial difficulties attending an effort to fully disentangle the social from the political, it seems to be a necessary endeavor if the value of political society relative to other human goods and associations is to be accessed and assessed.

So, to recapitulate, "human flourishing" draws on the Aristotelian-Thomistic ethical tradition that emphasizes the rational cultivation of human capacities in an effort to fully enjoy the goods to which they are naturally inclined. "Constituent" denotes being part of the essence of something; a constituent part of the good life partially *defines* what is meant by living well. And, finally, the political common good contemplates the full range of benefits, activities, customs, processes, and institutions that make up the sum total of political life—as distinguished from other forms of nonpolitical association.

Why Answer This Question?

To some degree, the need to address the intrinsic goodness of political association within the context of the natural law tradition is, at best, counterintuitive. Notwithstanding the aforementioned observation that the paradigm of "human flourishing" necessarily gives fundamental primacy to the individual, it is in many respects very difficult to harmonize this qualification with arguments from both Aristotle and Aquinas that strongly privilege the political community. Indeed, if constitutive goods define what we mean by that which they constitute, it often seems that for both Aristotle and Aquinas the political community dominates human existence. The flourishing of the individual, while important, seems to find its content and meaning within the context of the greater political whole. Aristotle, for example, argues that "the city is prior in the order of nature to the family and the individual," as the whole is necessarily prior to the part. In an analogy that calls Aquinas's gloss mentioned above into question, Aristotle likens the part-whole relationship he has in mind to that of body and limb. A man cut off from the city is like a hand severed from the body.[23] Interestingly enough, Aquinas does not demur from this analogy in his commentary; on the contrary, he says that by this Aristotle *proves* the priority of a whole, since the form of parts does not remain the same when the matter of the whole has been destroyed.[24] The force of this analogy for Aquinas, too, seems to indicate that a man cut off from the city ceases to retain part of what is essential to the human form. As Aristotle says, such a man is not human at all, but must be either a beast or a god.[25] Moreover, Aquinas retains this part-whole language throughout the *Summa Theologica*. In arguing that all law must of its very nature be directed toward the common good, Aquinas reasons, "Since every part is ordained to the whole, as imperfect to perfect; and since one man is part of the perfect community, the law must needs regard properly the relationship to universal happiness." He goes on in the body of this article to cite Aristotle's identification of the state as a "perfect community."[26] At other times, Aquinas speaks of the individual as *belonging* to the political community.[27]

The political community and its common good for both theorists, then, follows very naturally as a controlling or more "divine" end, and politics is the controlling science. Aristotle opens both his *Nicomachean Ethics* and *Politics* with strong affirmations of the primacy of political life. The highest good belongs "to the most sovereign and most comprehensive master science, and politics clearly fits this description."[28] This same kind of encomium is repeated in his striking introduction to the *Politics*; the city's good is "most sovereign" and all-inclusive.[29] Here again, Aquinas gives repeated indications that he follows Aristotle on this point. His commentaries give evidence that he is persuaded by Aristotle's logic on this point, and this is further confirmed by his affirmation in his own short treatise on government, *De Regno*, that "the good of the multitude is greater and more divine than the good of one man."[30] Moreover, his classic definition of law—an "ordinance of reason for the common good, made by him who has care for the community, and promulgated"—establishes an essential link between legal and political authority and the common good.[31] Thus, a good deal of evidence seems to indicate that for Aquinas as well as Aristotle, the political common good exists as a comprehensive human end that, well beyond being simply a component of human flourishing, includes, orients, and most fully realizes all other modes of human goodness.

However, enough has already been said to indicate that this is far from an uncomplicated picture for either theorist. Although it is clear that in important ways the individual exists as a part of the political whole, "man is not ordained to the body politic, according to all that he is and has."[32] Indeed—to leap ahead to the twentieth century—some of the most important developments of contemporary neo-Thomism have centered on a reevaluation of what has been taken to be the primacy of the common good in Thomistic political theory. Largely provoked by the "personalism" of Jacques Maritain, a sharp dispute arose in the 1940s between two prominent Thomists, Charles De Koninck and I. Th. Eschmann, concerning the Thomistic pedigree of emphasis on personal goods vis-à-vis the common good in the new personalism.[33] Maritain's subsequent contribution to this debate, *The Person and the Common Good*, apparently intended to clarify his position, is often broadly suggestive, while still lacking clarity in specifics.[34] For the purposes of this project, however, Maritain does indicate clearly enough his view on the instrumentality of political life. The key distinction for Maritain is that between political society and the state. The good of political society, he argues, while not absolute, is an "honest good," that is, a good sought for its own sake. As such, it is an "infravalent end," characterized by "reciprocal subordination" with the goods of the person.[35] While the state is the "topmost authority" of political society, its function is organizational and essentially instrumental: "The human person as an individual is for the body politic and the body politic is for the human person as person. But man is by no means for the State. The State is for man."[36]

One of the most prominent commentators on Aquinas of the past thirty years, John Finnis, has argued forcefully for what is, in effect, an extension of Maritain's instrumentalization of the state to include *the whole of the political common good*, and he has advanced this as the authentic position of Aquinas. Finnis argues that "the political community—properly understood as one of the forms of collaboration needed for the sake of goods identified in the first principles of natural law—is a community co-operating in the service of a common good which is instrumental, not itself basic."[37] I will call this his "instrumentality thesis." In consequence, the political common good, for Finnis, is primarily *conditional*: "A set of conditions which enables the members of a community to attain for themselves reasonable objectives, or to realize reasonably for themselves the value(s), for the sake of which they have reason to collaborate with each other . . . in a community."[38] Very significantly, Finnis has redrawn the demarcation between instrumentality and essential human goodness put forward by Maritain. For Finnis, it is the whole of political community, not simply the state, that serves an instrumental function to more fundamental (or "basic," in the argot of the "new natural law"[39]) forms of human goodness. It is important to recognize, however, that Finnis is not relegating human sociability as such to an instrumental status.[40] Rather, the *political* common good is simply one of several, for example, the common good that exists in virtuous friendship and the common good of families. Thus, Finnis argues that for Aquinas man is clearly a *social* animal, meaning that his flourishing is inextricably intertwined with the goods of certain basic human associations, but he is not essentially a *political* animal. Although we necessarily rely on the broader political community in order to secure and facilitate individual and social goods, it does not itself realize any further human good not already experienced in smaller human communities.[41] Here Finnis relies on a distinction between two senses of "natural" indicated at the outset of this paper: (1) organically or conditionally *necessary* to the sustenance of life, and (2) intrinsically constitutive of full human flourishing operating according to a rational principle.[42]

Finnis has staked out a new position in Thomistic political theory. Paul Sigmund has called Finnis's magnum opus on Aquinas—*Aquinas: Moral, Political, and Legal Theory*—the most comprehensive and significant explication in print of Aquinas's work in these areas.[43] Since the publication of his seminal book *Natural Law and Natural Rights*,[44] Finnis's work has provoked copious and fruitful comment, particularly with respect to his rearticulation and defense of the "basic human goods" foundation of Thomistic natural law.[45] Surprisingly, however, Finnis's instrumentality thesis—one of his most provocative given that he takes it to describe a political position "not readily distinguishable from the 'grand simple principle' . . . of John Stuart Mill's *On Liberty*"—has received much less consideration.[46] Although, as Robert P. George has pointed out, Finnis's Aquinas is by no means a liberal theorist by contemporary standards since almost all traditional morals legislation is sustainable under Finnis's version,[47] nonetheless, in Finnis's hands Aquinas takes a notably modern turn. Moreover, Finnis's position is becoming increasingly influential (in substance, if not always directly acknowledged) in contemporary natural law theory and Thomistic interpretation.[48]

Consider, for example, the prominent study by Mary Keys, *Aquinas, Aristotle, and the Promise of the Common Good*. In arguing that Aquinas reworked Aristotelian politics primarily by emphasizing a universal common good grounded in natural law, Keys follows Finnis in replacing a *political* human nature with a decidedly *social* nature. By Keys's lights, Aquinas viewed the political good as fundamentally contingent, relative, and thus very problematically connected to unqualified human flourishing. Of course, Aristotle himself wrestles with the contingency of political regimes and their ability to fully realize the human good simpliciter for all citizens. Aquinas, Keys argues, is unsatisfied with the Aristotelian solution (an embrace of regime relativity, she argues) and consequently "*redefines* the political or civic character of human nature more fundamentally in the function of human sociality and its ethical requirements."[49] Natural law privileges the universal social nature of man over the *intrinsic particularity of the political*. Although Keys recognizes that for Aquinas law implies a community, a particular group, she contends that the clear emphasis is on the larger common good of the universal human community. Cosmopolis replaces polis.[50] Now, certainly Aquinas subjects the pronouncements of human law to the transcendent and universal tenets of the natural law.[51] But Keys's position seems to require the further premise that insofar as political community is inherently particular and relative it has no intrinsic telos or natural orientation to human social goods. Since political community is not itself guided by intrinsic purposes constitutive of human sociability, it seems inescapable that regardless of the political community's strict necessity, it is substantively instrumental to the human social good. This is the nub of the argument for both Finnis and Keys, although Finnis places greater emphasis on the subpolitical common goods shared among friends, families, and religious communities and Keys emphasizes the transpolitical character of a universal common good defined by natural law.

Together Finnis and Keys illustrate what Mark Murphy argues is a persistent—and as yet unsatisfactorily resolved—problem for natural law theories of the political common good. On the one hand, Murphy argues, the subpolitical challenge contends that friends and family (for example) simply count for more than does the political community.[52] One might argue (as does Murphy) from the specialness of these relationships, which seem to inherently provide strong rational grounds for preference and protection, or (as does Finnis) from the ability of these relationships to objectively realize goods of greater significance to human flourishing. On the other hand, the "superpolitical" point of view challenges the rationality of the political community's limited common good. From this perspective, Murphy explains, "The good of persons [is] fundamentally and non-derivatively the object of practical concern, [and] any principled difference between the good of members of one's political community and the goods of non-members [must be rejected]."[53] Finnis has argued along these lines, "If it now appears that the good of individuals can be only fully secured and realized in the context of international community, we must conclude that the claim of the national state to be a complete community is unwarranted."[54] Mary Keys's privileging of the superpolitical point of view in her interpretation of Aquinas addresses the issue from a more abstract ethical position, but the outcome is the same: a significant derogation of the role political life inherently plays in realizing the human good.

Thus, politics is assailed from above and below—by the greater intensity of sharing in human goods provided in the latter case and the greater extension of human concerns required in the former. This dilemma undoubtedly characterizes all political philosophy, but, as Murphy points out, it is particularly problematic for natural law/natural right theories inasmuch as they *ground* the authority of law in its ability to promote the common good of the polity.[55] To the degree, then, that rational reflection undermines decisive commitment to the political common good, it would seem that authority of law itself is called into serious question.

It is not necessary here to give a full review of Murphy's treatment of this dilemma and all his reasons for concluding that the theoretical difficulties persist for natural law theories of the common good. The discussion of Finnis's and Keys's respective work should suffice for that. One point that Murphy makes should be highlighted, however, because it demonstrates the limitations of one particular kind of argument for the primacy and intrinsic human goodness of the political common good. An argument from the inclusivity of the political common good bases its superiority on its comprehension of the good of the many rather than the good of a few or of one.[56] Both Aristotle and Aquinas give indications that the greatness of political society is based on the greatness of its extension. For example, Aquinas states that "the good of the multitude is greater and more divine than the good of one man."[57] The problem with this argument is that it suggests very little. A common good based on inclusivity only entails an aggregation of individual goods. That the political community protects *more* goods seems to require that the common good be pursued only as a modus vivendi. But, this, in turn, would seem to derogate the qualitative status of the common good and thus its importance relative to other human goods. This is precisely the kind of argument that Finnis makes about the qualitative status of the political common good. The political common good is "complete" insofar as it extends to everyone in the community and provides the matrix they and their various subpolitical associations need to flourish.[58] But at most, as Finnis consistently argues, this entails a conditional, instrumental understanding of political society. This is not to say that the inclusivity argument achieves nothing, and I do not mean to imply that either Aristotle or Aquinas employs it exclusively. It does, however, suggest that arguments of this nature must be employed very carefully, without expecting them to do more work than they are able. More important, it also indicates what kind of argument is needed in order to demonstrate the intrinsic goodness of the political common good—or any association for that matter. What is needed is a qualitative understanding of the association as such. What are its aims? What kind of activity is required to achieve them? Are these ends, once achieved, and the activity whereby they are achieved, perfective of human capacities? If so, how? And finally, which capacities do they perfect, and what is the value of these virtues relative to other human virtues? With these questions in view, the argument of this work proceeds as follows.

Given the prominence of his argument, and moreover, its substantive merit as a cogent normative and interpretive presentation of the political common good, I begin by giving sustained critical attention to Finnis's argument against the intrinsic goodness of the political common good. Whereas previous critiques of Finnis have tended to focus on his inability to account for various passages in the Thomistic corpus that seem to strongly privilege the political, none of them have addressed the structural features of Finnis's account that he takes to anticipate and dispose of such objections. I have attempted to remedy this situation by taking Finnis on his own terms, giving careful consideration to his methodology and dual structure of the common good. I do find Finnis helpful on many points and, in fact, rely upon his dual structure of the common good in articulating formal characteristics of the political common good in Chapter 3. Nevertheless, I argue that Finnis's instrumentality thesis emerges as an unjustified conclusion of his argument, and that this mistake follows from a crucial elision Finnis relies upon between saying that the law does not aim at cultivating all-round virtue and saying that it does not aim at cultivating virtue simpliciter. From here, I turn to develop a positive account of the intrinsic goodness of political association.

My overall method is basically Aristotelian in its attempt to understand the thing that is political community by taking it apart, as it were, and developing an understanding of the whole that is informed by its constituent parts.[59] This methodology is guided by a twofold conviction: first, that the nature of the parts will tell us something important about the whole (this is particularly true of *ordered* wholes[60]), and second, that the whole is more clearly seen when contrasted with its constitutive parts. I do not achieve this by a substantive analysis of each of the political community's parts—moving from reproductive to household relationships, then on to civil society (businesses, civic and religious groups, etc.), and ultimately political associations. Rather, my argument is both formal and substantive. It gives equal attention to the relationships among the various parts and the substantive goods of those parts. This dual character of the argument has necessitated that I focus on pivotal ideas and associations. Perhaps the clearest example of this is that my account of subpolitical associations, while treating friendship in various ways throughout, only directly addresses the social "building block" of the family. This is a justified focus insofar as Aristotle and Aquinas each in his own way took it to be *the* building block. This is a position that I take my argument not simply to assume but to strengthen. And, in fact, as the discussion moves from the family to the city, it will become clear how different ways of characterizing the familial good profoundly affect how one understands the political. Still, there is much more that could be said about personal friendships and the important realm of civil society that lies (on something of a continuum) between the family and the political community. However, I think the formal arguments developed here are well worth the time and effort. For essential to the logic of critical reconstruction is not only understanding discrete parts as they are in themselves, but also how exactly they fit together and relate to the whole. My aim has been to advance this dimension of the Aristotelian methodology as well.[61]

The first piece of my positive account, Chapter 2, explores the substantive goods of familial association—giving particular attention to the classical concern with the family's particularity, on the one hand, and the modern concern with its inequality, on the other. Drawing upon the parent-child relationship as a primary example of Aristotle's "other self," the argument highlights the essential connection between parental love and a moral framework conducive to the cultivation of a truly virtuous character, namely, one that sees and acts according to the inherent desirability of virtue. Moreover, the inherently *educative* character of parental love imbues the family with an inherent rationality, not merely an affective or emotional importance. A crucial aspect of this chapter is that it puts a fine point on a fundamental problem encountered when articulating the substantive value of the common good. The problem is this: intimate relational goods of family and friendship exert not only an affective primacy in individual preferences but also instantiate very rich experiences of virtue and flourishing. Thus, the claim of political community to be anything more than an instrument to these realms of private life is subject to serious question. Although I rely in important respects on the thinking of both Aristotle and Aquinas about the family, a crucial fissure emerges between them that grows as the argument progresses from the familial to the political.

Chapter 3 serves as a kind of bridge between Chapter 2 and the arguments I develop in Chapters 4 and 5. Here, I consider the formal characteristics of all common goods generally (including the common goods of friendship and families) and then specifically the formal characteristics of the political common good. I argue that common goods are both aggregative of individual goods, on the one hand, and, on the other, distinct loci of social practice—such that promoting the good of an association per se may factor intrinsically and decisively in the determinations of practical reason. Two key theses emerge in this argument: first, an *inclusivist thesis*, that is, whatever the common good of political society is, it must *include* the distinct and irreplaceable goods of associations like friendship and family. Second, the *distinctiveness thesis*, that is, an adequate account of the political common good must in part include the unique and distinctive good of the political community per se.

This brings the argument to the substantive account of the political common good developed in Chapters 4 and 5. In Chapter 4 I focus on the nature and possibility of civic friendship, a bond that both presupposes and transcends citizenship. For Aristotle, a unique form of friendship is possible in a shared life of virtue centered on the political association itself. Although Aquinas appropriates Aristotle's understanding of civic friendship in important respects, I argue that the rift between them widens in Aquinas's "affirmation of ordinary life" and the pluralistic account of human sociability that follows from it. Nevertheless, there are essential human virtues— justice, love, generosity—that are uniquely, if not exclusively, realized in the extended scope of political community. Even when relatively small associations gathered around a common civic life are abandoned, I contend that civic friendship still has an important political role to play insofar as it draws upon the repository of goodwill and common constitutional commitments embodied in the community itself. This, in turn, highlights the essential significance of the political community's *distinctive good* (i.e., the good of the community per se) to an overall account of the common good and, moreover, preserves the intrinsic value of the political common good against the superpolitical challenge of a universal human community.

These claims are expanded and strengthened in the final piece of my argument (Chapter 5), in which I explore the substantive social goods that spring from the life of a healthy political culture. This move requires explanation for a couple of reasons. First, instead of Aristotle and Aquinas and their modern-day exponents, I shift focus to the work of Edmund Burke, a thinker often thought to be at odds with the natural law tradition. Why the switch? Second, given that civic friendship seems to represent the apex of political flourishing—focused on the quintessential social virtue of justice— why say more? Why wade into the murky conceptual waters of political culture if civic friendship effectively answers the question of unique and intrinsic goodness?

The short answer to the second question is that my argument for civic friendship culminates in what is effectively a direct appeal to political culture. I describe a "repository of goodwill" that contextualizes the actions of political friends, but this is nothing if not the history, customs, ideals, and so forth that make up a political culture. The idea begs for further elaboration. At a deeper theoretical level, I also think that the argument from civic friendship does not quite get the job done. Not because it fails to pick out an intrinsic good, but because it stops short of describing dimensions of political life that are absolutely essential to understanding its goods. Civic friendship focuses our attention on the present association of active citizens; political culture requires a historical and generational analysis. It understands community as something extended through time, expressed in long-standing customs, preserved in institutions, and memorialized in shared remembrances. It draws our attention to political goods realized in the common life of a people sustained and cultivated over time. And this is simply what human community is, a generational enterprise. Therefore, any attempt to describe the political common good apart from a people's political culture will be incomplete, and significantly so.

This brings us back around to the first question. Here, the answer is simply that Edmund Burke understands the goods of political culture and the generational nature of community as few others do. Aristotle and Aquinas make gestures in this direction, but it is an underdeveloped area of their respective writings and of the natural law tradition more broadly. Therefore, Burke is necessary to finish the argument. Yet, his thought is very much in keeping with the natural law tradition. I am persuaded by the work of the many scholars over the past sixty years who find in him a deep affinity with— even reliance upon—natural law and natural rights.

Burke's work expounds what I call (drawing on his own language) a *tradition of reason* and a *tradition of the moral imagination*—both of which uniquely emerge in the institutions, laws, customs, history, and icons embodied in particular political communities. By way of illustration, I look to the example of Abraham Lincoln's powerful reliance on the Declaration of Independence in the American confrontation with slavery. Participation in a community of this sort—in a broad sense of political participation that I will unpack—represents a unique ennobling and intrinsic fulfillment of human social capacities. Although I do not take political society to be the most important domain of social flourishing, it does hold out unique and tremendously significant goods. Taking the right measure of these goods, in turn, is necessary to an adequate theoretical justification of the value of patriotism.

Finally, by way of conclusion, I turn to the very practical question: What kind of political activity does my argument entail? If politics is an intrinsic good embodied in a society's architectonic association, does my argument put us in an essentially Aristotelian position—subordinating and subsuming all other forms of association to the state? I think not. Instead, if we rightly account for the intrinsic and incommensurable goods of subpolitical associations like the family, expressed in the inclusivist thesis, we must recognize the principle of limited government as a necessary component of a just society. At the same time, fully appreciating the goods of political association realized in civic friendship and political culture does establish a compelling philosophical basis for understanding active patriotism as a key dimension of human well-being.

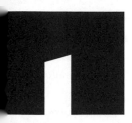

Critical Assessment of Finnis's Instrumentality Thesis

The aim of this chapter is to provide a critical "ground clearing" of perhaps the most influential account of the political common good in contemporary natural law theory. I will begin with a general statement of John Finnis's position and then will explain the contours of my own approach to his argument before beginning a detailed consideration of its merits. A central conclusion of Finnis's position is a distinction between public and private that precludes on the basis of principle governmental regulation of "secret and truly consensual adult acts of vice."[1] On a more fundamental level, he argues that Aquinas views the state's role as both limited and instrumental. It is limited in that state action is only rightly directed toward the maintenance of a "political common good" or "public good"; that is, a state of temporal tranquility conducive to the flourishing of individuals, families, and churches. And this "public good" is, in turn, instrumental in that it does not inherently instantiate a good constitutive of human flourishing.[2] The political community as such, then, is not an end sought for its own sake, but only for the sake of and to the degree that it facilitates other goods. This contrasts with a tradition of moral paternalism that viewed the government's role as that of moral instructor, responsible for inculcating virtue and eradicating vice, not only in the public life of the community but also in the private lives of citizens.[3] According to this traditional view, the state takes a direct part in shaping virtuous citizens qua individuals. This, in turn, contributes to a civic common good—thickly conceived in the Aristotelian sense of a communal life of virtue[4]—that instantiates a level of human flourishing aptly described as "complete." The polis or civitas, generally speaking, is the whole of which individuals, families, and various associations are parts.

There are, of course, numerous limitations and qualifiers necessary here to fully cash out the differences between the traditional view of the state and that for which Finnis argues. But the general dividing faults are clear enough: In Finnis's view the state's "completeness" as an association in virtue becomes a comprehensive, but fundamentally secondary, association in which other, more basic goods are facilitated. The state is complete in extension, but not as an end of the good life. Consequently, the role the state plays in bringing about the good life is likewise secondary. Governmental responsibility, and thus authority, only extends to persons and events as they appertain to the public interest in justice and peace, social aims that for Finnis are mainly conditional and coordinative.

The general aim of this chapter is to give consideration to the interpretive methodology according to which Finnis structures his argument. None of the previous analyses of Finnis's political thesis have given any attention to this basic structural component, yet it is perhaps the most important and interesting element. Finnis himself is very careful to provide a particular orientation to his investigation, though the degree to which this course holds constant is somewhat ambiguous. Nevertheless, Finnis's basic methodological claim (which I will explain shortly) is provocative and, I think, repays careful consideration. Pursuant to this general aim, I have addressed myself to two particular aspects of Finnis's argument, namely, his articulation of a principled distinction between public and private, and his specification of the aim or purpose of law. Consideration of the first will be comparatively brief but nonetheless important to my argument. I will finally turn to consider a significant aspect of Finnis's argument that does not appear to fit into the initial methodology. Throughout, my basic contention is that Finnis's explicit methodological orientation predisposes him to infer more about the nature of political community and association from the limited operation of law and government than can be legitimately derived. This mistake, in turn, underlies a basic assumption about the aim or purpose of law that ultimately requires the conclusion Finnis reaches concerning the instrumentality of the political common good.

Finnis's Interpretive Methodology

Before turning to the details of Finnis's argument, let me limn his methodology. For Aquinas, the fundamental question concerning the legitimacy of state authority is its relationship to the common good. His famous definition of law states that law is an "ordinance of reason for the common good, made by him who has care for the community, and promulgated."[5] The common good is the ordering principle of all law justly conceived, and to the degree that law strays from this end, it is defective and only called "law" in a limited sense.[6] However, Aquinas is less than clear on what exactly the nature of this common good is. As Gregory Froelich has pointed out, whereas Aquinas provides an extended treatise in the *Summa Theologica* on the nature of individual goodness, he provides no such comparable discussion of the common good.[7] Rather, we are left to piece together his view from various texts (examples primarily) in which the idea is used in many different ways. On Finnis's account, however, this difficulty seems to be the product of a methodological decision by Aquinas to stipulate that the state[8] (or civitas) is a "complete" community in a purely formal sense, that is, "a community so organized that its government and law give *all* the direction that properly can be given by human government and coercive *law* to promote and protect the common good."[9] The result of this formalism, Finnis maintains, is that the basic question about the nature of the common good becomes "substantially equivalent" to the question of the appropriate means of governmental regulation. That is, the question "Can a state's common good, being the good of a complete community, be anything less than the complete good, the fulfillment—*beatitudo imperfecta* if not *perfecta*—of its citizens?" is answered by asking, "What type of direction can properly be given by governments and law?"[10] Given the paucity of direct comment on ends (i.e., the nature of the common good of political community), any interpreter of Aquinas is forced in large part to consider his discussion of means (i.e., the appropriate scope and methods of governmental regulation), but it is a significant move to treat them as equivalent by making one the interpretive key to the other. Before saying more about this, let me delineate further several discrete aspects of Finnis's basic question and the bifurcated answer he proposes to it.

In asking whether the common good of the state can be less than the fully virtuous flourishing (*beatitudo imperfecta*) of individual citizens, Finnis places a number of importantly distinct issues on the table. First, the question concerns the state's relationship to an individual's full internal possession of a virtuous character. A law may require that a virtuous action be performed, but should it—is it even able to—demand that the external action be motivated by a truly virtuous frame of mind? Second, the question concerns the state's legitimate interest in the whole gamut of virtuous activity. Does the common good equally concern "self-regarding" virtues such as temperance and "other-regarding" virtues such as generosity and justice? Third, an inquiry into the link between the common good and complete human flourishing requires an understanding of the relationships and associations essential to that flourishing. If it is clear that the family, for example, is integral to complete human virtue, then the investigation must necessarily address not only an individual's virtuous character but also the familial relationships and context that serve as an essential object of virtuous action. As Aquinas argues, particular objects or contexts for virtue create separate species of virtuous action.[11] And since understanding various species of virtue is necessary to a full account of *beatitudo imperfecta*, the nature and requirements of basic human associations are also at issue here. Finnis's argument, therefore, turns not only on the law's concern with the internal workings of the individual soul or a distinction between personal and other-related virtue, but also on the particular character of political relationships and interactions. A pivotal question, then, is this: Does the political community constitute an essential locus of human virtue?

Understanding Finnis's treatment of this issue is complicated by the nuanced answer he offers to his initial question. In answer to the query "Can a state's common good . . . be anything less than the complete good . . . of its citizens?," Finnis argues yes and no. This reply is based upon two different ways of conceiving the political. His primary answer is yes, the *specifically political* common good for which the government is responsible is less than the complete natural good of individuals. The primarily conditional character of this "public good" has already been remarked. On the other hand, Finnis answers no, allowing that the "common good of the political community" includes the complete good—or "all-round virtue"—of all its members and constituent associations.[12] Thus, Finnis wishes to maintain a distinction between the political and the *specifically* political. He denotes the former with the terms "political community," "state," or "civitas" and conceives its good as nothing less than the "common good of the whole of human life."[13] The *specifically* political, on the other hand, describes the common good particular to the domain and activities of government. Finnis calls this the "political common good" or "public good," and his argument especially aims to demonstrate the limitedness and instrumentality of this good. But as I shall argue, Finnis's differentiation of "the common good of political community" and the "political common good" is highly problematic when it comes to clarifying and assessing the character of political life and its relationship to human flourishing.

This fundamental difficultly is closely entailed, it appears to me, by the basic methodological equivalency Finnis constructs between the end or purpose of political community and the appropriate purview of governmental regulation. Notice that by deriving the common good of the state (by which he means the whole political community) from the operation of government and law, Finnis has substantively subsumed consideration of what political community is into a description of legal regulation. Now, it is clear that Finnis wishes to avoid such an outcome by maintaining the category "common good of the political community," but as I will contend, this conceptual distinction has no real substantive content that does not reduce to an account of government and law or, in the opposite direction, dissipate into the universal good of humanity, whose good is common (temporally speaking) only by way of logical predication.

A Limited Political Common Good: Delineating Public and Private

Let me begin by briefly recapitulating the various components of Finnis's case for limited government. Finnis is fundamentally concerned with distinguishing the scope and goals of parental authority from those of government. Given that Aquinas unequivocally affirms that both authorities seek to inculcate virtue, can we assume that the law, like parents, aims to educate citizens "into complete, all-round virtue and fulfillment?"[14] Whereas this conclusion is initially plausible, Finnis argues, a number of factors preclude it. At the most basic level, all human law evinces a twofold difference from divine law. Divine law ordains men, not only to one another but also in relation to God, and thus it comes within its domain to regulate all those things whereby man is rightly related to God—including precepts related to the intellectual virtues and interior passions. Human law, on the other hand, because its purpose is only to order persons with respect to each other, is likewise limited in jurisdiction. It only properly regulates external acts pertaining to social interaction.[15] Finnis next adduces the public/private distinction to show a further restriction on the class of external acts that government properly regulates. Insofar as Aquinas indicates that the object (or subject matter) of at least some acts of virtue will only be ordainable to private goods, a further narrowing of the particular purpose of law (i.e., the common good) is entailed. The existence of private goods for which the law is not directly responsible necessitates a diminished scope to that common good for which it is. Additionally, Finnis points to the ecclesial community, as well as the personal goods of religious faith and worship, as goods that fall outside the jurisdiction of government and thus indicate a constrained political common good.[16] These factors, Finnis reasons, combine to form a conception of the public good much "thinner" than the fullest sense of peace in Aquinas's writings. In that substantial sense, peace expresses the unity of persons joined in fully virtuous activity and desire.[17] Specifically political peace, by contrast, is only that "peaceful condition needed to get the benefits [*utilitas*] of social life and avoid the burdens of contention. It is a peace which falls short of the complete justice which true virtue requires of us."[18] Just law, therefore, cannot rightly require *real* virtue of citizens (cannot say "be a just person"), but only regulates external actions; nor is it directly concerned with the "all-round virtue" of citizens, but only the interactions among people regulated by the norms of justice. In these important respects, legal authority differs from parental. For although it is true that parents do not actually require virtue itself,[19] their sensitivity to the outward manifestations of virtue allows much greater precision in successfully cultivating a virtuous soul. Moreover, the authority of parents *does* embrace virtue all round, including those "self-regarding" acts of virtue (e.g., most acts of temperance and friendship) that fall outside legal purview.[20] In contrast, Finnis argues, Aquinas's articulation of a limited public good entails that governmental regulation of conduct is, in principle, excluded from encroachment on "secret and truly consensual adult acts of vice" or "truly private conduct of adults." Instead, government is responsible for the "public realm or environment."[21]

Now, the core of Finnis's case for limited government is the distinction between public and private goods, and the great onus of this distinction rests on Aquinas's response to the question "Whether human law prescribes acts of all the virtues?"[22] He answers that whereas certain actions of *every virtue* will be rightly prescribed by law, not *every act* of every virtue will be. Aquinas reasons thus: because the end or purpose of the law is the common good, the objects of acts of virtue ("that on which the action is brought to bear"[23]) must be referable to that good. Acts of virtue whose objects are only referable to a private good are not properly enjoined by law. Aquinas is clear in saying that whereas various acts pertaining to all virtues will be ordainable to the common good, at least *some* acts of every virtue will be ordainable only to a private good. In the case of courage, Aquinas explains, courageous acts may be done for the common good, as when one goes to war, or for a private good, as when one defends the rights of a friend. There is, therefore, a class of "private" acts; that is, those acts of virtue whose objects cannot be rightly referred to the common good. So although Aquinas refers to legal justice as a "higher" or "supreme" virtue, which directs acts of virtue to the common good of a "perfect community,"[24] a state's laws must also recognize and promote as constitutive of that common good particular individuals pursuing particular goods by means of particular virtues. In contradistinction to what is "common" or "public," Aquinas calls these goods pertaining to individuals as such "private."

Although it is clear that Aquinas makes this principled distinction between public and private, its precise nature and scope is not altogether plain. Still, in various places Aquinas specifies a number of private goods, which in combination begin to clarify the kind of distinction he has in mind. Temperance, although certainly at times and places referable to the common good, is a virtue Aquinas particularly identifies with the individual's good.[25] Moving beyond the person, we just saw that Aquinas considers friendship, too, a private good. He also excludes liberality and friendship from the scope of justice, as having "little of the nature of anything due in them."[26] Additionally, Aquinas indicates that there is a distinct domestic good, to which law should relate in an indirect manner. Prohibition of acts of gluttony in the Old Law, for example, was left to parents as being "contrary to the good of the household."[27] This domestic good, while concerned in part with daily necessities of life, acquires a profound importance for Aquinas, inasmuch as marriage appears to be the highest form of friendship (*maxima amicitia*).[28] It realizes not only the pleasantness of sexual union between the two but also a fellowship in the whole of domestic activity and interaction.[29] Thus, Aquinas places what he takes to be the highest form of friendship at the core of the domestic good. Issuing from this foundational union, in turn, children extend the intimacy of friendship within the home. They are at once a chief common good of the marital friendship as well as distinct persons with whom spouses will grow in friendship as they fulfill their duties of care and education.[30] Finally, the ecclesial community also constitutes a particular or "private" association within the political community, given its direct ordination to an eternal end transcending the competence of human government and law.[31]

Finnis appears to be well justified, then, in insisting on an important principled distinction between public and private goods for Aquinas. The basic character of this distinction is that it fundamentally inheres in acts; it is a differentiation between: (1) acts whose objects may be referred to the common good, whether immediately or mediately, and (2) acts whose proper objects are so directly connected with private goods as to be unreferable to the common good.[32] Additionally, it seems evident that Aquinas attaches the distinction to acts inherent in particular relationships—friendship, most basically, and by extension the complex of relationships within the family. This is not to say that the household becomes entirely insulated from the law's influence or is spatially defined as "private," but Aquinas does give strong reason to identify it as a particularly private good, among whose relationships the law intervenes indirectly and secondarily.

Finnis's argument on this point holds sway against critics such as Michael Pakaluk who are inclined to a much more Aristotelian reading of Aquinas's political theory. By Pakaluk's lights, it appears that Aquinas is fully Aristotelian, save for the addition of charity, which, if anything, serves to expand the scope of law, drawing individuals and families into a "complete harmony of persons" instantiated in the political community.[33] Whereas Pakaluk argues that there are a number of Aristotelian-Thomistic safeguards against totalitarianism (e.g., that there are real differences in kind of authority, which entails that higher authorities only "correct and direct" lower ones[34]), it is far from clear that any of these rise to the level of the Thomistic affirmation that there are private goods that are not rightly ordered to the common good. In this respect, one thinks of Aristotle's recommendation that in the best regime the state's "child-supervisors" should regulate the "explanations and stories" that young children are told in the home.[35] Although Aristotle apparently has some appreciation for the natural affection of the parent-child relationship, and thus for its effectiveness in putting children on the path to virtue, it is clear that he does not identify the family as a locus of private goods in the way that Aquinas does, and consequently subject only to indirect guidance and assistance by law.[36] Finnis's insistence on the public/private distinction, then, is importantly helpful in clarifying Aquinas's view of appropriate state regulation.

At the same time, it is evident that Finnis misidentifies the nature of Aquinas's principled line between public and private. Whereas Aquinas locates the distinction in actions intrinsic to specific goods, and identifies it to certain degree with particular relationships, Finnis ultimately argues that "secret," "truly consensual," and "adult" combine to clarify the "privacy" Aquinas has in mind.[37] Moreover, privacy would also seem to take on a spatial connotation for Finnis insofar as he contrasts "truly private conduct" with the "public realm or environment."[38] These criteria are perhaps clearer than the abstract principle Aquinas propounds; however, insofar as they specify "realms" or "environments" of strictly principled privacy, they run afoul of the Thomistic principle. The salience of this mistake for our purposes is that it focuses the account of limited government on a primary aspect of what the law *does*, that is, maintain general conditions of peace and justice, instead of the diverse ends that delineate law's jurisdiction, that is, various private and public *goods* instantiated in actions and relationships. In consequence, the emerging description of political society itself derives almost entirely from the means or operation of government rather than from an assessment of the goods inherent to political life. This becomes clearest as Finnis turns to consider the relationship between law and virtue.

The Aim of Law: All-Round Virtue and Virtue Simpliciter

Finnis's misspecification of the principled distinction between public and private is closely connected to a deeper substantive difficulty in his account, namely, what Aquinas takes the essential aim or purpose of law to be. It will be my argument that Finnis's specification of the particular purpose of law and government has, in turn, very significant implications for his final assessment of the goodness of political life. In order to evaluate Finnis's conclusion that the political common good is instrumental to other goods more basic to human flourishing, it is necessary to be clear on his account of the aim of law. Clarity on this point, however, is not a simple matter in light of Finnis's nuanced distinction between the political common good, on the one hand, and the common good of the political community, on the other. It is an important matter, however, inasmuch as the end or purpose of an association defines its character. My guiding concerns throughout this analysis are: First, how specifically does the law cognize virtue? And second, what difference does the answer to this question make for how one understands the political?

After having presented his basic case for a limited political common good, Finnis turns to consider what are perhaps the most problematic texts for his interpretation: "Those many texts . . . which flatly say that law and state have amongst their essential purposes and characteristics the inculcation of virtue."[39] How should such texts be understood given the law's limited responsibility only for the societal conditions of justice and peace? The answer, Finnis avers, is that in order for the government to be a successful guarantor of justice and peace, it is necessary that citizens not merely be constrained or coerced by law, but that they *personally adopt* the government's aim of promoting and preserving justice. But in order for citizens to consistently act in a just manner, they must ultimately cultivate the internal dispositions and habits of the virtue itself. Thus, if the state is to successfully achieve its purpose, it must necessarily intend not simply to externally compel citizens to just actions, but that they actually *become just persons.* Consequently, Finnis concludes, "it is a legitimate hope and important aim [finis] of government and law that citizens will come to . . . act out of that particular virtue of character."[40] Furthermore, because "practical reasonableness is essentially all of a piece" government also has a "legitimate interest" in citizens cultivating other virtues, and this interest is ultimately strong enough—though not unequivocally—to support maintenance of a public moral environment in which such virtue can develop.[41]

So the law's *interest* in virtue generally follows from the essential unity of all virtues, and thus its necessary connection to the virtue of justice. The virtue of justice, in turn, qualifies as an appropriate *aim* of government because having truly just citizens is necessary to *consistently just activity*, which is necessary if government is to achieve its essential function of maintaining the conditions of justice and peace. Now, I want to contend that there is a significant lacuna in Finnis's argument here, so I will restate what I take to be the critical claim: the rationality of the law's aim at cultivating the virtue of justice in citizens derives only from the necessity of virtuous citizens (who have themselves adopted the purposes of government) to the government's successful maintenance of the conditions of justice and peace that circumscribe its proper activity.[42] Finnis is careful to specify that he takes the virtue of justice to be a finis (i.e., end, purpose, aim) of law, and this is just the word Aquinas employs.[43] However, Finnis is equally careful to insist that virtue *as such*, as distinct from actions merely in keeping with the requirements of virtue, only comes within the purpose of law because of its necessity to the public good. Virtue is a legitimate goal for the legislator because it serves this further end.

At this juncture Finnis's distinction between the political common good and the common good of political community becomes critical. For although the legislator's cultivation of virtue finds its justification in the public good, this good itself is part of a larger complex of goods—individual and common, private and public—that together comprise the common good of the political community. In Finnis's nomenclature, the political community (or "state," or "civitas") is simply the "whole large society" that comes under the political organization of a particular legal system.[44] *Its* common good is all-inclusive—the sum total of the *beatitudo imperfecta* of all the constituent members of the political community, both individuals and those essential human associations, such as the family, that reasonably desire participation in political society for the sake of the flourishing this "complete" community enables.[45] Consequently, the public good that government maintains is "for the sake of individual and familial well-being and cannot be identified and pursued without a sound conception of individual and domestic responsibilities."[46] Thus, in an important sense, law and government are for the sake of the complete virtue that *beatitudo imperfecta* signifies, and the ultimate reason for law cannot be fully realized without an understanding of the diverse kinds of flourishing essential to the individuals and associations that comprise the political community. However, in moving beyond the particular specification of the purpose of law to the purpose of the political community as a whole, the role of law and government with respect to virtue fundamentally alters, Finnis argues. Beyond the end of the public good, law no longer regards virtue in the same way (as is already evident in the derogation to an *interest* in virtues other than justice and the somewhat tenuous affirmation of public morality). Because political community is comprised of individuals and families that themselves seek political life for their own "unrestricted purposes," according to distinct kinds of practical reason in pursuit of goods that are "irreducibly diverse," the law's relationship to virtue becomes essentially indirect—oriented by a "sound conception" of human flourishing, but no longer "aiming" at it, that is, taking it as an end for which the legislator acts. Thus, beyond the political common good and for the sake of its conditions, the law no longer *leads*[47] to virtue but instead *facilitates* the virtuous life of all.[48] This all-inclusive good, Finnis allows, is "in a sense *the* common good of political community," but this would seem to be an importantly qualified sense, given that it is not, strictly speaking, political.[49] The specifically political—that for which individuals and families, and so on, find it reasonable to engage in political life—is instantiated in the political common good, and the virtuous conditions realized at this level are the terminus of *the legislator's* purpose toward virtue.

Now, the essential point of Finnis's argument here is to demonstrate the ways in which law and government are not competent or concerned to make citizens "*really* good persons *all round*,"[50] but I want to argue that there is another critical aspect of the law's relationship to virtue that slips into Finnis's account with insufficient justification. That is this: there is a very important difference between saying that law, on the one hand, neither (a) simply requires that citizens be virtuous (as opposed to that they perform virtuous actions) nor (b) regulates the complete range of virtuous actions that comprise full human flourishing, and on the other, that law does not (c) cultivate those virtues related to actions that it *does* rightly regulate for the sake of the individual person—that is, aim at virtue simpliciter—simply for the sake of the perfection it realizes in the soul of the individual citizen. Consider the straightforward command that citizens pay their taxes.

Aquinas's analysis of such a command would begin by differentiating the twofold manner of the law's intention to virtue: first, the *aim* or *purpose* [finis] of the lawgiver, and, second, the *matter* that the law concerns [*id de quo praeceptum datur*]. The aim of the lawgiver, Aquinas says, is simply "to lead [*inducere*] men to something by the precepts of the law: and this is virtue." The intention relative to the matter of the precept, on the other hand, is "something leading or disposing to virtue, viz. an act of virtue." The real virtue that is the purpose of a law and the act of virtue that the law enjoins are not the same, just as generally an end [finis] and what is for the sake of an end [*ad finem*] are distinct.[51] In the case of taxation, then, the law simply requires that citizens submit a tax return with the appropriate amount made payable to Uncle Sam. However, Aquinas thinks that such compliance only represents part of a good legislator's intention. The *goal* is that in paying taxes, citizens acquire a just disposition of character that inclines them to act freely for the good of the community. Such citizens would contribute to the public weal apart from being required by law to do so. Finnis's description of the law's relationship to virtue makes sense of this inasmuch as he takes the real virtue of justice to be a legitimate aim of law. The law does not just seek to induce virtuous acts but by means of these acts to induce to virtue itself.

Finnis's account, however, foregrounds a further question: *Why* does the legislator aim at cultivating real virtue? For Finnis, the legislator is only justified in answering "So that citizens will reliably perform those actions necessary to the maintenance of the justice and peace for which I am responsible." He does not answer "Because it is good for citizens to be just inasmuch as it perfects an aspect of their innate capacities and thus contributes to their happiness." The legislator's concern with virtue, then, essentially refers to a further end. Virtue simpliciter, for its own sake, which necessarily entails cultivation in the individual soul (insofar as human virtue is the concern), is not an appropriate aim of law since *justifying* such a goal requires reference to a further end, that is, the conditions of the public good. Thus, Finnis finds no direct connection between the law and the individual for the sake of that person's own virtue.

Now, I do not intend to argue either (a) that the legislator does not take the conditions of justice and peace (as distinct from the acts of virtue that ideally comprise them) as an appropriate purpose of law, or (b) that it is illicit for an authority to intend the virtue of subjects *for the sake of* securing such conditions. Insofar as the remedial functions of law seek not to make citizens just, but to repair the effects of their having been unjust, the law is essentially concerned with securing conditions of justice. Moreover, given that such conditions directly contribute to the common good of human persons, a legislator is not amiss in conceiving virtue as a means (because not a *mere* means) to those conditions he is responsible to maintain. At the same time, it is clear that aiming at virtue simpliciter is at least conceptually distinguishable from aiming at it for the sake of further ends. It seems perfectly reasonable, in fact, to say that an authority aims at virtue simpliciter and as a means to conditions of the common good. These purposes are not mutually exclusive.

Consider a simple example within the familial context: a parent's requirement that children remove their toys from the living room floor after play. Certainly the good of household order is the immediate aim, and insofar as order is partly constitutive of the common life that the family shares, a whole complex of domestic activities and relationships is in view. It also seems true that any parent would anticipate that this simple requirement would begin to mold a child's character by creating a general habit of orderliness and by fostering a regard for the interests of others—both generally and particularly with respect to their immediate family life—which over time would contribute to the mature possession of a just character. And just as it is right for a legislator to intend the citizen's virtue for the sake of the public good, there seems nothing wrong with saying that a parent desires a child to cultivate these virtues of orderliness and justice for the sake of the family's common good. If a family is to achieve its potential as a closely knit partnership in the goods, virtues, and joys of daily life, it is evident that each member must come to engage that community freely and fully, and to exercise their virtues for the sake of the common flourishing it realizes. Yet, at the same time, a parent's intention is informed by the belief that the familial good instantiates something good for the child. Therefore, the intended virtues can also be intended for the child's own sake—or, to say the same thing, for the sake of the virtues as perfective of the child's character. Because it is good for the child himself to be orderly and to contribute to the order of the common family life, a parent's directives naturally regard the virtue of the child for its own sake, virtue simpliciter. So both the common good of the family and the good of the individual child as such naturally fall within the intention of an attentive parent.

Limited to the familial context, Finnis should have no objection to this example, and, therefore, should generally accept the distinction I wish to advance.[52] However, as I remarked at the outset, Finnis is particularly concerned to demonstrate essential differences between legal and paternal authority. So perhaps my example is inapt. Indeed, I have already accepted an important part of Finnis's argument that strongly indicates that law does not concern itself with individuals as such. Because Aquinas's public/private distinction requires that the virtuous act that the law enjoins be ordainable to the common good, it would seem that the law is not directly concerned with virtue as such (i.e., as it perfects the individual) but rather with the specific virtue of justice, which specifically regards the individual qua citizen and orders actions according to and for the sake of those goods for which government is responsible. Of course, since these conditions themselves are oriented to full human virtue, the law's commands ultimately refer to the happiness of individuals. Yet, this is an indirect, instrumental relationship that does not give the legislator a concern for the individual per se. Finnis observes that Aquinas recognizes a distinction between legal and paternal authority inasmuch as paternal authority alone deals not just with the child's interaction with others, but with matters that pertain to the child as such, for example, the fully "self-regarding" acts of temperance that Aquinas takes to be outside the purview of law.[53] So even though neither parent nor king can simply require *real* virtue and, therefore, both are constrained by limited means in their pursuit of this end, it is likewise clear that for Aquinas, parental authority takes a unique responsibility for the individual as such—for the child's "all round virtue." A parent does not regard a child only as "family member" but is also responsible for the child's well-being and education in every aspect of life. Because a parent's responsibility extends beyond the common good of the family to include each child individually, parental authority has a fundamental connection to the individual as such that state authority does not have (at least not in the first instance). The law is simply not concerned with the individual in the same way that a parent is. Parental authority takes cognizance of both "family member" and "individual person." The law, on the other hand, only cognizes "citizen." Therefore, Finnis might want to object, the distinction I am suggesting is inapt to the analysis of law.

All of this (save the conclusion) is correct or can at least be conceded for my present purpose.[54] However, it falls short of addressing the point I wish to urge about the law's aim at virtue simpliciter. It is important, I think, to distinguish a couple of ways we may wish to answer the question, "Does the law regard the individual as such?" In the sense that Finnis demonstrates, Aquinas does not take the law to regard the individual as such inasmuch as government is not responsible for securing the full range of virtuous acts that comprise individual flourishing. Moreover, it is those activities and relationships of an immediately personal nature that Aquinas naturally takes to pertain to "private goods." Whereas parental authority may address these self-regarding activities and goods, state authority is at best indirectly concerned with them. Because the state's responsibility extends only to those actions bearing on the common good, the law, most precisely, regards *citizens*; it is not responsible for the virtue of individuals per se. Or, to put it another way, the whole concerns itself with its parts qua parts; it is not directly responsible for the flourishing of its parts qua distinct wholes, which have functions and goods particular to themselves.[55] It is important to notice, however, that this limitation only concerns the scope of state action, that is, what the law does. Aquinas's distinction between public and private defines the class of acts the government may properly regulate, and it therefore seems appropriate to say that with respect to *jurisdiction* or *means*, the law does not directly regard the individual but is concerned with him qua citizen. On the other hand, Aquinas recognizes a basic distinction between what the lawgiver does (or requires) and why he does it.[56] An act of virtue is commanded, but the full cultivation of virtue is intended, giving rise to the further question why the law intends virtue at all. Here the question is not answered by differentiating among the acts of virtue that the law is justified in requiring or by specifying what particular virtue at which the law may be properly said to aim. The question is, for the sake of what or whom does law intend those virtuous acts and qualities that it *is* justified in addressing? And at this level of description it seems very plausible to say that the law *does* regard the individual directly insofar as the virtue of justice is desired directly and precisely for the contribution to the individual's character that it is. So even if we say that civic virtues or justice are all that law properly requires, insofar as they contribute to what we take to be genuine flourishing of the individual, it is possible for the lawgiver to desire them for the sake of the individual. In this way, the law regards the individual qua individual with respect to its *end* or *purpose*. It just does not do so by requiring the whole panoply of virtuous acts that instantiate the individual's full flourishing. However, one cannot infer from the fact that an authority has a limited role in cultivating an individual's virtue whether or not that authority performs his partial task for the sake of the individual himself, that is, cultivates virtue simpliciter, or whether he acts exclusively for a limited end inherent in the description of his jurisdiction.

There is, therefore, a notable conceptual gap between the substance of Finnis's arguments demonstrating that the law does not aim at the complete, all-round virtue of its citizens and his inference that it also does not inculcate virtue for the sake of the individuals that come within its jurisdiction. One may grant all that Finnis carefully lays out—that law only promotes virtue indirectly inasmuch as the internal aspects of real virtue are beyond its control; that human law only orders external interactions between people; that its jurisdiction is further significantly constrained to acts pertaining to the common good; that the ecclesial community, individual faith, and worship are beyond its purview; that the law's concern with peace does not extend to "the complete justice which true virtue requires of us"; that its precise aim is at the virtue of justice; and thus even that the law is neither responsible for nor directly intends the complete, all-round flourishing that comes within parental jurisdiction—and still maintain that the law aims at virtue simpliciter, not simply for the sake of conditions the lawgiver is responsible to secure, but for the sake of the good it does to individual human persons as such.[57]

One may wonder if this conceptual distinction is substantively important. Does it tell us anything about the nature of the common good for which the lawgiver is responsible to say that he or she intends the virtues pertaining to it for the sake of individual citizens? There is much that may be said about this relationship, and I do not intend to explore all aspects of it here. I do want to draw attention, though, to what seems to me to be a significant oversight necessarily entailed in Finnis's account of the way that law aims at virtue. This oversight particularly relates to Finnis's conclusions about the instrumentality of the specifically political. For it would seem that if an authority does not promote the virtues specific to the association under her care for the sake of its individual members, she does not take the common good for which she is responsible to be intrinsic to human flourishing (i.e., she takes it to be merely instrumental). This inference is problematic for Finnis because if, as I have argued, Finnis does not adequately demonstrate that the law does not aim at virtue simpliciter, by concluding that it does not, Finnis effectively decides the question of instrumentality before setting out to prove it.

Consider a simple illustration. A professor, convinced of the necessity of personal dialectical engagement to the learning process, takes the seminar discussion class he teaches to be the kind of association essential to the basic human good of knowledge. He takes an essential part of human flourishing, then, to be involved in the kind of shared pursuit of understanding that he wishes his class to be, and he considers achievement of this goal the common good for which he is responsible. The full and informed engagement of each member in this process realizes at once the common good of all, inasmuch as it contributes to the dialectal process, and the individual good of each, inasmuch as participation in this particular kind of common good realizes a part of what it is for humans to flourish. Of course, the professor must recognize myriad limitations on his responsibility. In the first place, his common good is a limited one. His students have other pursuits, responsibilities, virtues, and so on, that are necessary to the whole complex of human goods of which he takes his own common good to be essential. His responsibility, and thus authority, is limited to requiring of his students only those sorts of activities that pertain to the class. Moreover, his authority does not practically extend to *making* the students mentally engage in the group discussions, much less to securing the level of insight and interaction necessary to achieve their common progress in understanding. Thus, his ability and authority to promote the good for which he is responsible is substantially limited, it would seem. Nevertheless, in addition to those structural requirements that provide the requisite order for class proceedings, he gives directives to the students designed to further the class objectives, for example, writing assignments that require that they read and think about texts before coming to class and required contributions during the discussion. Now, obviously if students do only what is strictly necessary to fulfill the requirements, his real objectives will not be accomplished. The prospect of commonly gained insight depends upon students actually engaging the ideas, the dialectical process, and one another as they seek better understanding. Thus the common good depends on each student's real acquisition of the virtues pertaining to the class. Insofar as this is the case, it seems fair to say that he desires that the students be virtuous for the sake of the common good of the class. Because this particular set of virtues is necessary to the good of the association for which he is responsible, he is right to intend that students be diligent in reading and thinking, attentive to the logic of unfolding arguments, and justly considerate of classmates by being punctual and respectful in discussion *so that* the common learning, which is the point of the association, can progress. At the same time, given his understanding of the common good itself, it would be incomplete to say that he did not intend all of these same activities and virtues for the sake of the students themselves individually. His understanding of *this* association as a kind intrinsic to human flourishing entails that the virtues necessary to the associational good are likewise simply perfective of the individual as such. Insofar as human goods are associational, the relevant associational goods are human. Given that the desired human good is instantiated in the group itself, it seems necessary to say that the professor intends the virtue of each student simpliciter.

Because the fundamental flourishing of the individual is not taken as a further end but is pursued in the group itself, the professor aims directly at the good of individuals.

What I think this illustration makes clear is that if an authority takes the common good for which she is responsible to be intrinsic to human flourishing, then she will promote the virtues specific to that association for the sake of its individual members. From this it necessarily follows that an authority that does not promote the virtues specific to her association for the sake of her individual members does not take the common good for which she is responsible to be intrinsic to human flourishing. This creates a problem for Finnis since it indicates that a substantive conclusion about the nature of political association (i.e., that it is instrumental) logically follows a premise about the law's relationship to virtue that he failed to demonstrate in relevant part (i.e., that the law does not aim at virtue simpliciter). Whereas one may grant Finnis's point that the law does not regard the individual qua individual with respect to the range of virtues it commands—giving principled scope to the exercise of both individual and domestic prudence—it does not follow from this that the law does not regard the individual qua individual with respect to its end, cultivating virtue simpliciter precisely because the common good that it promotes is partly constitutive of human flourishing.

Of course, there remains the challenge of Finnis's distinction between the political and the *specifically* political, or, the common good of the political community and the political common good. What should we make of Finnis's further claim that the law *is* ultimately for the sake of virtue simpliciter insofar as the political common good is a necessary support to the full flourishing that occurs within the political community as a whole? As I have noted, in order to fulfill this auxiliary function, Finnis allows that the legislator must "ascertain and adhere" to the truth about human fulfillment and morality, ensconcing a "sound conception" of individual and familial responsibilities in the law.[58] In this sense political community is as thick as *beatitudo imperfecta* itself since it includes the complete complex of goods that comprise human flourishing. Doesn't this provide a way for Finnis to affirm that political life is *for virtue* and a substantive account of the political that does not reduce to government and law? It does not.

The first reason for this follows directly from the argument I have just made. It is precisely the *legislative aim* at virtue that matters to our understanding of the nature of that association that comes within the legislator's care. Although political community, as Finnis understands it, includes all the virtues of human flourishing, it represents no common aim or purpose toward them. Rather, the political common good facilitates the "unrestricted purposes" of individuals and families.[59] The common good of political community represents no unified purpose other than that of the legislator, and Finnis is clear that this purpose terminates in the political common good. Virtue simpliciter, then, remains in no sense a *political aim* or a *common* good of the political community.

Neither is the related substantive conflation of political community and government/law mitigated. Insofar as the political common good is "interdefined with the jurisdiction of state government and law" and this is the only unified purpose that the members of political community share, political life as such is all but entirely reduced to the operation of law and government. Now, it is true that government intends for citizens themselves to "adopt its purpose of promoting and preserving justice," but Finnis gives no indication that this purpose extends beyond the jurisdiction of law and government (since the political common good represents the only shared purpose of political community). Political life, it would seem, then becomes simply a partnership in freely doing what the law commands, or perhaps what the law could command. But this is what one would expect if the lawgiver does not take himself to be inculcating virtue simpliciter since it follows that political association is then simply instrumental. Citizenship becomes freely fulfilling the instrumental purposes of the law.

One wonders, then, why Finnis labels this all-around flourishing the common good of a political community. The community seems to be political only insofar as it falls under the authority of a particular government, and the government itself has no direct or essential connection to that flourishing (except insofar as Finnis is willing to allow that restorative justice might be essential to the basic good of societas[60]). The goods are common in a logical sense, of course, since they are shared perfections of human nature, but insofar they bear only slight connection to political community per se, it is difficult to see how the relevant community does not simply dissolve into the universal human community.

It is evident, then, that Finnis's account of the common good of political community (the "no" answer to his basic question about the scope and nature of the state's common good) does not adequately address the difficulties raised by his explicit methodological decision to answer this question by examining the kind of law governments are justified in propounding (this is the "yes" answer, and the main thrust of Finnis's argument). There is, however, a final twist in the discussion, one that raises a doubt about the real impact of his initial methodological commitment.

An Aristotelian Ascent?

In the final move of his argument Finnis turns to reconsider, apparently ab initio, whether there is a principled reason to constrain the state's authority. "Are there good grounds for judging that the state's specific common good is this limited public good of justice and peace?"[61] His aim here seems to be to determine if there is a good particular to political community that does not reduce to the limited and instrumental political common good. It is evident that Finnis is after the essential nature of political life per se, as distinct from all other forms of human association, since he quickly moves into an Aristotelian ascent from the nature of the family to groups of families and finally to the polis, asking in the process what makes political community "complete." That is, what makes it different in kind, not simply a larger aggregation of associations with greater—though essentially the same— objectives? *This* kind of methodology would seem to be directly contrary to an illicit inference of the purpose of political community from the operation of law and government. It becomes clear upon examination, however, that Finnis carries the same interpretive commitments forward into this reconsideration and, consequently, that the assumptions and substantive conflations I have identified continue to shape his conception of political society.

The upshot of Finnis's investigation is that "the common good which is interdefined with the jurisdiction of state government and law seems indeed to be an instrumental good." The crux of this conclusion is that "the need which individuals have for the political community is not that it instantiates an otherwise unavailable basic good."[62] So although law and government make political community "complete" in that they provide the final stratum of all things necessary to the successful cultivation of basic human goods, the goods themselves (i.e., education, friends, marriage, virtue, etc.) are already realized by individuals and families, Finnis argues. Save the remedial operations of law that restore justice between people, nothing essential to human happiness is added by law and government.

Within the space of a single paragraph, however, Finnis makes an essential transition in this argument. The question, remember, concerns the good of political community itself. This is the purpose of the Aristotelian ascent—to get at the basic nature of the political. At the critical point, however, Finnis simply shifts from speaking of the "complete community" or "political community" to simply a description of the functions of law and government, concluding that the common good "interdefined" with the jurisdiction of government and law is instrumental.[63] Now, if Finnis were to include in this common good the whole complex of political activity, association, identity, and so on, in which citizens engage and that presumably falls within the jurisdiction (not to say control) of government insofar as it is publicly shared, there would be no substantive conflation here. This kind of common good would generally represent all that we mean when we speak of political life and association, and could be understood as "interdefined" with the jurisdiction of law and government. However, this is manifestly not what Finnis has in mind. If it were, at least some discussion of the nature and value of this kind of political association would be required before concluding that it is merely instrumental to human flourishing. Instead, Finnis immediately concludes that the political good is instrumental, having only described it in terms of the operation of law and government. The unavoidable conclusion, then, is that he simply refers to the political common good under its previous description, and that description, as we have seen, collapses the substance of political association into an account of government and law. Moreover, Finnis's account of the political common good necessarily entails instrumentality since it excludes what would be necessary to concluding that political association is intrinsic to human flourishing, namely, that the legislator takes himself to be cultivating virtue simpliciter. Thus, Finnis's Aristotelian ascent culminates in the same conflation that characterized his explicit methodology at the outset. It is clear that here, as well as there, he intends a conceptual distinction between political community and the operations of law and government. Nevertheless, at both points of his argument the conceptual distinction substantively collapses. The "political" becomes the "specifically political," which in turn reduces to the legal or governmental.

Conclusion

Recall that Finnis's basic question, "Can a state's common good . . . be anything less than the complete good . . . of its citizens?," requires that he address at least these three subsidiary issues: the state's relationship to an individual's internal possession of a virtuous character, the state's legitimate interest in the whole gamut of virtuous activity, and finally, the nature of associations in which individuals flourish—particularly the character and value of political association as such. Therefore, insofar as he takes his basic question to be equivalent to asking, "What type of direction can properly be given by governments and law?" Finnis sets out to analyze and define these three issues through an account of the appropriate operation of law and government. This methodology—which Finnis attributes to Aquinas[64]—does not reduce, strictly speaking, to a simplistic derivation of the end of law from its means. Clearly, even Finnis's description of the kind of direction government rightly gives progresses in part by steadily narrowing the purpose of law to the temporal, then to the external, then the interactive, and finally to the common or public good. At the same time, it is evident that by taking the command of law as the interpretive key to the state's common good Finnis's analysis runs off course. In the first place, his specification of the private/public distinction attaches to a description of what the law does (i.e., the conditions it secures) rather than to the activities and relationships intrinsic to diverse goods, as for Aquinas. This focus on the operational aspects of law compounds in Finnis's articulation of the law's relationship to virtue. Finnis suggests that we understand what the law directly does, most importantly the conditions of justice and peace that it maintains, as the sole good that it seeks, its purpose. This is evident inasmuch as the law's aim at the virtue of justice derives justification from this further end. Finnis takes the aim of law to be virtue for the sake of just conditions, exclusive of virtue simpliciter. However, in so doing, he necessarily assumes far too much about the basic nature of political community per se, effectively determining the issue of instrumentality from an unargued premise. Perhaps it is too much to say that this all necessarily follows from his initial methodological framework, but there does appear to be a single thread throughout. Finnis is consistently inclined to answer questions relevant to the nature of political community as such with an account of the operation of government and law. The paucity of direct theorizing about the political common good may suggest such an approach, but it is ultimately inadequate. What is needed, then, is a fuller account of the substance and content of the shared political life for which government is responsible.

Where to begin? Given that political community is a composite thing, comprised of many parts and yet bringing them into important unity, let us begin by following Aristotle's method of understanding the character of the whole in light of the nature of its constitutive parts.[65] The family is the fundamental building block of society and—along with religious institutions—the association that most calls the unique and intrinsic good of political society into question. As one of the most vital loci of human flourishing, it makes the claim plausible that political society merely serves as an instrument to its flourishing. Therefore, building to an adequate assessment of the goods of political community requires that we begin by taking measure of familial goods. Then, in light of these goods of intimate association, we can more clearly see the unique social goods that political society affords. To such a discussion I now turn.

The Familial Good

Philosophers and political theorists have long taken the family to present great promise, as well as deep problems, for politics. Putting to one side the (relatively) mundane fact that "reproductive labor is socially necessary labor,"[1] the particular character and strength of familial bonds raises pointed questions about the nature of political community and its relationship to the various associations that exist within its jurisdiction. All types of subpolitical association (e.g., friendships, ecclesial and civil associations) raise such questions, but the difficulties are uniquely acute in considerations of family life. The primary reason for this is the peculiar—and peculiarly strong—form that the human experience of belonging takes in the family.[2] Whereas friends may over time come to regard each other, according to Aristotle's famous formulation, as "other selves," family relationships intrinsically form an intricate matrix of organically, biologically linked persons. Family members, to use the literal Greek and Latin syntax, are of each other in a unique and potent way.

The argument of this chapter will proceed as follows: first, to consider the basic difficulties that arise from this experience of familial belonging; second, to give particular attention to the nature and complications of belonging as it characterizes the parent-child relationship; third, to reflect on the relational significance of this parent-child belonging, particularly as it addresses the fundamental concerns about the family we begin with; and fourth, in order to demonstrate the immediate political and policy importance of this philosophical consideration of human sociability, to bring this investigation into dialogue with contemporary liberal theorizing about children's rights and education.

At the outset, a couple of caveats are in order. It should be apparent that I do not attempt to deal with the family in toto. I am not concerned with the marital relationship per se, but only (and briefly) as it relates to the parent-child relationship. Nor am I concerned with gender roles in the family, neither the role that gender plays in structuring the family as a whole nor its significance to rearing children. Given the sources from which I primarily draw (viz., Aristotle and Aquinas), it is obvious that this is a significant historical abstraction.[3] However, it is an abstraction I am comfortable making given that the different ways in which fathers and mothers experience connection to their children is not central to my argument, nor, in the final analysis, is that connection strictly biological. (So although I take biological reproduction to be the central case of the human experience of belonging I want to consider here, it is an experience and commitment of interconnectedness that characterizes adoptive relationships as well, and can come to exist between friends.) Moreover, I agree with Susan Moller Okin in maintaining that "nothing in our natures dictates that men should not be equal participants in the rearing of their children."[4] So although Aristotle and Aquinas gave greater emphasis to the role of fathers in the lives of their children (particularly with respect to education), for my purposes here, it does no violence to their thought largely to prescind from gender differences in order to speak of the *parent-child relationship*.

The Twofold Problem of Familial Belonging

The philosophical and political concerns with familial belonging may be helpfully distinguished according to two basic elements: particularity and inequality. The first of these finds expression in the earliest elaborations of Western political philosophy by Plato and Aristotle, while the latter is primarily a modern concern (which I will treat within the context of contemporary liberal theory). However, it too derives from problems of which Aristotle and subsequent commentators were well aware and that they explored in the process of unpacking the basic character of familial association. Let us consider these difficulties in turn.

PARTICULARITY AND THE ARISTOTELIAN DILEMMA

The community of women and children recommended in Book IV of Plato's *Republic* is, of course, infamous for its rejection of natural family relationships. Socrates proposes a radical restructuring of sexual and familial relationships in an attempt to transfer the particular preferences of home and hearth to the common identity and well-being of the city. The problem, as Socrates saw it, is that the fierce loyalties and intimate relationships of the nuclear family preoccupy citizens with individual concerns, thereby diverting attention from the common good. The basic relationships of the family, therefore, must be reworked in order to harness the possessive power of the family for common benefit. "Marriage, the having of wives, and the procreation of children must be governed as far as possible by the old proverb: friends possess everything in common," Socrates opines.[5]

Equally famous is Aristotle's sensible refutation of Socrates's utopian deconstruction (which Plato himself significantly moderated in *The Laws*). While still maintaining and expounding the classical commitment to the primacy of political life, Aristotle defends the very great importance of the nuclear family—not only as a necessary or inevitable component of human life but as itself a seedbed of social virtue. Debunking Socrates's vision of tight civic unity, Aristotle observes that political brotherhood in reality relies upon familial fraternity. When the family ceases to be, citizens will not call all men "brother"; they will simply cease to have brothers. Individuals will not count the common stock among their possessions; rather, the powerful human motivation for what is possessed and held dear will be lost. Political ties, Aristotle insists, presuppose familial attachments.[6] This critique suggests a marked rejection of the Socratic problem, relying instead on a basic fecundity in familial life to animate political loyalties. And indeed, there are other significant lines of Aristotle's argument that support such a reading.

For instance, Aristotle is notably sensitive to the importance of the parent-child relationship to one of the city's primary objectives, that is, the moral development of children.[7] Although Aristotle is convinced of the necessity of good laws to providing parents with the social structure, punitive force, and ethical insight required to keep children on the path to virtue, he also gives strong support to the role of parents in this process. Parents, Aristotle argues, are not only most inclined to pursue the moral education of their children but are also uniquely suited to directing the process. The natural affection that develops within the family inclines children to heed parental instruction, and the intimate knowledge that parents have of their children allows them to tailor instructions and discipline according to the needs of individual children. Thus, for the *best* youth (those well-disposed to virtuous activity) legal force is unnecessary and the particularity of parental knowledge might be thought preferable to the moral generalizations of the law.[8]

This argument, it is important to note, serves as Aristotle's transition from his discussion of individual and social ethics to his treatise on politics. Cities in general have no real concern for the moral education of their citizens, Aristotle observes. This is not to say that he is sanguine about the prospects of familial training in virtue. On the contrary, just as most states neglect real virtue, Aristotle notes that most men live isolated and self-centered lives, capriciously ruling households in Cyclops fashion. Nevertheless, it appears that the moral concern and effective guidance of parents supplies the impetus for moral education, and concern for friends widens immediate familial concerns.[9] From this vantage point, families are naturally oriented toward what it is that good laws should aim to do, and thus it is no surprise that in the opening chapters of the *Politics* Aristotle gives the family pride of place in the associational development culminating in the city. Communication in rational pursuit of the good and the just characterizes not just the city but the household as well.[10] The family, then, is not just the seedbed of social concern, or simply the source of particular knowledge and affection essential to effective education, but it would also seem to be a locus of *rational* discourse definitive of the good life. The combined force of these factors prompts Ernest Barker to suggest that for Aristotle, "Of the vast majority it is true, that the love of their family [and their professional work] is, and is quite rightly, the sum of their life.[11]

Yet this assessment seems to overstate the case, for there is much in Aristotle's analysis that cuts the other way. In particular, it obscures the degree to which Aristotle appears to subsume other pursuits and associations into political community. For all his appreciation of particularity and familial belonging, it becomes notably overshadowed in Aristotle's thought by the broader dimensions of his ethical and political concerns. Thus, there is much to support Jean Bethke Elshtain's complaint that Aristotle presents a "functionalist view" of the family, that is, that it is merely necessary to the polis but not an integral part of the good life.[12] We should recall that even in his discussion of the educational effectiveness of fathers, Aristotle ultimately deemed the legislator's grasp of universal principles to be superior for moral education. While intimate knowledge may alert us to exceptions from the general rule, it is still preferable for care (and education) to be guided by one in command of scientific universals. One with particular knowledge of a person may be able to contrive effective, perhaps in some cases superior, medical care, but it is still better to have one's illness treated by a physician. Likewise, Aristotle takes the scientific knowledge of the legislator to be superior, and solicitous fathers should study the rational science of morals and law.[13]

Furthermore, Aristotle's almost exclusive focus on the material, commercial concerns of the household in the *Politics* seems to belie his inclusion of the family in activities essential to the good life. It is remarkable, in fact, that he never fulfills a promissory note (made at the end of Book I) to investigate how moral education should be conducted within the home. Instead, he gives strong indication in Book III, chap. 9, that the associations of family and civil society exist simply as means to the noble pursuits of political life, and his articulation of the best regime in Books VII–VIII suggests that moral education in the home is best if monitored by the state's "child supervisors."[14] Such an innovation seems to reverse any secondary status of politics suggested in the *Nicomachean Ethics* X.9, instead making the parental role subsidiary to the aims of political citizenship. The family's importance, then, follows from and is essentially contingent upon its necessity and utility in political life.

In sum, while it is apparent that Aristotle rejects Socrates's theoretical deconstruction of relationships of belonging in the family, it is not altogether clear that he views them finally as constituting much more than an instrumental means to the aims of political life. Although he defends the particular bonds of the family against communistic innovation, the intrinsic value of these bonds is unclear. To say that political bonds require familial attachments does not entail that such attachments possess equal or greater importance. They may turn out to be subsumed by the broader purposes of the city and valuable only to the degree that they support those ends. Likewise, the special knowledge of intimate relationships appears for Aristotle to be finally subordinated to the universal dimensions of rational science, and, above all, this subordination effects education of the young. Here again, the belonging and particularity of the family may engender certain benefits, but these seem ultimately superseded by the more capacious, objective character of political life. There is significant evidence to be marshaled on both sides of the issue in interpreting Aristotle. Suffice it here to say that he was aware of the difficulties involved and provided important resources to sort them out.

These are three areas, then, where the particularity of familial relationships seem to pose problems: (1) in a love of one's own that cuts against commitment to the political common good; (2) in affective attachments that undercut rational commitments to the universality of goodness; and (3) following on this, in the particularity of intimate practical knowledge that needs clarification and systemization in a broader, universal science.

Although contemporary liberal theory has very different preoccupations than the premodern concern with particularity and the common good, the distinctions can be overemphasized. There are persistent difficulties woven into the fabric of human relationships and thus traceable in the history of moral and political reflection. One sees in the contemporary dispute between John Rawls and Susan Moller Okin, for example, an effort to square the particular, intimate arrangements of domestic life with the political or common interest in securing women's civil rights. The question persists: can or should intimate familial arrangements be squared with external moral and political commitments? Rawls, citing the practically secure place of the family in the "basic structure" of society, is disinclined to interfere in the domestic realm by directly subjecting the family to the requirements of political justice.[15] Okin, in contrast, rejects such passivity, insisting that political justice is, in fact, impossible apart from true familial justice, and thus that the law should mandate equitable social and economic treatment of women in their domestic relations. "Without just families," Okin argues, "how can we expect to have a just society?"[16] In similar fashion, contemporary debates about public and private education in large part concern reconciling political requirements and desiderata with the social and moral commitments of private associations—most often families.

The current concerns with the experience of familial belonging, however, take on a particularly modern character in their focus on the inequality in the parent-child relationship. As we will see, Aristotle and Aquinas are sensitive to this dynamic, but the modern commitment to individual freedom and autonomy invests it with distinctive political urgency. Contemporary liberal theorists are inclined to treat familial "belonging" not in the relational and affective sense of personal interconnectedness but rather as it connotes possession or parental rights. "Belonging" in this sense highlights the fundamental inequality and possibility of dominance that exists in the parent-child relationship (Okin, Gutmann, Fineman, West, Reich, Dwyer, etc.). These two senses are importantly related, though the relationship is seldom explored. Very often, as is a well-discussed tendency of liberal theory, the parental rights that "belonging" denotes are rebutted with articulations of children's rights or matched by a defense of communal interests. If belonging is understood in any relational sense, it is as an emotional commodity of sorts to be categorized and dispensed much as food, clothing, and shelter.[17] Children have a need for it, and the family, as an association that "specializes in emotion,"[18] is probably best suited to address that need. But once that box is checked, so to speak, you should move on to talk sensibly about children's *real, prospective* interests as maturing adults and future citizens. For many contemporary theorists, then, "belonging" tends to be treated as either a highly suspect form of possession or a merely affective, albeit necessary, commodity.

Along these lines, Susan Okin is concerned that in addition to masking the inequality of gender roles in the family, the inequalities present between parents and children serve to normalize unjust social paradigms for impressionable children.[19] Amy Gutmann gives a much more strident analysis of this dynamic, arguing that families *intrinsically* stunt the development of children by (at least) "implicitly foster[ing] disrespect for people who are different," necessitating the intervention of the state to equip children with the skills necessary for "rational deliberation among ways of life"—particularly those different from their parents. The family produces people ruled by "habit and authority" rather than citizens with the capacity for autonomous self-government required for self-fulfillment and good citizenship.[20] The concern of liberal theorists with the self-preferential and perpetuating modes of traditional family life is twofold, Gutmann explains: first, *political liberals* worry that the basic virtues of tolerance and openness upon which liberal democracies rely is undermined (and here we have another iteration of the particular/universal problem); and, second, *comprehensive liberals* share the deeper fear that the autonomous intellectual maturity that healthy human development requires is vitiated in the radically unequal and fundamentally self-serving parent-child relationship.[21]

By suggesting that these contemporary concerns are frequently expressed with an insufficient attention to the complexity of relational belonging—focusing only on its negative potential for possessive domination—I do not want to imply that no genuine problem is raised. Certainly, in relationships of belonging close identification between the parties introduces the possibility of viewing the other, whether consciously or not, primarily as an extension of oneself or effectively as a means to one's own enjoyment or personal aims. The very personal identification parents often have with their children amplifies this possibility, and there is little reason to think that the intensity of parental love altogether precludes it. Moreover, it is not difficult to see that the extreme inequality of the parent-child relationship creates the possibility of such misguided possessiveness going unchecked and having long-term ill effect. Children are simply very vulnerable, and they are particularly vulnerable to their parents.

One need not tend toward criticism of family relationships to recognize this point. Alasdair MacIntyre has helpfully analyzed much the same worry in terms of the process whereby children move from all but entire dependence upon their parents to the mature exercise of independent practical reason.[22] Due to their complete dependence on adult caregivers, every child quickly learns from experience that desire satisfaction requires pleasing adults. In this significant way, the desires of children are filtered through the desires and aims of their parents for them. Due to this and the close affective bond between parent and child, a child will not necessarily clearly differentiate between personal desires and those presented to him by authority figures. Yet such a differentiation, MacIntyre argues, is not simply necessary to self-awareness or independent self-perception. It also necessarily precedes the further ability to distinguish between oneself and one's current desires or "subjective motivational set." And in order to function independently as a practical reasoner, one must be able to distinguish present desires or felt needs from one's true self or true good objectively conceived and work to transform those desires to conform with one's rational good. Thus, MacIntyre observes that "failure as a practical reasoner to be able to separate oneself from one's own desires characteristically results from a failure to make oneself sufficiently independent from those on whom one was dependent in infancy and who initiated one into practical reasoning."[23] So whereas MacIntyre would not generally support Gutmann's critique of familial education, and would explain the problem more in terms of filial dependence than parental self-interest, both theorists share a concern with the intrinsic inequality of parent-child relationships and the deep challenges it poses for finally achieving mature adulthood.

The reason for their *disagreement* at this point, of course, springs from contrary underlying theories about the nature of rational inquiry and autonomous moral agency. What is for Gutmann the oppressiveness of habit and authority is for MacIntyre the rationality of tradition. Expanding on Aristotle's basic insight that all rational inquiry necessarily proceeds on the basis of some starting point, MacIntyre contends that rational inquiry cannot be adequately conceived apart from a tradition in which the standards of rational justification emerge and are vindicated in the debate and experience of that tradition.[24] Therefore, raising children within a particular tradition does not inherently deprive them of the exercise of independent rationality but is a necessary preparation for it (when rightly done). Leaving this basic dispute aside, however, we see in MacIntyre's affirmation of "the ordinary good mother"—despite an educational process "fraught with imperfections"—a fundamental demur from the common identification of familial belonging with possessiveness and self-interest.[25] In MacIntyre's account, the love, recognition, security, and instruction that ordinary parents provide their children not only serve to meet emotional needs and provide a sense of self-worth but also essentially inform a relational environment in which a child's rational maturity and independence are fostered.

These differing assessments of familial belonging highlight an important fact that accounts for the focus on relational and ethical analysis in this discussion: it is clear that much of the contemporary concern with familial belonging in its *political dimensions* follows from conclusions about its basic character in *ethical and relational dimensions*. Contemporary theorists are often stuck in the difficult position of acknowledging the practical necessity and affective primacy of the family, while seeking to undo or circumvent by political means the damage parents do to a child's personal development. Family may be necessary as an importantly emotionally charged environment, but it is also, perhaps precisely for that reason, a realm of possessive belonging in which the inclination to control or manipulate requires that its vulnerable members be given "safe haven."[26] Stanley Hauerwas helpfully summarizes the dilemma the family poses for the liberal tradition:

> In spite of our claim that the family is the bedrock of our society, the family has always been an anomaly for the liberal tradition. Only if human beings can be separated in a substantial degree from kinship can they be free individuals subject to egalitarian policies. Thus we assume . . . that it is more important to be an "autonomous person" than to be a "Hauerwas" or a "Pulaski" or a "Smith."[27]

In similar fashion, the political dimensions of what I have called the "Aristotelian dilemma" seem to follow directly from Aristotle's ambiguity about the value of particularity in familial belonging. Whether or not the family plays a fundamentally instrumental role in the city in large part turns on its connection to human flourishing. And that question turns largely on whether we take the intimacy, affection, and belonging of familial relationships to serve merely affective needs and desires or to be more directly connected to the rational human good. Thus, two primary questions need to be dealt with in considering the place of the family in political life: What is the nature of familial belonging, particularly in the parent-child relationship? And what are the goods realized in that relationship, particularly as they relate to achieving the full rational maturity of the child? As will become evident toward the end of my argument, this concern with full rational maturity is situated within a larger concern to adequately appreciate and account for a child's present actuality or being in addition to his/her prospective potentiality or becoming.

The Nature of Parental Love

For Aristotle, family relationships should be joined with those of the closest of friends in their fundamental difference from relationships of agreed-upon mutual advantage. As distinct from the myriad temporary alliances we form and dissolve on a regular basis—and even from the common good characteristic of citizenship—kin and comrades regard one another with a unique kind of disinterestedness.[28] There are, of course, very important distinctions between Aristotle's understanding of friendship proper and the relationship between family members. The greatest difference is found in the parent-child relationship inasmuch as it is a relationship of fundamental inequality. Brothers are the paradigmatic case of friendship (and the best of friends are wont to liken themselves to brothers).

On the other hand, although we may not wish to identify the parent-child relationship as the central case of friendship, it may well be the highest case of the love according to which friendship is centrally defined. As Lorraine Pangle points out, it is in describing the love of parents for children that Aristotle first employs his famous formulation of friendly love as regarding the friend as an "other self."[29] (In this respect, it is notable that in his comment on Aristotle's remark that all familial friendship depends upon parental friendship, Aquinas seems to expand the point by saying that *all* friendship refers to parental friendship insofar as it is the nearest to self-love, from which friendship is fundamentally derived.[30]) Parents, indeed, have a unique basis for this kind of relationship insofar as their children are literally "of themselves," springing from the genetic union of father and mother and remaining biologically dependent upon mothers for some time.[31]

The immediate organicity of the bond, in fact, generates conceptual (and experiential) difficulties with the relationship. There is an important distinction, it would seem, between the relationship of *belonging* that derives from the physical generation of children from their parents' bodies and the personal differentiation entailed by the formulation "other self." "Belonging" at least suggests the possibility of simply being regarded as part of or appurtenant to a possessive whole. Aristotle raises this possibility, in fact, with a startling analogy: "For that which has sprung from a thing belongs to its source, for example, a tooth, a hair, and so forth belongs to its owner." Both share the characteristic of generation in some way from one's body, and the source, Aristotle says, "does not belong at all—or only to a lesser degree—to that which has sprung from it."[32] As Aquinas puts it, parents view their children as existing as part of themselves (*utpote pars existens*) or as separable parts of a whole (*sicut partes separabiles ad totum*).[33] Now, the force of this worry is certainly mitigated by its context. After all, Aristotle's point is that parents love their children *more* than children reciprocate precisely because parents are aware of and intimately experience a child's connection to themselves. And, as I noted, Aquinas is quick to draw essential connections to friendliness in general, not just relationships within the family.

At the same time, it is a mistake to move too quickly over the difficulties posed here. The experience of belonging—an immediate awareness that this child is *of oneself*—poses the risk of failing to take adequate cognizance of distinct personhood. A child's existence as a *part* of one's self is, of course, merely "so to speak," but it is rooted in a real biological priority of parents that plays itself out relationally. Genuine ethical concerns are naturally raised by these physical and psychological realities. If I perceive this child as a "separated part" of me, am I not inclined to view her good as appurtenant to my own and shape it according to my own wishes? (Here the difficulties of inequality are also evident in the part/whole analogy.) Or, if the child is "of me," that is, generated from my body, do I not have a right, as against the state, the community, or perhaps the child herself, to continue to direct and shape her personality and education? (It perhaps exaggerates the issue somewhat to say "I" rather than "we" brought her into existence. Surely the reality of "we" is an important factor here, and I will address it shortly.) Whether or not these impulses rightly characterize common parental responses, they are the sorts of worry that often motivate criticism of "parental rights" or an "expressivist" model of the family.[34] The basic concern, it would seem, is that the self-preference to which all people are generally prone is in important respects exacerbated in parental relationships—and that at the expense of vulnerable children. And while there are crucial differences in their characterization and interpretation of the relationship, I think that the description of parental belonging Aristotle and Aquinas develop give reason to consider these concerns carefully.

It would seem that if the close relationship of parent and child opens a unique possibility of movement from the *self* to the *other*, it also must necessarily open the possibility of subsuming the other into the self. [35] If this child is so identified with me as a parent that in loving her I love myself—or love myself *by* loving her—what keeps the essence of familial belonging from being primarily a matter of self-love? (And if it is in essence a matter of self-love, to state the modern concern, are we justified in identifying the interests of parents and children in the institution of the family?)

IDENTIFICATION AND REFERENCE

This set of issues is importantly related. However, any adequate consideration must also begin by making a distinction between the issues of *identification*, on the one hand, and those of *reference*, on the other. That is to say, taking another's good to be "part of" or "appurtenant to" my own may mean either (a) that I perceive or consider X's good to partially comprise my own (insofar as a description of my goodwill entails a description of X's good), that is, in a fundamental sense I *identify* with X; or (b) that I *refer* X's good to my own insofar as I take X's welfare to be important or valuable insofar as it contributes to my own overall good. Now, the identification with another described in (a) and self-love are importantly related insofar as (for both Aristotle and Aquinas) a natural will toward one's own happiness "causes all other willings, since whatever a man wills, he wills on account of the end."[36] At the same time, this cannot be simply or ultimately reduced to pursuing another's good only as it *inures* to one's own good (in other words, self-love does not reduce to reference) inasmuch as it is possible to *identify* oneself with another. Identification of this kind does not entail an effective conflation of personalities, goods, or even interests such that no practical distinction between persons so united may be cognized. Rather, the point is that in such a bond between persons each party pursues the other's good as his/her own (i.e., the good for X is part of my good) and pursues his/her own overall good as *in part* good for the other (i.e., I desire my own good in part as "good for X").[37]

This is, of course, a vexed ethical issue about which much ink has been spilled. However, we must at least acknowledge that to fail to differentiate these relational dynamics at the outset is to beg an important question. It is precisely in consideration of the basic character of human relationships that the question of the true nature of the "other self" must be answered. There are, then, two important distinctions immediately implicated here: first, that between (a) *identifying the goods of two persons* in friendship and (b) *referring another's good* to one's own; and second, that between (c) identification *of goods* in friendship and (d) a closer identification *of personalities or self-conceptions.*[38]

To return to the fundamental relationship of identity between parent and child, it is clear that parental regard for children is in large part insensitive to the distinction between (c) and (d). Parents not only incorporate the good of their newborn children into their own hopes and plans for future good but also more directly identify physically and personally with their children. The unfolding of Aristotle's description of parents and children draws attention to the way in which the relationship is first an *enlargement* or *expansion* of the self, rather than, as the formulation "other self" might denote, a "standing outside" of oneself in consideration of the other's goods. Children are not simply sloughed off, nor are they simply observed and cared for; rather, as Aquinas puts it, they are "separable parts," still included by the whole in itself.[39] The physical dimensions of this, as we noted, are apparent in a child's issuance from a mother's body and the extreme physical dependence he has upon parents. There are, as well, physical traits that mark the relationship and remind parents of their connection (often intensifying it), even as physical dependence lessens. Moreover, dependence requires that parents provide and care for their children intensely and persistently, making them not only their chief benefactors (to use Aristotle's characterization) in generation but also in the whole trajectory of their health and well-being. The profundity of the connection here must necessarily affect the strength of the identification. The parent-to-child relation is more than a matter of *reflecting* oneself (as significant as that is), for as Aristotle notes, a beneficiary *actualizes* what the benefactor is in *potentiality.*[40] Insofar as parents perceive qualities and attributes (e.g., physical traits, personal idiosyncrasies, and proclivities) that they recognize in themselves, a child reflects and expands their self-conception. But, in addition, insofar as a child is the *product* of parents' creative activity on their behalf (procreative and educational), children reveal something of what parents are. (This is, of course, a complicated relationship, one that parents are likely to exaggerate or minimize in differing ways, yet few are likely to gainsay its fundamental significance.) Thus, children constitute an essential expansion or elaboration of the self and are included in one's self-conception.

In addition, or perhaps as a compounding effect, it is helpful to consider this identification in light of the relational psychology that MacIntyre calls attention to in his discussion of the process by which children attain rational independence.[41] As noted earlier, MacIntyre observes a fundamental identification of desire that develops between parents and children and follows readily from a child's early realization that satisfaction of his desires requires pleasing his parents (or other adult caregivers). MacIntyre convincingly argues that such dependence results in a powerful unconscious identification of a child's "subjective motivational set" with that of his parents. This is itself a basic, if easily unobserved, form of dependence from which children must separate if they are to adequately develop characteristics of independent practical reason.

It does not detract from the force of MacIntyre's assessment to note that this psychological identification is, to significant degree, bilateral. That is to say, parents identify their children's desires with their own; they do in fact easily adopt and pursue them *as* their own. If children discover that their desire fulfillment is dependent upon parental desires, by the same token, parents often find it impossible to be satisfied themselves apart from fulfilling their children's desires. The tail often wags the dog.

Now, this does not mean that parents always pursue or fulfill their children's desires any more than they are necessarily constrained to act on any of their own. The point is that the strong identification parents feel with their children very often leads to a proximate adoption of their needs and desires as the parents' own. There is, of course, a basic asymmetry here insofar as adults possess the requisite physical and financial resources to meet needs and desires, and children are ultimately dependent upon that. Yet this is substantially mitigated by the fact that, as Aristotle observes, parents have a much greater awareness and experience of their connection to their children and thus tend to love them more than can be reciprocated.[42] There is also often an underlying asymmetry to the degree that parents have developed the virtues and capacities of practical reason necessary to separate their desires (and thus their children's desires) from a rational consideration of all parties' long-term and objective goods. Yet, here again, the intensity of parental love, the closeness of one's children to the bone, may well require from them another degree of restraint and rational objectivity altogether.

The point here is that the close, often subconscious, identification of desires and motivations that affects the self-perception of children (and thus raises concerns about their independence) *also* profoundly affects the self-perception and "subjective motivational set" of parents. Procreation of a child is in an important way an *enlargement of the self* before it is a creation of *another*. Recognition of this degree of psychological identification—the way in which parents really do perceive and act as if children were a part of themselves, as belonging to themselves—should alert us to a unique set of dangers, as well as a unique set of advantages. Let us briefly consider each in turn.

IDENTIFICATION: DANGERS AND BENEFITS

I think the most salient dangers are twofold: indulgence and projection. As noted, it is immediately clear that parents who have not themselves cultivated the virtues of practical reason will tend simply to react to their child's desires as they react to their own, and pursue the child's interests in the same way that they pursue their own (to the degree, of course, that this identification maintains). This may involve crass indulgence or more sophisticated calculation—essentially incorporating a child into one's own perception and pursuit of goods, however that plays out in individual cases. However, the main concern would seem to run the other way, insofar as identification entails not simply the *inclusion* of a child's desires in one's own, but also the *attribution* or *projection* of one's own desires to the child. If children are prone to internalize their parents' desires for them, common experience alerts us to the fact that parents are themselves often likely to *project* those desires. This does not seem to be, in the first instance, a *reference* of a child to one's own desires or purposes, but rather a failure to adequately differentiate the distinct desires of two separate persons. Inclusion of a child's desires in one's own "motivational set" easily results in this sort of conflation and further tendency parents have toward "vicarious experience" in their children.

Now, obviously moral education requires a certain level of imposition of a parent's desires upon the child in a way that directs her toward goods. By the same token, this overlay of desires, which for a parent, to tweak Aristotle's point here, is felt more acutely because of greater awareness of their basic connection, presents challenges corollary to those that MacIntyre develops from the child's perspective. Moreover, once we have acknowledged this point about *identification*, it is not hard to see its further connections to problems of *reference*. An inclusion of a child within one's self-conception, an incorporation of her desires into my own and identification of my own desires with hers, all seems well-tailored to the further step of incorporating a child within one's own plans or purposes and acting in such a way as to ensure that this child's good becomes a part of my own—that is, ultimately serves my own ends.

The basic recognition of these problems—both of identification and reference—may lead us to question the general plausibility of MacIntyre's description of the parent-child relationship, particularly whether or not he is justified in speaking in terms of the "ordinary good mother." However, for reasons that begin to come clear in consideration of the *positive aspects* of parent-child identification, I think that he is.

Despite these difficulties, the degree of identification in parent-child relationships presents substantial goods. We may recall what was noted at the outset: Aristotle first associates the love of "another self," which is essentially constitutive of friendship, with the love of parents for children. The reason for this (Aquinas reasons) is that it is precisely this experience of identification—experiencing a child as a "separable part" (or "separated part") of oneself—that bears the closest (*propinquissima*) resemblance to love of oneself,[43] and Aristotle takes self-love to be the basis of all friendship. Now, we cannot address here the fundamental difficulty of Aristotle's theory of friendship—whether a good man is related to a friend as he is to himself, thus making self-love the basis of friendship—but we need not. Our concern is to understand the relationship between the self and the other as it manifests itself in familial belonging (and perhaps then better understand and assess Aristotle's claim about friendship).

Briefly, then, there are five characteristics that Aristotle identifies with friendly relations: (1) wishing and doing good things for a friend; (2) wishing for the existence and life of a friend for his or her own sake; (3) spending time with a friend; (4) having a unity of desires; and (5) sharing sorrows and joys.[44] Aristotle says that (5) is most often found in mothers and (2) is a feeling common in mothers toward their children, as well as in friends who remain so despite quarrelling. Characteristics (4) and (5) have been central to the analysis thus far, but it is (2) that makes the essential point here. The fundamental relational good of belonging, as it concerns a state of identification, involves perceiving and acting with the same recognition of another's goodness, simply rooted in her *being* and *continued existence*, which one intrinsically has toward oneself. As with oneself, this is not an assessment or evaluation of worth. It is simply an appreciation that refers to no other end, takes cognizance of no other attributes, than simply what it is to *be* that person. Mothers, Aristotle says, display this to the degree that they would delight in observing and knowing about the lives of their children even if completely unobserved themselves.[45]

This kind of "joy" in another's existence—first of all rooted in a basic identification of selves—not simply a unity, of course, but something more than a union—is of immediate and obvious value.[46] I will have more to say about this further on; suffice it to say here that commentators of all stripes acknowledge its importance to providing children with at least "a sense of their own value and a confidence in their ability to fulfill their intentions."[47]

Yet, as I have tried to demonstrate, there are genuine difficulties in an iden-tification of this kind. Despite the foundation for a real unity of persons, children exist as separate persons, and particularly because of the inequality of the relationship, are vulnerable to being overwhelmed or in some senses subsumed.

Up to this point, however, we have proceeded by narrowing the focus (as much as possible) to one angle or aspect of the relationship, that is, parental belonging specifically insofar as it is characterized as an identification with one's child in an *expansion* of the self. This considers a child insofar as she might be viewed as a *part* of a whole. We cannot, of course, entirely prescind (even in a limited consideration of *belonging*) from an important fact: chil-dren are individual persons whose existence, in whatever way it pertains to their progenitors, is unique and distinct. This fact must necessarily inform a full understanding of what belonging might be, for in reality parents do not abstract from the fact of a child's distinct existence. Nor, for that matter, does Aristotle isolate *belonging* from its larger context. The elements distin-guishable in the concept "other self" are not hermetically sealed; they are, in fact, proximately related. Therefore, in order to fully understand a child's identification with the self, we must think about her existence as an *other* self—issuing from parents, but established in separate existence as an *other*. Let us then turn to such a consideration.

CHILDREN AS DISTINCT "OTHERS"

Despite Aristotle's strong statements about the obligations and debt of gratitude owed to parents,[48] we should remember that the observations about belonging we have just discussed occur within the context of an argu-ment about parental *knowledge* and personal connection. It is not primarily a point about the substantial relationship between parents and children. Of greater importance, however, is the fact that Aristotle is brought in one seamless thought from his strong characterization of physical unity to estab-lish a fundamental discontinuity between the two, begetter and begotten. "So we see that parents love their children as themselves: offspring is, as it were, another self, 'other' because it exists separately."[49] There is simply the patent physical fact that here exists a separate being, one who despite ances-try and extreme dependence, exists as a distinct, perceiving self who biologi-cally and mentally functions as a "self-integrating organism."[50] To recognize this fact is to encounter a relationship that coexists with the child himself, as it follows from who he is. Self-perception implies no relationship (except in-sofar as one might be said analogically to regard oneself[51]), nor does perception of the *other*. In perceiving a distinct human person as *of oneself*, however, one perceives an *other self*, a relationship created by the other's existence.

Furthermore, one immediately encounters the fact that this person is the combined creation of *two* parents—distinct from each in part because the genetic expression of both. In the definitive sense of *possession*, a child belongs to neither parent by virtue of his distinct personhood. Yet, even in the partial sense entailed in the closeness of the physical and personal bond, a child belongs exclusively to neither parent because he belongs in this way to both equa*lly*. Consider: my perception of an *other* self is not only informed by separate consciousness of the child, but by apprehension of this child as himself united to another person. A separate person exists who—contrary to being simply a part of me—I must understand *myself to be a part*. In procreation, two persons contribute equal parts in the generation of a new human being. This is not an *expansion* of the self as was implied by the perception of a child as being *of me*. It is to be united *of oneself* to what is outside of or beyond oneself, inasmuch as the child is equally *of the other parent*. In this way, the parental relationship is not simply a connection between oneself and another insofar as one perceives a child to belong to oneself. It is in a fundamental way a *drawing out of oneself* inasmuch as a parent perceives himself to be both a part of this child *and* connected of himself to the child's other parent. Inasmuch as parents each give of themselves to create a person to whom each is intimately connected, they are correlatively connected to each other (in important ways *dependent* upon each other) and bear responsibilities not only to the child but also to each other.

The relationships of belonging, therefore, run not simply from each parent to the child, but because two equally contribute *of themselves*, from the child to each parent and ultimately between parents. Thus it is that a father does not simply encounter in a child a reflection of himself but a reflection of the mother as well. Often times physical and personal resemblances are combined in such a way as to reflect both parents simultaneously, so that what is in a sense an expression of self-love (delighting in a child as *my child*) becomes substantially and experientially indistinguishable from delighting in another—both the child himself and the other parent.[52]

Recognizing one's child as an *other* self further entails that the relationship cannot be reduced to an ultimate stance of self-regard. Aristotle's account of benefaction might be applied in this way to unequal relationships of giving and receiving: benefactors realize their *own* potential in the good they bring into actuality. Benefactors love a beneficiary because they love their own existence.[53] Whereas there is an element of real truth here, it might suggest what I think is a false dichotomy between the respective goods of giver and receiver, for benefactors such as a parent or ruler most fully realize their own potential *precisely* in maximizing the capacities and goods of those within their care. According to Aquinas's classic definition of law, this is essentially what it *means* to have authority, and as Aristotle notes, the greatness of rulership is measured relative to the excellence of the souls within one's care.[54] Thus, clear-sighted benefactors realize that even loving their own existence qua benefactor is essentially united to the good and flourishing of their beneficiaries. Nevertheless, as a practical matter, there is often enough a tendency to collapse the interests or goods of intended beneficiaries into one's own self-interested motivations. As I noted previously, such overreaching may well follow from the close personal connection between parent and child, but the dynamics of *otherness* under consideration serve as a powerful corrective.

Because a child is one's own, he is immediately loved for his own sake, that is, simply *as* and *because* he is. *From identity with the self follows love of a child's being or actuality.* At the same time, a salient feature of childhood is that children are in essential part a bundle (so to speak) of undeveloped potentialities. Therefore, to love children for that which they are simply entails loving them for what they will and can become. To perceive a child as other is to perceive him as a person with unique abilities, capacities, and desires, which may be widely divergent from one's own. Thus, from the love of a child's being and acknowledgment that it is other and distinct from one's own follows a particular attentiveness to identifying and cultivating a child's innate capabilities. *From apprehension of the other follows a love for a child's unique potentiality.* That is to say, parental love is essentially educative, intensely concerned with children realizing all those abilities and goods of which they are capable. And in this way parents are most concerned with moving beyond the simple identity of selves and dependence in which children are born to a mature state of self-possession and independent exercise of human virtues. In this vein, MacIntyre describes the transition from dependent to independent practical reason: "Yet what those adults have to teach the child if the child is indeed to become an independent practical reasoner, is that it will please them, *not* by acting so as to please them, but by acting so as to achieve what is good and best, whether this pleases them or not."[55]

Clearly this is the kind of educative aim that many contemporary theorists, Amy Gutmann chief among them, view as simply beyond the ken of family life. Such independent capacity for critical evaluation of one's upbringing could hardly be an attractive objective for parents who "desire above all to perpetuate their particular way of life."[56] MacIntyre himself immediately acknowledges that "all adults find it difficult and some find it impossible to teach this."[57] There is no doubt that it is an intractably difficult task, both because of the imperfection of the parties involved and the inequality of the relationship. Yet, as I have noted, MacIntyre possesses a fundamental optimism in the capacities of the "ordinary good mother" to achieve this end. I have endeavored to demonstrate that the fundamental tendency of parental belonging, while certainly subject to missteps or even abuses, justifies this optimism.

The reason for this stems from a basic understanding of parental belonging as an outwardly oriented relationship. Children are unique in their immediate extension of an individual's self-conception and inclusion within the individual's own good. Whereas this opens the possibility of inadequate differentiation or respect for a child as a separate person, it also gives rise to a powerful love and delight that, in a sense, takes for granted the goodness and worth of a child.

Parents are, moreover, intimately connected with their children as *others*. Insofar as children exist separately and as the unified creation of two persons, they are themselves a *part* of other persons. If experience of a child as part of oneself suggests the idea of belonging, recognition of oneself as a part of others completes the circle in *mutual belonging*. Perhaps the perplexities of genuine friendship—coming to identify the other with oneself—are in the first instance precisely reversed in parenthood, that is, coming to see what is *oneself* as *other: another*. Unlike the case of friendship, however, parties do not perceive and appreciate each other first as distinct individuals, in time coming to regard each other as "other selves." Rather, the relationship must develop within a context in which identities are interconnected more than any other. If this is the case, then the experience of parenthood tends toward friendship in an outward motion, as it were. Individuals are, in a profoundly personal way, drawn out of themselves to regard, love, and care for what is of themselves but must also be recognized as other.

We should be careful to say that this is initially a matter of *perception of the good*, not yet an *ethical* matter of directing others toward oneself or referring their goods to one's own. (This recalls the distinction between *identification* and *reference*.) Friendship does serve to draw one out of oneself, but in order for that to happen (affectively and in the will) we must first come to *perceive* goods. Another way to put this is that unity causes love, love causes seeing, and seeing, in turn, causes love.

Positive Effects of the Relationship of Mutual Belonging

NEED FOR BELONGING

I have up to this point focused primarily on the nature of the parent-child relationship from the viewpoint of parents, as it has been the main task of the argument to clarify the character of parental love. It is worth shifting perspectives in order to consider a few ways in which familial belonging positively affects the maturation and education of children. In so doing I begin to address the Platonic and Aristotelian quandaries about the relationship between the family and state. This is, however, only a beginning. A full consideration of the relative importance of familial and political associations and of their respective insulation or authority relative to each other requires consideration of further issues I cannot raise here. Nevertheless, I do hope to shed additional light on the goods realized in familial relationships, which in turn suggests a general approach or orientation to the political questions.

The first thing to remark on is the correspondence between the parental belonging I have discussed and a child's need *to belong*. Aristotle thought that because they are less aware of their origins, children tend to love less than they are loved.[58] This may be true, but at the same time people evince a deep need to be connected with their biological origins, in particular their parents. It is a desire for relationship with those persons from whom one's existence was generated that if unsatisfied in childhood persists into adulthood.[59] In other words, the fact of belonging—that despite subjective independence as human persons, who we are is organically linked, even derived, from others—gives rise to a profound need *for belonging*. It is an awareness that the *self* is immediately and intimately connected to an *other*, that the other is part of one's self. Thus, the experience of *other self* and the relationship of belonging (i.e., you are a part of me) also runs in the other direction.

This is one aspect of what it means to be an embodied being in a particular place and time, standing in intrinsic relation to others—"'stuck with' a history and a people." "Without the family, and the inter-generational ties involved, we have no way to know what it means to be historic beings."[60] It would be a mistake, of course, to describe this simply as a desire for *knowledge* of one's origins. The need is most immediately relational. Just as a parent's personal identification with a child gives rise to a simple delight and appreciation in the child herself, children evince a basic need to be loved, appreciated, and connected to those with whom they are so identified. Jean

Bethke Elshtain makes a corroborative point in her argument that a child's successful structuring of self and other requires long-term relationships with "specific beloved others"—either parents or their "permanent not temporary surrogates."[61]

It is also important to note that the relational dynamic goes somewhat beyond the primarily Kantian concerns of philosopher Jeffrey Blustein's treatment of the parent-child relationship. In Blustein's account, parental love and affirmation serve to provide children "a sense of their own value and a confidence in their ability to fulfill their intentions."[62] Whereas I think that the elements Blustein (and others) emphasize are critically important to the healthy maturation of children, it is also easy to speak of the parent-child relationship in these terms as, in a sense, conferring a status on an autonomous moral agent—that is, confident self-possession—rather than as constituting a relationship integral to the person.[63] These elements are not necessarily opposed, but the concern with a child's individual self-conception stops short of recognizing the relational character of self-identity.

Such insensitivity is particularly marked in Robin West's concerns with the nature of familial relationships. West provocatively argues: "Family love is intense, and we need it to survive and thrive. It is also deeply contingent on the existence and nature of family ties. Children are loved in a family *because* they are children of the parents in the family. The 'unconditional love' they receive is anything but unconditional: it is conditioned on the fact that they are their parents' children." In contrast, the "welcome respite" of a school environment affords a child the opportunity to be regarded and respected as an independent individual, that is, simply for herself.[64]

There are a couple of things to say in response to this. In the first place, West elides an important distinction between a *cause* of love and an *object* of love. As we have spent a good deal of time considering, it is indeed the case that parents love their children in the first instance *because* they are their own. The parental relationship explains why this parent has an immediate, intimate love for this child. However, in loving *someone* and in seeing them as lovable, the object of love itself becomes a further and primary cause of love. Seeing causes loving. This marks the movement from *self* to *other* that organic familial connections affect. Whereas it is hardly likely that a parent would come to love a child in abstraction from their relationship—this is always a special cause of love—it is equally unlikely that a parent does not come to appreciate a child for who she is and to see the goodness of hidden attributes, or even of those that do not immediately inspire affection. West's contrast between a parent's basically self-regarding love and a teacher's care and regard for a child irrespective of their relationship presupposes that parents never come to regard and appreciate their children as *other* selves. Why should anyone be concerned that a natural relationship is the *cause* of love if it directs the lover to see and delight in the beloved in her own right?

This raises what is, perhaps, a more fundamental assumption in West's account, namely, that being regarded for or in oneself entails being regarded independently of any relationships one might have. It seems that in West's view regard for this child simpliciter cannot include or take cognizance of her natural relationships. In essence, it entails an atomistic self. The problem with this view is perhaps best revealed by asking West: if, as she says, paternal love is "deeply contingent" and "anything but unconditional," under what conditions might it be true that *this* mother and father are not the parents of *this* child? The answer is none, of course: to contemplate different parentage is to contemplate a different person altogether. Thus we must acknowledge that to consider persons apart from their natural relationships is to consider not human beings, but conceptual abstractions.

West may reply that her point is that parents regard children under a particular aspect, that is, *relative* to themselves. Yet (putting my first criticism aside), why shouldn't that qualify as regarding a child according to something that is inherent to any accurate and fully meaningful description of who she is? Inasmuch as a child deeply experiences and grows to understand this relationship, would it not constitute a profound affirmation and appreciation of who the child is? If the argument I have advanced is persuasive, indeed it would.

PARENTAL LOVE AND EDUCATION

If parental belonging uniquely addresses needs related to a child's cultivation of a sense of self, it is also true that the character of parental love has a uniquely powerful *communicative* effect that can serve to rightly orient children to virtue. This dynamic transpires, I think, at a couple of different levels (or, perhaps, develops in relational stages).

As I have already noted, Aristotle appreciates the educational utility of the parent-child relationship, inasmuch as parental affection and care engender affectionate response and the willingness (generally) to comply with parental instruction. I may say further that constancy in such care over time creates a relationship and general environment of security and trust in which children are released from "felt needs," and the range of activities worth pursuing for their own sakes is expanded.[65] In one sense, this fundamentally liberal stance toward activity is facilitated by affection, security, recognition, and the freedom to independently conceive and pursue activities (i.e., play). This may be thought of as the *liberal environment* of the family.

In another, deeper sense, however, the parental relationship not only facilitates a liberal environment but *communicates* the independent desirability of goods and virtues to which parents direct their children out of love. Here too, I think we can helpfully differentiate a couple of levels. In the first place, the experience of being loved would seem intrinsically to communicate to the beloved that the lover desires his good, and thus pursues things for his good.[66] Children who perceive a parent's delight are thus oriented to something recommended to them by the parent *as good*, and thus worthy of pursuit simply on its own merits, that is apart from the recommendation. Thus, as an educative matter, the simple fact that love underwrites the process itself communicates something about what is being learned. Now, this dynamic occurs in some sense across the spectrum of human relations insofar as they are naturally characterized by goodwill,[67] and its force would seem to increase through the influence of several relational factors: (1) the degree to which one is appreciated *for oneself* (as in the movement between friendships of utility and pleasure); (2) the degree to which good is desired "on account of" the beloved (i.e., not for the further reason of self-regarding good, which pleasure friendship entails); and (3) the intensity according to which the love is felt.[68] Factors (1) and (3) are perhaps most easily and immediately communicated in the parent-child relationship owing to the sheer pleasure parents derive from their children and the extreme ends to which this often takes them—frequently with only subsequent consideration of the costs. These aspects of parental love are powerful, but (2), I think, takes us to a deeper communicative level, one that more complexly unfolds in the course of a parent-child relationship.

What I have in mind here is characterized, in the short term, by the conflict and disparity between action and expectations that inheres in any educative endeavor, and in the long run, the possibility of unrealized potential and disappointed hopes faced in every life. In essence, the nature of the day-to-day educative enterprise, as well as the long-term goals parents have for their children, affects a powerful and deeply communicative dynamic in the relationship. We may well allow Aristotle's point that familial affection aids moral training, while still acknowledging that the process is fraught with conflict. We should *expect* conflict insofar as moral education itself presupposes the need for some degree of formation and curbing of unruly desires. We should, moreover, *desire* it insofar as it is a natural part of the necessary differentiation of personalities and desires necessary to a child's maturing independence. It is, nevertheless, difficult, and in such moments of moral guidance, a clear difference emerges between one's love of a child simpliciter and one's love and delight in a child as good, virtuous, pleasant, and pleasing. It is in this disparity that one encounters the fundamental difficulty MacIntyre notes in orienting a child *to the good*, in the final analysis, whether it pleases one's parents or not.

The pivotal point in this process seems to boil down to a parent's simple recurrence to (and intentional communication of) the love that simply takes for granted the goodness and worth of a child as an *other self*. It is never easy, of course, to put aside inconvenience, frustration, and anger in order to access this deeper and more abiding "joy" in a recalcitrant child or rebellious youth (even while ensuring that appropriate consequences for bad behavior are met). However, to the degree that parents succeed in cultivating and tapping into this basic interconnectedness with their children, the underlying communicative aspects of the relationship take on a fundamentally liberal character: Children are not required to perform virtuous acts or develop virtuous habits as a means to being pleasing (even though virtue is inherently pleasant) because they are recognized to be good and lovable despite being nonvirtuous and noncompliant. Inasmuch as they are loved apart from virtue, the required virtue is commended to them as itself good and lovable—not as something that makes them lovable, but as a good desired for them because they are loved. Thus, by means of a relationship of belonging, virtue is presented as its own end, something worth pursuing for its own sake. *It is the liberality of familial love that informs a liberal stance toward virtue.*

Over the long haul, the force of this liberal love is felt in its unstinting permanence, the preference for one's child despite failure in achieving those objectives and hopes in which parents are so heavily invested. It is natural and important that they should be so invested (at least in a general sense). It is clear, moreover, that even in disappointed hope, love that is concerned with cultivating and realizing the goodness of a child's potential never relents in assisting toward these ends. To love a human person simply entails this prospective quality.

At the same time, love that is committed to a child "come what may," with a "systematic refusal . . . to treat the child in a way that is proportional to its qualities," simply rests in one's child as he is. And it would seem that the communicative force of liberal love in this wider context would serve, in an analogous sense, to structure one's life with a liberal stance toward virtue and achievement—even as the love and approval of parents diminishes in immediate significance as a child enters adulthood.

There is a further point to be made here. On the one hand, I have pointed to the communicative importance of quotidian interactions, and on the other, formation of an overarching structure to one's long-term goals. The two poles are connected, the content and outlook of virtue inculcated, by the routine practice of virtuous actions performed in a virtuous way—by what Aristotle called habituation. Miles Burnyeat helpfully emphasizes that this habituation is not merely the establishment of rote activity or predilection. Rather, there is an important "cognitive slant" inherent in the process of habituation.[69] Careful habituation succeeds in establishing a kind of experiential knowledge, an understanding of "the that" of virtue; that is, it establishes by experience that performing acts of virtue is in fact pleasant. At this early stage, one need not, indeed cannot, understand "the why" of virtue—the full explanation of human capacities and goods that provides the full context, defense, and specification of virtue. However, it is Aristotle's point that in order even to get to this explanatory and refining phase, one must begin with a certain degree of knowledge, since all moral inquiry necessarily begins from some fundamental starting point. This is the task of habituation: providing the basic experiential knowledge of the desirability of virtue that provides a starting point for mature analysis, refinement, and understanding.[70] As Jacques Maritian explains connatural knowledge, the line of thinking within natural law theory that develops Aristotle's "cognitive slant," "It is not rational knowledge, knowledge through the conceptual, logical and discursive exercise of Reason. But it is really and genuinely knowledge, though obscure and perhaps incapable of giving account of itself, or of being translated into words."[71]

The additional point, therefore, is that the communicative character of the parental relationship serves, over time, to effectively communicate an important kind of experiential knowledge about the independent goodness of virtue. Virtue, liberally pursued within the context of parental education, is cultivated and ultimately *understood* liberally. This does not, of course, obviate the importance of further discursive reflection on the character and content of virtue, but it does clarify the importance of the educative dynamic within the family. It is not simply a domain of affective primacy, no matter how necessary and beneficial we are willing to allow that emotion is. On the contrary, the inherent tendency of ordinary familial relationships serves to provide children a basic orientation and knowledge of virtue that is required in the fullest rational account of a virtuous soul. And, as we will see, if the family is a vital locus of rationality uniquely suited to promoting real human flourishing, its relative independence and integrity must be maintained in any persuasive account of the political common good.

Concluding Remarks

In conclusion, let us turn to reconsider the remaining worries about familial association in light of the arguments I have just advanced.

INEQUALITY

Clearly, the inequality of the parent-child relationship cannot be gainsaid, and it does, in some respects, raise questions concerning the welfare of children. Contemporary theorists seem in part to be motivated by a commendable desire to protect children and to look for ways to redress this vulnerability. Equally clear, however, is that the vulnerability is an intractable characteristic of the human condition, that is, the reality of birth and gradual maturation. The question, therefore, is how that vulnerability is best to be protected, given that any context whatever will be marked by substantial inequalities. Despite theorists like West's supposition of a "safe haven" in the public realm of independent, individual respect, it is difficult to see how relationships with peer groups and teachers alleviate the problem. (This is, of course, not to say that interaction with teachers other than one's parents and friendships developed even in relatively early youth cannot profoundly affect children for the good, and motivate them to virtue in ways they do not encounter within the family.)

The underlying problem with much liberal theory, however, is the competing-rights paradigm brought to bear on the problem. Parental interests are often treated as simply "expressive" or "self-regarding," which naturally means that they will often militate against a child's long-term good. Therefore, immediate emotional needs met in the family have to be balanced against securing more enduring interests. As I have argued, this paradigm simply misconceives the basic character of parent-child relationships. These relationships unfold not toward possessive subordination of a child's good but toward a fundamentally friendly stance toward one's children as *other* selves. For the ordinary good parent, it is precisely the experience of the inequality of the relationship, the vulnerability of their children, and the awareness that each choice they make on a son or daughter's behalf may affect them profoundly—and certainly will so affect them in the aggregate— inspires in most parents a desire to achieve their best selves, not simply for themselves, but in the interests and for the good of their children.

THE KNOWLEDGE PROBLEM

As I noted at the outset, a basic aspect of what I have labeled the "Aristotelian dilemma" (one among many dilemmas) is the value of special parental knowledge and guidance of one's children relative to the universal dimensions and principles that are the study of the legislator. Robert Reich gives contemporary expression to this basic worry by noting the high contestability of parental claims to have *real knowledge* of what the best life is for their children. Perhaps a broader, more objective perspective distilled in political life affords the state a better claim to such insight.[72] I do not take the discussion here to be fully dispositive of this issue. It is not an issue, in truth, subject to full disposition, contingent as it is upon vagaries of time, place, and especially persons involved. However, the discussion here does, I think, substantially favor an underlying formal principle of subsidiarity. My reasons for thinking so are as follows.

First, as I have just restated, it is a mistake to view the set of questions raised in the relationship between the family and the state as a somehow turning on a basic distinction between spheres of emotion and of rationality, respectively. To do so is not only, as I have argued, to underestimate and simplify the solidly rational orientation and aspirations of family life but is to inflate the claims to objective knowledge obtainable in the public sphere. Second, and perhaps more to the point, the nature of familial love is inherently, ineluctably educative. To love a maturing human person simply is to love his or her developing capacities and unfolding potential. Moreover, this educative relationship exists between parent and child from the outset of the relationship, such that, prior to a child's reaching majority, any unwelcome educative activity intended directly for children is an interposition. The very great goods inherent in the parent-child relationship require that such interference be pursued, as William Galston recommends, only in cases of clear abuse.[73] As a practical matter, this would seem to require close curricular and administrative oversight by local school boards.

CIVIC EDUCATION

Aside from what has already been said, a suitable answer to the question of state interests in education of youth largely goes beyond the scope of this chapter. It requires an articulation of the good of political community not yet undertaken. It is worth noting, however, another fundamental problem in much of the rights-based liberal theory we have discussed. In addition to the desire to safeguard children, very much of it is guided by the civic interest in educating future citizens. This is a reasonable and worthy goal; however, if not pursued in an appropriate manner, with deference to parental guidance of education, it runs the risk of taking an unreasonably *prospective view* of the child.

Philosopher of childhood Gareth Matthews has written about the tendency in dominant theories of moral education to take a strongly prospective view of children, that is, to view them primarily in terms of their future potential and to treat current activities and educational efforts as largely directed to meeting future developmental goals.[74] This is, of course, a very important part of childhood, but if unbalanced by an appreciation for the current state and existence of the child that in itself fully actualizes a unique part of what it is to be human, we are likely to miss the importance of today by thinking only of tomorrow. And this, in addition to simply missing the meaning of the moment, itself undermines the future good we're seeking. An application of Matthews's work to these problems warns against treating children as *future citizens* in a way that undermines their current well-being as children. Rights-based theories are particularly prone to this mistake because of the tendency to view parents' and children's interests as in conflict with each other.

The primary objective of my argument in this chapter has been to give a substantive account of the familial good. In so doing I have sought to be specifically responsive to long-standing political worries that derive from assessments of the family's affective particularity and relational inequality. Over against a picture of the family that paints it as simply a necessary locus of affective attachments largely directed toward the self-interest of adults, I have emphasized two counter-theses: First, parental love is basically *outwardly directed* inasmuch as self-love is brought to intimate engagement and appreciation of another person and deep concern for his or her distinct good. Second, parental love is *inherently educative*—and thus rationally driven—insofar as in loving a child parents are drawn into a careful and sustained consideration of human goods as they seek to cultivate or educate (literally, "to lead out") a child's potential talents and capacities. Moreover, parental love is rational in effect as well insofar as its unconditional character is essential, perhaps absolutely necessary, to rightly orienting children in a fully rational stance toward virtue. Thus, the fundamental character of the family, deriving as it does from the parental relationship,[75] belies the concerns of its detractors.

Accordingly, the family must be regarded as a primary and irreplaceable locus of substantive human flourishing. Familial love not only structures relationships within the family, in creating an association of mutual regard, affection, and shared good, it creates an experiential knowledge and appreciation of mutual cooperation. Family life makes the possibility of a genuine common good plausible. Thus, it is often, and rightly, referred to as the first school of social virtues. And, of course, it does have an important role to play as part of the broader political society. This is evident not only from its material insufficiency and dependence but also from the positive outward orientation of its educative drive and the generous nature of the love that animates it.

In the following chapters, I turn to consider that broader political good specifically, first, by delineating its formal characteristics as an association of associations (Chapter 3), and second, by articulating its substantial nature as realized in civic friendship (Chapter 4) and political culture (Chapter 5).

Formal Characteristics of
Political Association

Every association, Aristotle tells us, is formed for some purpose; there is
some end that it seeks.[1] The concept of a common good is, of course, most
closely associated with the purpose or raison d'être of the political community, but it is a concept of much broader application. Common good identified with political community is taken to be *the* common good because of
its claim to supremacy, as in some sense embracing all goods within a community and thus taking priority over them all as the architectonic good.[2]
Yet, this is not an unproblematic claim. Basic to Aristotle's account of associations is the recognition that associations, whether friendships, families,
clubs, polities, and so on, are quite different in character. The political community, he is keen to point out, does not merely differ in number or extension from other communities. It takes on a qualitative difference in kind.[3]
Yet if it is different in kind, realizing a good and mode of interaction that is
fundamentally distinct from other associational goods, how is its claim to
supremacy to be sustained? Perhaps other goods outstrip the political common good as, for example, Aristotle's central case of virtuous friendship appears to be better—more intensely instantiating human good—than civic
friendship. Or, if we ground the political common good in its greater inclusivity of disparate (and perhaps better) goods, in what sense is its greatest
good actually common or its most common good that great? Greater exten-

sion of goodness seems to entail attenuation that diminishes the qualitative value of any commonness.

This brings us back to the point with which natural law theory is much preoccupied, namely, the apparent fact that political community does not have a monopoly on common good and many of the goods realized prior to political community seem superior to its good. Its claim to supremacy must be articulated and evaluated within a general context of human sociability in which real common goods are created and enjoyed within a range of human associations. Thus, any account of *political common good* must orient itself within a broader framework. To this end, let us first ask the question, what do we mean by a *common good*? Remember that the goal at this point is not to specify what precisely the substance of various common goods is, but rather what the formal characteristics are of goods that should be recognized as common. These formal questions provide necessary background to substantive questions, that is, those specifying what exactly the content of the common good is. Given the complexity of human associations—the various purposes and modes of interaction they involve—we must first be clear about precisely what we mean by "common good." Then we can ask if political community plausibly realizes one. That question will be taken up in the next chapter.

What Is Meant by "Common Good"?

Gregory Froelich's tripartite analysis of Aquinas's account of the common good provides helpful structure to the range of issues raised in this question. Additionally, Mark Murphy reworks and elaborates Froelich's analysis in illuminating ways. Froelich identifies three basic kinds of commonness in Aquinas's thought: those by predication, by causation, and by distribution or enjoyment (i.e., common *goods*).[4] A good common by predication is one that can be attributed to multiple persons, although the people do not share in their possession of it.[5] Commonness in this sense is simply a logical concept, insofar as all those referenced possess the same attribute. We may say, for example, that all Olympic athletes are healthy, and in a sense excellent health is something they have in common. Yet, what we have identified is a property that each possesses individually, since groups as such do not enjoy physical health. The health that each athlete enjoys is not one and the same, but is common only insofar as it is a property descriptive of the kind of thing each athlete is. Knowledge and happiness work in a similar manner (though such attributes require a high degree of generality to be predicated broadly).

Now, although commonness by predication does not precisely denote a *shared good*, it is foundational to the idea of the common good insofar as the very possibility of sharing in goods, or pursuing common states of affairs that facilitate individual goods, requires a common human nature. If the natures of two creatures are so disparate that they can share no good by predication, there is no possibility of common good between them. This difficulty underlies Aristotle's question about whether one would desire the ostensibly greatest good for his friend, that is, becoming a god. To wish such a thing would be to dissolve the friendship by eliminating the possibility of common good between two radically different kinds of being.[6] A direct political example of this relationship is evident in the marked attenuation of the common good in the modern period. In the work of Thomas Hobbes, for instance, the dilution of human nature entails a dilution of the potential for common good. Hobbes's minimalist notion of the common good as a mutual assent to sovereign power for the sake of personal self-preservation is directly connected to his remarkably reductive account of human nature in terms of primal passions—most basically, the fear of violent death.[7]

For the moment, let us pass over Froelich's second category of commonness by causation to consider the third: commonness by distribution. Aquinas most often marks this usage by a plural construction, common goods (*bona communia*), in order to identify particular material goods. Common goods are assets or resources that are cultivated, protected, or managed in common but are distributed or enjoyed independently. Such public resources as water are immediately necessary for life, and thus, as Aristotle argues, explain the very existence of a community.[8] Yet, they are instrumental goods, and if the community is to exist for something more than mere life, its common good must extend to something inherently choice worthy.

Here Mark Murphy helpfully modifies Froelich's analysis by expanding this notion of distributable resources to include common purposes that are effectively, if not literally, distributed.[9] Murphy defines the category according to the intentionality of the members, which controls the character of the common *action*, rather than according to the distributive character of material goods. Distribution in Murphy's sense occurs when the end result that motivates each member of a group to action is not shared. Now, there may be a single state of affairs that each party desires to achieve—construction of a public road, for example—but this purpose is basically distributed, Murphy argues, if each party desires the road only as a means to her own travel. Evidently, this is nothing other than Aristotle's friendship of utility:

common action is undertaken for the sake of separate ends.[10] Because the association was not intended for common benefit in the first place, when it ceases to serve the purpose of any individual member it may be broken off without fault (assuming termination is conducted in a way suitable to the terms of the agreement). Of course, that each party intends the road to facilitate her own travel does not preclude the possibility of a truly common purpose. One may intend such a good for the "good of all," or the "good of the community" and as a means to one's individual good. What is necessary to exceed a distributed commonality is that members' conceptions of the final end sought essentially converge. Such convergence obtains either in the case where each member acts for the good of all members (including herself) or in the case where each member acts for the good of the group per se.

Aristotle's pleasure friendship falls into this category of distributed good, but it presents a more difficult case. It would seem to be essentially a good common by distribution insofar as each party engages the other ultimately for the sake of personal pleasure. "The friend is loved not because he is a friend, but because he is . . . pleasant. . . . Consequently, such friendships are easily dissolved when the partners do not remain unchanged."[11] At the same time, the nature of such relationships, unlike friendships of utility, depends upon *mutual* enjoyment, or "good play of the game."[12] Friendships of pleasure require that both parties really enjoy the interaction, and thus achieving one's own objective intrinsically requires attentiveness to the other's objective. Mere cooperation will not do. Pleasure friendships, therefore, require a greater concern for the good of other members than do utility friendships (or, goods common by distribution). Thus, each party does in an important sense aim at the pleasure of both, and the good is not distributed. At the same time, insofar as the common interaction is immediately sought for divergent ends—most importantly, the pleasure of the other is not sought for the other's own sake—the purpose of the relationship is fundamentally distributed.[13] The appearance of true commonality in this case turns on the distinction between intrinsic and extrinsic common goods, about which more will soon be said.

It is evident that intentionality is the decisive factor here. Even goods that require material distribution to achieve their purpose, a public reservoir for example, may be the object of genuine common good if treated as such—created and managed either "so that everyone has the water he/she needs" or "to serve the community." Both cases are importantly distinguishable from the case in which community members simply cooperate to secure their own source of water.[14] Conversely, members' intentions may transform an endeavor that seems inherently common—construction of a public park, for example—into an essentially distributed good if the purpose of the association is for members simply to secure their own personal recreation and aesthetic enjoyment. In one sense we might take the nature of the good to be inherently common, insofar as the park is publicly (i.e., commonly) owned and maintained, and as such is indivisible. On the other hand, if members of the community build the park, each for the purpose "so I can have a place to walk my dog," there is really no common good sought because no single state of affairs is desired by the members. As Murphy puts it, what is really pursued are distinct aspects of a single state of affairs.[15]

In contrast, commonness by causation entails that the motivating purpose of members' actions is a shared end. Such common good may not necessarily entail a high degree of shared life. Thus, Finnis's primary description of the political common good as a set of conditions instrumental to other social and individual goods may fit this description of community to the degree that members act to secure the necessary conditions "for the sake of all" or "for the good of the community."[16] Instrumentality itself does not entail a distributed good as long as there is a shared purpose in acting for the instrumental good. This point draws our attention to the distinction briefly mentioned earlier between intrinsic and extrinsic common goods. Pleasure friendships, I noted, present the possibility of goods sought that are inherent to the association itself but that are nonetheless common only by distribution, that is, as the association serves the friends' separate desires for enjoyable companionship. The inverse case is that of goods common by causation (i.e., a single thing or state of affairs motivates members' coordinated action), which are nevertheless extrinsic to the association itself. Finnis's version of the instrumental political common good is perhaps the most controversial case of such a good, but we have already touched on clear examples. Assuming the purpose is truly common, provision of a public utility or construction of a community park are both examples of common goods extrinsic to the association itself. Neither the park nor the utility is inherent to the common action itself; the reason for the group's association is something other than the association.

By contrast, the common good of an association such as a book club exists precisely in the common action of the members in reading and discussing texts, enjoying each other's company, and attaining the insight that comes from shared inquiry and reflection. If the intention of the members vests in a common object—the pleasure and growth of all members as a group and/or as individuals—we have entered the domain of what Aristotle identifies as the central case of friendship. Unlike friendships of pleasure, virtuous friendship is based upon love of another person's intrinsic character, the "other self," for her own sake. The goodwill that frequently characterizes human relationships in a general sense becomes established in a friend's character as a disposition to act for the other's good.[17] Moreover, the good that is sought is common inasmuch as each takes the other's good to be part of one's own, and since this love is reciprocated, recognizes one's own good to be part of the friend's good. Thus, friends come to desire their own good, in part, as a good for the friend, and vice versa. "The reciprocity of love does not come to rest at either pole."[18] So the aim of the association takes on the character of a truly common good.

In addition, most of all the good shared by friends of this sort is the activity of friendship itself. Inasmuch as friends delight in the goodness of each other's character and share the "mark of a good man" in working hard to achieve the good, their interaction ("nothing characterizes friends as much as living in each other's company") becomes a shared pursuit of the good life. Moreover, the friendship itself becomes a significant part of that shared purpose.[19] This distinction brings us to what we might designate as another level of community, inasmuch as the good sought inheres in the association itself. (Although common action for a common end is all that is required for true community, when the community itself embodies the end sought, we can recognize a higher degree of commonality or shared life. More will be said about this below. Recall that pleasure friendship, although it seeks a good intrinsic to the relationship, is not true community because a shared end is not the object.)

This central case of friendship points up a difficulty with the analysis thus far. In the course of getting at what counts as the formation of real community, a real common good, I have interwoven the concepts of friendship and group community. This is helpful insofar as virtue friendship instantiates the greatest degree of commonness, and derogation from the central case, moreover, often characterizes the common goods of wider communities. Yet, reaching the central case of friendship—those oriented to a common pursuit and sharing in a good life—brings out a fundamental discontinuity between friendship and broader community, or at least another line of analysis that must distinguish the two. The distinction is that between intensive and extensive common goods.

Despite a common misconception that having many friends is a great thing, Aristotle points out that real friendships are actually rare. This is in part due to the scarcity of virtue. But it is also due to the fact that even in the best conditions we simply do not have resources for extensive life-sharing. Even those with a mutual desire for friendship, Aristotle notes, cannot *be* friends without time and familiarity—having "eaten the specified measure of salt together."[20] Moreover, the close identification of lives, the love of another as oneself, and the intimacy that entails, simply cannot be widely shared. This is, of course, the central point of Aristotle's critique of Socrates's familial communism,[21] and I have attempted to elaborate that point in my discussion of familial association. Overextension does not simply attenuate; it substantively precludes a vast range of vital interpersonal goods.

We must recognize, therefore, that different associations are characterized by disparate ends and distinct modes of association, and thus they realize incommensurable goods. This is not to say that there is no continuity between the central case of friendship, for example, and civic friendship. Civic friendship is plausibly a reciprocated disposition to act for the good of fellow citizens. But such continuity raises its own problems. If the good sought inheres in the association itself—what seems to be a higher degree of community or common good—the greater the extension, the more the good itself is attenuated. Conversely, the closer an association's connection to the good of individual persons, the narrower its extension. From this vantage point, the most important goods (affectively and rationally) are those allowing the greatest opportunity for real friendship and common life. Of course, some goods are *only* found in extension, for example, effective defense, reliable and efficient long-term material provision. What the full range of these goods is, how they are realized, and what their merit is relative to other human goods, is our main topic of inquiry. Here two points are important to note:

1. Intensive and extensive goods are often fundamentally different and incommensurable.
2. To the degree that they share common characteristics, the goods of wider communities seem simply to attenuate those of closer communities.

In summary, then, common goods are spoken of in a number of related, but distinct, ways. Goods common by predication—denoting a shared nature—explain the existence of more specific common goods and may provide a general sense of a group's purpose. Common *goods* address the material exigencies of human existence, yet in an important sense they may be more the object of common purpose than associational goods that are distributed by intentionality. Commonness by causation does represent common intent, and thus a truly common end, but here a heightened degree of community is reached when the end sought is at least partially intrinsic to the community itself. This ultimately directs attention to the intensiveness of common good attained in virtue friendships vis-à-vis the extensiveness of goods realized in wider community relationships. Putting this final distinction aside, we have arrived at the following definition of common good per se: a common good exists most basically when common action is undertaken for a truly common aim, and most fully when the unity of the group itself is one of the intrinsic goods sought.[22]

The Political Common Good

This distinction between intensive/extensive goods is key to our understanding of the formal characteristics of the political community since political community is defined according to its extensive properties in a couple of different ways. First, classical political thought formally defines political community as possessing a full sufficiency for life—a qualitative extension. Other subpolitical associations are characterized by an outward trajectory of need—for existence, preservation, daily necessities, occasional necessities, defense, and so on—culminating in the political community's provision of the complete range of needs for life. This sufficiency is both material and intellectual or spiritual, as the city possesses not only that which is necessary to life but that which is necessary to living well. "The end, then, of the city is living well, but these other things are for the sake of the end, and a city is the community of families and villages in a complete and self-sufficient life, which we say is living happily and nobly." Such flourishing is essentially located in the rational communal pursuit of the good and the just.[23] The second extensive claim of political community is quantitative, that is, it secures the good not simply for one person but for a multitude of people. "So even though the good be the same objective for one man and the same for the whole state, it seems much better and more perfect . . . to procure and preserve the good of the whole state than the good of any one man."[24] The political common good claims to be *the* common good, rightly ordering individuals and other associations to a common purpose, because it realizes the full sufficiency of the good life and extends that good to a whole people.

A much-disputed difficulty emerges with this characterization. If the city indeed possesses this degree of completeness, it would seem to be that for the sake of which other associations exist, insofar as self-sufficiency is the goal of human association and the city attains the height of self-sufficiency. It is easy to interpret Aristotle at least as holding the view that individuals and associations are in a fundamental sense "realized" in the city, insofar as they are incomplete parts in a larger whole.[25] The flourishing of individuals and associations is most realized qua parts of the political whole. Aristotle's rebuttal of the Socratic political communism in the *Republic* cites the necessary diversity of the city, but this does not necessarily preclude taking the goods and functioning of subpolitical associations to be basically instrumental to the political whole. This reading is significantly bolstered by the classical usage of the body metaphor, and Aristotle's compact argumentation gives plenty of opportunity to integrate ideas about the completeness of the city with the body politic.[26]

The difficulty is further compounded by the idea that political science is the architectonic art—concerned with the last end in human affairs—that directs and uses all other arts for its own end. "Since [political] science uses the rest of the sciences, and since, moreover, it legislates what people are to do and what they are not to do, its end seems to embrace the ends of the other sciences."[27] The highest practical art, then, seems to direct individuals to their role as citizens and subpolitical associations to an instrumental function in fulfilling the city's purposes. These difficulties are not fully answered by noting that the city is merely a unity of order[28] because the problem is not generated simply by conceiving of the city as a natural, organic substance. The problem emerges in articulating the extensiveness of the city's common good—as an association embodying the highest end of human action and the fulfillment of other associations.

There are a number of challenges that arise in response to the claims of political community—the superiority of the contemplative life, the incompetence of government on a range of issues central to the human good, the basic equality and dignity of human persons that precludes subsumption into larger wholes[29]—but I think perhaps the most powerful one is implicit in the distinction between intensive and extensive goods that the common goods of friendship and family illustrate. This distinction is also most important to our purpose here to articulate the formal structure of the political common good. The response is this. Given the great importance of these intensive associational goods as a means and intrinsic end of human flourishing—things inherently worthwhile—what are we to make of the thought that they are in some sense completed in the political community and thus ordered to its own purposes? Is this a plausible account?

The real goods of friends and family generate a normative claim in the face of political supremacy: any contention by political community to represent the supreme common good—that controlling in human affairs—must be grounded in a substantively inclusivist account of essential subpolitical human and associational goods. That is, the plausibility of the political common good turns upon its including as substantively constitutive elements, not merely as embraced, incorporated, or instrumental parts, the essential goods that precede it.[30] The claim is that these associational goods are worth seeking for their own sakes, not simply as means to a higher good (*bonum honestum*). The intensive goods of friendship, family, and so on are such that it is very plausible to say that higher associations are sought not to fulfill them but to support them, to provide what is lacking in lives already rich with purpose and human goodness. The "greater" goods, therefore, are only such if they add to, not transform, smaller associations. If the political common good did not entail this inclusivist element, what real normative force could it claim insofar as it distorted or subsumed basic, intimate human goods? It bears noting here, as I have elsewhere, that the force of the subpolitical claim does not flow simply from an affective intensiveness, that is, a claim that "Political community must include friendship because it is most important in my life." Such a claim might explain the necessity of Aristotle's observation that "Lawgivers apparently devote more attention to [friendship] than to justice," but more is required if the *normative moral claims* of political community are to be addressed.[31] The intensiveness asserted is found in the range of personal and associational goods—physical, emotional, intellectual, spiritual—that can *only* be realized in intimate forms of human association. (I should also reiterate that this point explains the great importance of the family discussion in Chapter 2 to an adequate understanding of the political common good. The "inclusivist thesis" presently under development requires that we appreciate the existence of substantial, unique, and irreplaceable goods of intensive associations like the family.)

Now, it is important to say that this is largely a formal point: the political common good must be in part the "good of friendship" + "good of family" + "good of church" + "good of civil associations." It does not tell us what those goods are and how they are necessarily preserved. Filling out that content requires the kind of investigation I undertook of the family in Chapter 2. And, of course, that discussion only touched on one dimension of the familial good. Much more work would need to be done to flesh out the substantial goods of friendships, families, religious groups, and so forth. Nevertheless, it is an important foundational orientation to acknowledge that whatever role the family plays as part of the larger whole, it must be consistent with the goods realized in familial relationships as such.

I think that this claim is, in fact, borne out in the logic of the political common good's primacy I discussed earlier. This primacy derives from the political community's formal connection to a final end—in both cases of qualitative and quantitative extension. "Full sufficiency for living well" identifies the city as complete and the greatness of self-sufficiency as being the best end. This would seem to necessarily entail that whatever is rightly judged to be essential to living well must be taken to be a part of the city's purpose. Yet clearly this cannot mean that it is realized in the political community per se. Very many of the associational goods of friendship and family are destroyed at that level of extension. Moreover, insofar as more intimate communities reach beyond themselves to make up for what they are lacking, the motivation to do so is destroyed if their essential goods are fundamentally transformed, such that the association becomes other than it is. This recognition is completely compatible with the idea that "full sufficiency" may entail adding or contributing previously unrealized elements to the goods of subpolitical associations. As Trevor Saunders describes it, the Aristotelian ascent entails that greater associations, which first issue out of necessity, come themselves to embody new potentials beyond those things contemplated in their initial formation.[32] Reason operates on necessity and reveals at each level of association new modes of interaction and flourishing. But this does not, cannot plausibly, entail that the essential goods of prior associations become something other than what they were before. In this case "full sufficiency for life" would not be obtained, but rather a new, fundamentally altered kind of life that would require justification as such.

In similar fashion, the classic Aristotelian identification of political science with the supreme end of human affairs is a purely formal argument. The supreme end of human affairs, Aristotle reasons, must belong to the most important and truly architectonic science. Because political science appears to be the most architectonic, directing those sciences below it to its end, its concern must be the supreme good. "Thus it follows that the end of politics is the good for man."[33] Now, this statement may be read in a couple of ways. First, it may be taken as a statement about what politics must be about, namely the human good and extending that good to many people. This reading works by connecting the architectonic or controlling characteristics of politics to the controlling end of human action, that is, the human good.[34] Second, the statement may be read as identifying the good for man by the end or aims of politics. The city's interest in and definition of citizenship specify the "good for man."[35] Here, Aristotle is deemed to be saying (at least on one level) that the concerns of the polity are the supreme good, rather than that the polity must be concerned with the supreme good. The former reading is more compelling, it seems to me, both interpretively and normatively. On the second reading, we must take Aristotle to be saying that because politics functions architectonically, its good must be controlling or final. This seems simply to assume the validity of the substantive primacy of politics as such, which there seems to be little reason for Aristotle to advance with no argument. On the other hand, the first reading serves to connect, on the basis of the general form of politics, the highest end of human action, that is, the human good, with the science that seems to be responsible for pursuing it—*without* making unjustified assumptions about what the content of that good is. The argument demonstrates that politics must be concerned with the human good (and extending that good to many people).[36]

The first reading is also more normatively compelling because it orients the purpose of politics to the human good, which is, as I have argued here, replete with nonpolitical goods, rather than defining the human good according to the interests and aims of political community. If politics is taken as a unique, architectonic association that addresses itself to understanding and promoting the full range of human goods—and itself contributing to that store of worthy ends—its claim to supremacy might be compelling. But as an association definitive of the human good per se, its claims simply run aground on both the objective dimensions of human goodness (i.e., those that are not defined according to the interests or needs of the political community) and the other basic associations that indispensably contribute to that goodness.[37]

This leads us to an important formal principle of the common good: it must be inclusivist, that is, including the good of each person, and including the distinct goods of each form of association within its purview that is essential to the human good—friendships and families most essentially. This means that in formally describing the common good of political community—that which motivates formation of the political community and which justifies its authority—we must say (as a matter of formal orientation) that it is aggregative, that is, the good of each person within the community and the good of each subpolitical association essential to their flourishing as human persons. Inclusivity also entails that the aim or goal of the association—particularly insofar as it includes goods distinct from its own functioning—must be distinguished from the association itself. The preeminence of the political community's aim does not entail its preeminence as a distinct association. The central thrust of the argument here may be restated as follows:

1. The ultimacy of political community depends upon its inclusivity.
2. Because of the essential diversity of human persons and human associations, inclusivity entails aggregation of subpolitical goods.
3. Thus, political community qua ultimate is not specifically political and qua specifically political is not ultimate.

The Common Good as Aggregative and Distinctive

This inclusivist character of the political common good is what I take to be most persuasive in Mark Murphy's argument in favor of an aggregative conception of the common good, which he advances to the exclusion of Finnis's instrumentalist account and the traditional view of the common good as "distinctive," that is, realized in the good of the political community as such.[38] By engaging Murphy's argument, which in important respects runs parallel to my own, we can see what additional formal requirements must characterize the political common good if we are to give it an adequate description. My aim here is to address what should be said about political association as such. In the preceding arguments I have moved toward a description of the common good that is diverse insofar as it must be described as aggregative of individuals and subpolitical associations. Now, the question is, is there anything more that must be said about political community per se? What is the status of political association in this overall common good? To that end, let's consider Murphy's argument.

His basic concern is this: given that natural law theory grounds the authority of law in its promotion of the common good, Murphy wants to articulate a concept of the common good that plausibly explains the allegiance owed to it. He contends that this is only achieved in an aggregative conception of the common good, that is, one in which the goods realized are the intrinsic goods of those within the political community. If it is a reason to adopt a law that it would promote X's good, the reason is even greater if it would, in addition, promote A's good and B's good, and so on. (This basically reproduces the element of quantitative extension mentioned earlier.) His view, Murphy contends, does not reduce to Hobbesian individualism insofar as the good that is common—the shared aim of all reasonable agents in the community—is conceived as the good of all; that is, A's good + B's good + C's good + D's good, and so on, extending to all individual members of the community. All reasonable members of the community will take promotion of their own flourishing and that of everyone else in the community as its common purpose.[39] So the end is truly common insofar as members of the community desire and act in part for each other's flourishing. Note that this view does not entail that the good of every individual in the community is realizable in practice. Rather, it establishes the aggregated good of all as a *regulative ideal* that guides individual and common action. It may be that particular circumstances require compromise or simply lead to irreconcilable interests, but this does not prevent community members from adopting the good of all as a goal or seeing the reasonableness of doing so. Murphy advances his account against the traditional view, represented by Aquinas, in which the common good is understood as a state of affairs that is the good of (or good for) the community per se. For Aquinas, Murphy contends this good is the condition of the community's justice and peace.[40] Although Aquinas and many recent Thomists understand the allegiance the common good claims "in terms of its place in one's own overall good," what the common good realizes is distinctive to the community as such.[41]

Now, Murphy does not deny the existence, in Charles Taylor's phrase, of "irreducibly social goods," nor does he doubt their intrinsic-ness to human well-being, as our earlier discussion made evident.[42] It makes sense to speak of the good of a community per se—any range of communities from sports teams to polities. Yet, recognizing that certain intrinsic human goods are basically social does not entail, Murphy wants to maintain, that we also accept the good of the community per se as providing a fundamental reason for action. On his welfarist account of practical rationality, "all fundamental reasons for action must be framed in terms of individuals' well-being."[43] Thus, Murphy resists a reconciliation of the two views that would identify the *content* of the common good as *both* the goods of individual persons (the good of each member of the community) and the good of the community per se. To give the good of the individual human person and that of the social group equally fundamental relevance in deliberation runs afoul of a basic commitment to the human good. Therefore, for Murphy, although we may recognize the intrinsic sociability of some human goods, the only persuasive account of the common good is framed in aggregative terms—the good of all individual persons within the community.

For reasons I have already stated, I think that Murphy is right in maintaining that any plausible account of the common good must be finally grounded in the good of the individuals who comprise the association. It is insufficient and implausible to maintain that the allegiance owed to law and the common good terminates in the good functioning and purposes of the community as such. If it cannot be followed up with an account of how the community is in fact good for human persons, allegiance to the common good is indeed in serious question.

However, I think that Murphy mistakenly conflates two distinct issues: on the one hand, *allegiance* to the common good, and on the other, the *content* of the common good. The issue of allegiance, that is, why a good deserves my respect and/or pursuit, is different from the issue of content, that is, of what does the good consist?[44] He is willing to acknowledge the existence of real irreducible social goods and that the goods of associations as such are epistemically accessible. That is, we can know what it means to advance the good of a group per se. Moreover, he takes at least some of these communities to be basically constitutive of human flourishing. Nevertheless, Murphy does not think we need an idea of a distinctive common good because it ultimately must recur to the good of each one aggregatively conceived. The distinctive common good, as a matter of grounding allegiance, is superfluous.

That may be true, but given what Murphy is willing to acknowledge about the nature of social goods, I think the question is whether the character of a common good (political or otherwise) can be known without a conception of the distinctive flourishing of the association. If such a conception proves necessary, then it would seem that knowledge of a basic good—human community—is contingent upon a distinctive common good: not just the good of everyone in the community, but the good of the community as such. If this is the case, even though one may have to concede that the distinctive common good is "parasitic" on the aggregative common good with respect to the allegiance issue, with respect to the epistemological issue (i.e., is the common good sufficiently knowable?) the aggregative conception is likewise parasitic on the distinctive conception.[45] In other words, it is unclear that Murphy's claim to general epistemic access to the human good, given what he has argued about the social nature of human flourishing, can be fully granted apart from a notion of the flourishing of associations as such. If such epistemic dependence indeed obtains, it would seem that distinctive common goods must be accorded some fundamental status in the structure of practical reasoning.

Propositionally, my argument runs as follows: the first four propositions are claims Murphy defends or recognizes as true; the fifth claim is what I take to necessarily follow.

1. Human community (or friendship) is a basic human good, a
   fundamental reason for action.

2. The most significant forms of community are characterized by *intrinsic goodness*, that is, the community itself is an inherent part of the good that is sought.
3. Intrinsically good sociability is irreducibly social in that it cannot be adequately described by the goods of the parties engaged in the association. The association or its intrinsic characteristics[46] are the relevant good sought.
4. It makes sense to speak of the good condition or flourishing of an association as such, whether it is a team, club, friendship, and so on.
5. It makes sense, therefore, to speak of the good of an association as such as fundamentally relevant to deliberation, insofar as it intrinsically and irreducibly instantiates goods—community and friendship—that are constitutive of human flourishing.

Whereas Murphy is willing to acknowledge the existence of irreducible social goods and the flourishing of associations as such, he resists the further inference that claims about what is good for an entity as such have fundamental practical or moral importance. If, for example, we consider justice as the well-ordered condition of a community as such, nothing is added to its choiceworthiness once the goodness of the community's members exercising justice toward each other has been bracketed. The justice of the community as such provides no normative pull.[47] In explanation he adduces what strikes me as a telling example: "Whether a vacuum cleaner is in good or bad condition is of no fundamental practical importance—it can only be made practically relevant by appeal to other reasons for action, reasons that are themselves fundamental or appropriately connected to reasons that are fundamental."[48] His point seems to be that simply being able to speak of the good of an association as an entity does not warrant its being given special status in practical deliberations. Entities of various kinds exist, such as vacuum cleaners, that it makes sense to speak of in similar ways and that are nonetheless entirely instrumental, that is, are only of practical importance to the degree that they serve external ends.

However, the problem with Murphy's analogy, it seems to me, is that it requires an instrumental function for each of the social entities he has under discussion. We may, of course, concede this in many cases. For instance, it makes sense to speak of the good functioning or success of a business partnership as such, but given its merely instrumental purpose—that is, it is sought only as a means to ends external to its own operation—such considerations do not count as being of fundamental importance to practical rationality. The fact that the distinct good of a business partnership may diverge from the individual financial interests of each of its members is not in itself reason to protect or promote the partnership as such. Can we say the same thing, however, in cases where the association in question intrinsically instantiates the basic good of community or friendship? In such cases, it would seem, the good functioning of the social entity bears an essential relationship to the human good and thus has some claim to being of fundamental practical importance itself.

Against Murphy's, the claim that I want to advance here is that in cases where intrinsic, irreducible social goods are realized in particular associations, understanding what the individual human good is becomes partially informed by the requirements and flourishing of that association as such. Thus, the distinctive good of the association per se becomes of fundamental practical importance. This follows necessarily, I think, from the fact that some basic human goods are social, and these goods are irreducibly social. Thus, the logic and flourishing of the association itself becomes of basic importance insofar as it is essentially constitutive and epistemically necessary to understanding the individual human good.

This point, that the distinctive character of basic associations becomes of fundamental relevance to practical deliberation, is helpfully illustrated in a couple of ways. First, recall Aristotle's careful attention in the *Nicomachean Ethics* not only to the intention of parties engaged in friendship but also to the objective requirements of various friendships. If the central case of virtuous friendship is to really exist, Aristotle argues, a condition of equality must obtain between the two parties. Spending time together in the activity characteristic of the friendship, too, is essential to the nature of the relationship. When friends are cut off by distance or distraction from the activity of the relationship, in time it will fundamentally change, and the goods it realizes will be altered.[49] A central implication of Aristotle's account is that there are a range of conditions necessary to the full functioning and realization of different kinds of friendship that are independent of the parties' good intentions for the relationship. What this requires if, for example, close friendships are to be maintained is an attentiveness to the relationship as such. Given that it develops from particular human capacities, perfections, needs, and limitations, friendship *is* something—a distinct and identifiable kind of relationship that cannot be reduced to, or generated solely from, personal intentions. This social fact requires something in addition to the "third point of view" that Finnis (rightly, in my opinion) describes as that characteristic of true friends, in which "one's own good and one's friend's good are equally 'in view' or 'in play.'"[50] It requires not simply that friends will and act in friendly ways toward each other, but that in some sense they are attentive to the friendship itself. If friendship is to be realized as part of an individual's good, the friendship itself must factor into the complex of basic goods that are arranged, ordered, and prioritized to achieve the best good, both for oneself and one's friend.

It may seem odd to speak of close friendships in this way, and certainly the activity of friendship upstages the relevance of attention to the relationship as such. However, it seems that the more extensive an association becomes, the more pronounced is this difference between the social goods intrinsic to the association and the association itself. Even at the relatively narrow extension of familial association, it seems that realizing familial goods requires careful attention to the family per se as a distinct association. One may ask, is it sufficient for the flourishing of a family for each person to have an aggregative conception of the association, that is, all desire each other's goods and their own? I think not. Concern for individual goods alone, as central as that is to the flourishing of the family—and constitutive of its good—is likely to lead to a diffused family life. Members may recognize the good of distinctly familial interactions as something good for the individuals of the family, but achieving that good seems to require practical deliberation from the perspective of the family—not as a unit that transcends the goods of its individual members but as one that contributes substantively to them. If it is the case that a complex of relationships and shared interaction constituted in *this* family contributes something intrinsically good to each of its members, achieving the good for each requires attentiveness to what those particular goods are, what conditions are necessary to their realization, and how they are to be fostered and protected in the long term. Additionally, if the associational goods are recognized as contributing constitutively to the basic flourishing of family members, it follows that the role each member plays within the group, as constitutive of and contributing to its good, becomes partially constitutive of his *own good* individually conceived. Thus, on this account, accurately describing the good and flourishing of Sir Thomas More requires inclusion of his familial roles, "Husband of Alice," "Father of Margaret," and so on. Insofar as these roles exist as part of a distinct familial association, the good of that association informs the content of those roles and thus part of what the overall good of Thomas More reasonably entails. The flourishing of basic associations like the family, then, is of fundamental practical importance.[51]

The upshot is that I am willing to concede Murphy's point (both on practical and metaphysical grounds) that the distinctive view is "parasitic" on the aggregative common good view when it comes to the issue of allegiance. Equally clear, however, is the epistemological dependence of the aggregative conception of common good upon a distinctive conception. If goods of community are taken to be intrinsic to human flourishing, the flourishing of those constitutive communities as such reveals, in part, the requirements and necessities of human flourishing. I take this to be, in part, the motivating idea behind Alasdair MacIntyre's essential link between individual goods and virtues and the goods of communities. "The identification of my good, of how it is best for me to direct my life, is inseparable from the identification of the common good of the community, of how it is best for that community to direct its life." While I do not share MacIntyre's additional view that "such a community is by its nature political,"[52] I do think that he is right to recognize an essential connection between individual and common goods. Moreover, as I will argue in the next chapter, I think there is room to affirm a unique, intrinsic contribution of politics to the range of social capacities without ceding to political community a subsuming or oppressive role in human life.

Conclusion

Regardless of whether we take the political community qua association to merit heightened protection as a distinctive common good for Murphy or a "group person" for Russell Hittinger,[53] the aggregative character of the common good requires a formal structure to the common good basically like Finnis's differentiation between the common good of political society (i.e., the all-inclusive good of everyone in the community) and the political common good (i.e., the specifically political domain of law and government concerned with maintaining conditions of justice and peace). The relationship between these two conceptions of the common good is, of course, of great importance, or perhaps more to the point, the relationship of law and government to the overall common good aggregatively conceived. Here I think Finnis is also essentially right in his description of the relationship. Government and law promote individual and subpolitical associational goods primarily indirectly, not through direct involvement in daily affairs but by ordering society according to a sound conception of individual, familial, and general social flourishing. It is, in fact, precisely a sound understanding of these goods and a responsibility to see them encouraged and facilitated in the political order that limits the scope of state involvement in daily affairs and allows for the general pursuit of one's own "unrestricted purposes."[54]

Apart from an aggregative conception of the common good, which takes cognizance of the full scope of human potential and the existence of "irreducibly diverse"[55] associational goods, the state is most likely to treat the political roles of individuals and subpolitical associations as the only, or the controlling, roles they play.

The specifically political common good, on the other hand, is that element of the political community structured around law, government, and the political participation of citizens. As will become clear, my main divergence from Finnis is to give a considerably wider scope to this specifically political good. Finnis, for example, has little room for either active citizenship, civic friendship, or political culture in his concept of the political common good. The thrust of my argument in favor of the intrinsic goodness of political life aims to expand this notion of the political, and thus the goods we take to be inherent to it. Such an argument revivifies the distinction that Jacques Maritain made between the state and political community.[56] For Maritain, it is the state (i.e., the institutions of government) that is instrumental to basic human associations, but it is instrumental not just to subpolitical associations but to the wider realm of political interaction as well. Although the state plays an important role in articulating and encouraging the practice of active citizenship among its members, the nature of political association cannot be reduced to this formal element. The constitutional identity of a people must not be understood simply in terms of formal political definition but according to a broader sphere of civic friendship and political culture. Finnis's instrumentalizing of the specifically political common good, as I argued in Chapter 1, largely follows from a substantive collapse of this political sphere into the domain of government and law. But, of course, defending the intrinsic value of this broader idea of political community requires some justification in light of (among other things) the size and diversity of modern societies, which would seem to significantly diminish the possibility of civic friendship. It is to such an investigation and defense that I now turn.

Civic Friendship

PARADOX AND POSSIBILITY

In turning to a discussion of the substance of the political common good, this investigation has come full circle. We have worked our way to an account of the intrinsic goodness of political community—something I argued in Chapter 1 that Finnis's discussion leaves incomplete. If I am successful in this argument, the result will be (as the previous chapter argued) that the good of the political community *as such* must be included as one of the constitutive components of the common good and fundamental in the calculus of practical reason. This does not entail that it is the only such good, or that due to its architectonic status it may justly subsume other fundamental social goods. Rather, my argument demonstrates that political association makes unique and intrinsic contributions to human sociability. But it does not *of itself* include all intrinsic aspects of that sociability, and so insofar as the common good of a political society is complete, it must be an association of associations.

So I turn to consider political community as such. Recall that I criticized Finnis for reductively speaking of the "specifically political" simply in terms of the operation or domain of law and government. I maintained that a complete discussion of political community must *also* account for actions of individuals and subpolitical groups in the process of associating. Additionally, it must account for the political culture that emerges over generations out of all these factors combined. This entails that law and government are only discrete parts of what we should recognize as specifically political community. This point is an essential one, I argue, because it is precisely in the free political activity and partnership of citizens—extended across generations in a healthy political culture—that the intrinsic value of the political common good is most clearly evident.

In this chapter I will focus specifically on *civic friendship*, discussing other important political concepts such as justice and citizenship to the degree that they relate to this relationship. I have chosen to focus on civic friendship instead of citizenship for a couple of reasons. First, civic friendship in important respects includes and exceeds citizenship insofar as citizenship provides the basic form of political relationships, and civic friendship perfects that formal relationship with the addition of a certain kind of friendliness. Second, and more important, insofar as a large part of the value of citizenship is realized in the expansion of knowledge and practical reason in the wider domain of political community, it is more vulnerable to the "superpolitical" or universalist challenge to the political common good. The breadth of knowledge gained at the political level clearly stands to be improved by looking beyond a particular polity.

Consider the central role political communities play in Alasdair MacIntyre's (Aristotelian) account of practical rationality. For MacIntyre, the identification of my good, how it is best for me to direct my life, is inseparable from the identification of the common good of the community, how it is best for the community to direct its life.[1] Thus, an adequate cultivation of practical reason requires exercise of political reason. Political community places pursuit of the individual good in its necessary and proper context. Nevertheless, MacIntyre argues that the full development of practical reason takes place within a *tradition*,[2] a form of rational inquiry extended over time that transcends particular political communities. Therefore, full rationality (and we may include theoretical reason too) transcends the borders of particular communities. Consequently, if we are interested in articulating the particular good of political communities, we shall have to look other than to their giving citizens access to more complete moral and theoretical knowledge. For this justification necessarily draws our attention beyond the political community itself.

In contrast, the relation of friendship turns on its particularity. It entails varying degrees of personal connection that cannot be replicated by any form of superpolitical universalism. Civic friendship requires *particular* communities grounded in *particular* political cultures. Thus, if the superpolitical challenge to political community is to be adequately met, civic friendship, rather than citizenship, presents the stronger argument.

Aristotelian Civic Friendship

Despite this initial rhetorical attractiveness, however, it is not altogether clear what might be meant by "civic friendship." Friendship seems to entail a close association and sharing of life between two people, something hardly characteristic of political association on any account. As Aristotle says, spending time together is most characteristic of friends, and yet citizens have little personal knowledge of each other.[3] Civic friendship, in fact, is not always readily differentiated from a kind of promiscuous gregariousness that often appears more obsequious than genuinely friendly.[4] Gilbert Meilaender pushes this general paradox a step further, arguing that civic friendship is a fundamentally incoherent idea. On the one hand, justice must be evenhanded and impersonal, but, on the other, friendship is intensely personal.[5] So it would seem that civic friendship is a misguided notion in practice and arguably a misbegotten idea in principle.

And yet, it would also seem to be an ideal closely allied with patriotism and civic virtue as the core of political life. As Aristotle observes, friendship holds states together, and lawmakers give more attention to it than to justice.[6] Moreover, the Aristotelian ideal, which Thomas Aquinas appears largely—if not completely—to adopt, holds the political community up as a partnership in the good life, understood as a life of virtue.[7] Aristotle explicitly rejects a utilitarian, contractarian view of political community, an option that seems plausible given these real limits on civic friendship. How then are we to understand what civic friendship involves? To what degree can politics accommodate a genuine relationship of friendship among citizens? What is the purpose of such a friendship? What is its object? And what is its primary mode of activity?

THE SHARED GOAL OF CIVIC FRIENDSHIP

Not surprisingly, Aristotle's explanation of civic friendship generally follows his explication of the end or purpose of the city. Just as he maintains that the city comes to be for the sake of life, but exists for the sake of the good life, Aristotle's account of the friendly relations among citizens recognizes both this utilitarian foundation and virtuous aspiration. Although he apparently identifies the primary case of civic friendship with a particular kind of "like-mindedness" in basic civic affairs, in some important senses its application seems to extend much further.

Aristotle is, of course, famous for his capacious notion of friendship as a relation that in some manner accurately describes the basically self-interested agreements of business partners as well as the full regard for a friend as an "other self" that can grow between people of virtue.[8] Every association, in fact, entails a basic friendliness, Aristotle thinks, since a commitment to a plan for common action, insofar as it is framed according to a just and fair treatment of all parties involved, entails a commitment to the good of other members of the group (encompassed in the common good).[9] Thus, between members of an association committed to pursuit of a common good, there exists a form of the mutually recognized goodwill that essentially characterizes friendship.[10] Moreover, insofar as there is a commitment to act for a particular person or group of people, we can take the goodwill involved to exceed the general feeling of benevolence we tend to have for kindred human beings,[11] but insofar as it falls short of affection or a regard for the other's good simply for his or her own sake, such relationships are friendships in a secondary sense.

Consistent with his account of the city's origins, Aristotle's explanation of civic friendship begins in human need and insufficiency. "Civic friendship," he observes, "has been established mainly in accordance with utility; for men seem to have come together because each is not sufficient for himself, though they would have come together anyhow for the sake of living in company."[12] It is not, however, the most basic needs of the city—safety, tranquility, material provision—that Aristotle associates most directly with civic friendship. Nor is civic friendship strictly an association of necessary compromise or capitulation. Aristotle thinks of it, rather, as a form of association that involves a certain amount of like-mindedness, "when citizens have the same judgment about their common interest, when they choose the same things and when they execute what they have decided in common." Moreover, their agreement concerns the most important matters of the city's operation, for example, requirements of office, alliances, and so on. This Aristotle calls "concord."[13]

Michael Pakaluk helpfully emphasizes that the citizens' agreement, or common judgment, represents more than the happenstance that might be inferred from "like-mindedness" (*homonoia*) or "concurrence of opinion" (*homodoxia*).[14] Communication and mutual recognition of agreement are essential to Aristotle's description of concord. This obviously anticipates the basic political principle—shared deliberation about the just, good, and advantageous—that explains the emergence of political community in the opening arguments of the *Politics*.[15] In one sense concord does naturally exist among good people insofar as they share a desire for the just and useful and remain constant in their desire for it. This *wish* for what inures to the common good, however, is necessarily realized in common political deliberation.

Lorraine Pangle draws attention to a second important aspect of concord: the way in which general goodwill can mature into stronger affection for fellow citizens as shared projects are undertaken and difficulties faced in common—as fellow citizens "enter sympathetically into one another's struggles and hopes" and thus increase the stock of natural goodwill.[16] As Pangle observes, Aristotle seems to signal this dynamic in part by following up his discussion of concord in the *Nicomachean Ethics* IX.6 with a consideration of the way in which benefactors grow in love for the recipients of their kindness. With every action for the city and for one's fellow citizens, civic friendship is naturally strengthened as common goodwill becomes attached to particular people, a particular community, time, and place. These affective components would seem to indicate at least the possibility of a true form of friendship, as citizens' concern for the common good matures into genuine regard for each other's welfare. However, Aristotle is rather direct in marking the basically utilitarian character of civic friendship of this kind, and in the *Eudemian Ethics* he gives explicit attention to the pitfalls involved in setting an unreasonably high expectation for civic friendship, that is, setting "moral friendship" as the standard for civic relationships that remain, despite a high degree of goodwill, essentially utilitarian.[17]

And yet, it is difficult to see that Aristotle's conception of civic friendship stops short at this simply utilitarian notion. Given the trajectory of the city as a community existing for the sake of the good life, it seems most likely that Aristotle would take the common deliberative pursuit of justice (and thus goodness) at the center of political life to follow this course, resulting in a notion of civic friendship keyed to the goodness and virtue at which the polis aims. This would not entail that civic friendship approximate the close personal friendship that exists between individuals; Aristotle explicitly rejects such a suggestion.[18] It does, however, suggest a development beyond the basically utilitarian concerns denoted by concord.

John Cooper argues that this is just the sort of progression that Aristotle articulates in Book III, chapter 9 of the *Politics*.[19] Aristotle's argument there is that members of merely utilitarian alliances are distinguished from citizens of cities inasmuch as they have no concern for the habits and virtues of others in the association. They are concerned only with avoidance of harm. In contrast, citizens are concerned with the good state of the laws, and thus with political virtue and vice. Aristotle's initial contrast perhaps suggests that citizens are concerned with fellow citizens' virtue *for the sake of* maintaining good laws. This is part of it, of course, but by itself it would not seem to differ substantially from the self-interest motivating merely utilitarian alliances. However, this concern with effective maintenance of the laws is not all that is involved, as Aristotle soon indicates. For civic concern with law does not terminate with each party securing personal rights or interests but rather in the goodness and justice cultivated in citizens themselves. Thus, the concern with the good condition of the city's laws is a concern, as Cooper puts it, "of each citizen for each other citizen, whether or not they know each other personally, and indeed whether or not they have had any direct and personal dealings with one another whatsoever."[20] He goes on to defend this shared concern for virtue as a plausible one, even in relatively unvirtuous regimes. Cooper adduces, very reasonably it seems to me, the sense of national pride and identity that seems to characterize political communities, even mass democracies. "This pride is not just in accomplishments, but even more in the qualities of mind and character that (are presumed to have) made them possible. . . . They want to think [of fellow citizens] as good, upstanding people, and definitely do not want them to be small-minded, self-absorbed, sleazy."[21]

Aristotle goes on to argue that this shared concern for virtue in the city is grounded in a shared familial and cultural life that is oriented to the complete and noble life of the city. This political life

> will not be possible . . . unless they do inhabit one and the same location and engage in intermarriage. That is why in cities marriage connections arose, as well as clans and sacrifices and the cultured pursuits involved in living together. Such things are the work of friendship, for the deliberate choice to live together is friendship. The end, then, of the city is living well, but these other things are for the sake of the end, and a city is the community of families and villages in a complete and self-sufficient life, which we say, is living happily and nobly.[22]

So here Aristotle adds to the *proper object of friendship* (i.e., concern for a friend's virtue[23]) the *mode of interaction* most characteristic of friends, namely, living and spending time together. At the core of Aristotle's description is this important distinction: he does not say that the friendly relationships and activity of civil society are simply necessary to the kind of mutual concern for virtue that defines the city; he understands such social interaction to be deliberately oriented to political community as its purpose. Each citizen does not "use his own household like a city" but instead orients life within the family to participation in life within the polis. This is because, for Aristotle, living well or nobly transpires specifically at the level of political community. The reason for this, as Gisela Striker has observed, is a rather narrow conception of practical intelligence that leads him to the conclusion that participation in government is an indispensable part of human happiness: "only political rulership will permit one to exercise [*phronesis*] for the sake of noble ends."[24] The good life is the political life, most centrally in the exercise of political authority, but also, as Cooper's description of political identity emphasizes, through participation in the life of the political community and the achievements of its most accomplished citizens. Thus, familial and cultural pursuits are, in the Aristotelian polis, deliberately taken to be for the sake of the city (though not simply collapsed into political association, as in Socratic communism). Aristotle apparently takes this extension of family life, cultural pursuits, and educational endeavors (spelled out in Book VIII's description of the best regime) to embody a form of life that is the highest form of political friendship.

To recapitulate, then, the Aristotelian view of civic friendship runs as follows:

1. Its incipient form is found in the reciprocated goodwill expressed in associations formed to achieve a common end according to a just and fair plan.
   a. If the common aim does not fairly include the good of each, it is not just.
   b. If the association is not just, there is no common good and thus no reciprocated goodwill.
   c. Thus, justice should be understood as the form of civic friendship.
2. Civic friendship centers on pursuing the ends of political life according to the political principle of deliberative discussion about the just, the good, and the advantageous. Thus, its trajectory follows the virtuous aspirations of the city.
   a. Civil discourse is motivated in important part by an affective goodwill, a sympathetic concern for the welfare of fellow citizens that increases as citizens invest themselves in common civic pursuits.
   b. Concord describes the common judgment citizens reach about matters important to political life through the process of discussion and debate.

3. In its highest form, civic friendship develops into a mutual, genuine concern for one another's virtue. In Aristotle's view, this seems to follow from a deliberate choice to share life—in relatively close, frequent association—as a political community and the political identity that emerges from such community.
   a. Civic friendship of this nature is oriented to living well and nobly, that is, living virtuously—political virtue being the most noble.
   b. Civic friendship grounds (by way of common identity) the participation of all citizens in the noble life of the best citizens, although all cannot personally achieve it.
      i. The common good is also grounded in each person being able to achieve as much as they are able.
      ii. However, insofar as nobility is associated preeminently with the city, the highest achievement of individuals will be in their contribution to the city.
      iii. Thus, it follows that all of life becomes, for Aristotle, a *means* to life lived and engaged *at the political level*.

Thomistic Modifications

Let us turn now to consider how Thomas Aquinas appropriates Aristotle's understanding of civic friendship. This is a vexed subject, and no small amount of the dispute, textually speaking, centers on Aquinas's short treatment of kingship, *De Regno*. Even though there are very notable departures in the text from a pure Aristotelian line,[25] at perhaps the most crucial points Aquinas's argument seems to simply appropriate Aristotle's discussion. So we see interpreters, wishing to emphasize the discontinuity between Aristotle and Aquinas, deemphasizing the text as not the "mature" expression of Aquinas's views[26] or as otherwise incomplete or unintended as a general theoretical treatise.[27] Conversely, Michael Pakaluk's strongly Aristotelian reading of Aquinas essentially relies on *De Regno*.[28]

Finnis attempts, unsuccessfully in my view, to advance a novel reading of *De Regno* that substantively cordons Aquinas's placement of "the virtuous life of the multitude" in the king's hands by specifying a limited and instrumental "public good" for which political authority is directly responsible. Notwithstanding my own general agreement with Pakaluk's interpretation of *De Regno*, I think it is mistaken to rely too heavily on the seemingly straightforward Aristotelianism of the text. (Here I have in mind, primarily, paragraphs 103–106, in which Aquinas argues that the purpose of the political community must be that of the individual, i.e., virtue.) It is remarkable that in just the passage where Aquinas directly appropriates the argument from *Politics* III.9 that the end of political life is virtue, he does not give the kind of further account that Aristotle does of what such a communal life looks like. Aristotle proceeds to articulate a kind of political friendship centered on the life of the polis and devoted to the high or noble pursuits of political life—indeed conceiving of subpolitical associations as intentionally directed as means to such a common political life—whereas Aquinas makes no such further explication of the politically focused nature of the common life.[29]

What this means is that we have relatively little idea of what Aquinas takes the "virtuous life of the multitude" to consist—specifically, what kind of political life is entailed. As Gregory Froelich observes, nowhere does Aquinas give us a treatise on the political common good, or in fact, even a complete commentary on Aristotle's treatise.[30] Another way this point may be made is by recalling the distinction mentioned earlier pertinent to Aristotle's account of civic friendship between the *object of civic friendship* and the *mode of interaction* characteristic of that friendship. Insofar as the object of civic friendship is an orientation to virtue—an intention toward living well in political community—it is clear that Aquinas shares the Aristotelian outlook. However, inasmuch as Aristotle fills out his view of political life with a mode of interaction focused specifically on the political life, and ultimately takes other forms of association to be means to this end, there is little indication that Aquinas follows him.

This distinction, in turn, seems to implicate a more fundamental one. It is noteworthy that the claims of the political community to primacy—"the end of politics is the good for man"[31]—is subject to two very different interpretations. The first makes the formal point that given the architectonic status of the political community, its purpose *must be* promoting the human good. From this it follows that the primacy of political community turns on its substantive inclusion of every type of good essential to human flourishing. A second reading appeals to the all-encompassing nature of politics and claims that its end—the purposes and requirements of the political community as such—represents the good for man. I argued in the previous chapter that the first reading is not only normatively superior, but in his commentary Aquinas spends some time making clear that he takes Aristotle to be saying the former.[32]

In the picture of political community developed in *Politics* III.9, however, Aristotle seems to be saying something much closer to the latter. Here political community is not described simply as an association that embraces and includes other substantive goods but rather as a community that subsumes those goods inasmuch as it represents their raison d'être and ultimate fulfillment. Therefore, we should ask: Has Aquinas simply gotten Aristotle wrong? Did Aristotle intend to say from the very beginning that the ends of political community determine the good for man, rather than vice versa? Is the principle of inclusivity, for Aristotle, really better described as one of subsumption? This is a plausible interpretation, but I think there is a better one.

For Aristotle, the character of political community ultimately takes on a subsuming quality, not because he does not think that political community must substantively include all subpolitical goods but because he attributes little *intrinsic substantive value* to subpolitical associations. They are, rather, instruments to the final political end. The reason for this, as noted earlier, seems to follow predominantly from Aristotle's narrow identification of human excellence with the high or noble things of politics and philosophy, and his almost exclusive association of the household—the locus of private life—with the provision of mundane necessities and nonrational affections and preference. Although Aristotle is justly famous for his acknowledgment of the different kinds of relationship and authority structures that exist in disparate associations, as well as the necessity of personal, affective relationships to the ultimate realization of the ends of political community, he evidently sees these goods as necessary components—rather than substantively constitutive parts—of political community. This interpretation, then, leaves intact the *formal* principle of the political community's primacy—all intrinsic individual and social goods must be substantively included in the political community—while reaching a subsumptive conclusion on the basis of *substantive* determinations about the purpose and value of subpolitical associations.

Contrary to Aristotle's commitment to the primacy of politics per se, Aquinas writes within a Christian tradition that recognizes the basic importance—at times even the countervailing primacy—of a range of nonpolitical social goods. John Finnis's work is particularly helpful in its emphasis on the range of these goods.[33] Most basically, the primacy of politics is delimited by the ecclesial community—the church's ordination of men to their final end. This recognition of the soul's ultimate belonging to God includes obedience in discerning and fulfilling one's vocation. Thus, religious orders, marriage, and so on, are choices that must be left to the individual and cannot rightly be determined by authorities, political or otherwise. Additionally, as we saw in Chapter 2, there is significant disparity in Aquinas's appreciation of the family. Not only does Aquinas recognize a basic difference in the possibilities of friendship between husband and wife, as well as the sacramental significance of the marital union, he also recognizes a basic rational principle animating family life in inclination toward and discharge of parental responsibility for education of children.[34]

Thus, contrary to Aristotle's insistence on the superseding nobility of political life, Aquinas's thought is infused with what Charles Taylor has called the "affirmation of ordinary life."[35] By this Taylor refers to the consistent commitment in the Christian philosophical tradition to the basic goodness and dignity of that realm of action devoted precisely to those things that Aristotle dismissed as "mere life." Now, central to Taylor's treatment is the Protestant, specifically Puritan, emphasis on the value of labor and thus of commerce to the modern notion of the self. Although Aquinas does not go so far as this, he is committed to the basic propositions that underlie this understanding of life. (Taylor himself indicates that the ideas developed and expanded by the Puritans had deep roots within the Christian tradition.) Thus, this affirmation of the basic goodness of a range of associations other than political community places particular weight on the idea of an association of associations. The architectonic status of political community does not entail the superiority of political life and interaction as such.

To put this in other words, for Aquinas the accent of the political community's completeness or perfection falls on its *extensive* qua*lity*, that is, its securing the human good throughout the community. This is a logical consequence, it would seem, of the affirmation of the goodness of subpolitical social goods. The importance of these other social (and personal) goods necessarily diminishes the *intensive significance* of the political good as a form of community that instantiates a kind of social goodness *perfective* of all other forms of association. M. S. Kempshall's argument corroborates this point: Aquinas is consistently reluctant to ascribe perfection to the political common good. Moreover, the basis of the political community's greater degree of perfection is its greater communication of goodness: "Degrees of perfection are degrees of increasing community, in that it is greater perfection for something to be good in itself and the cause of goodness in others than simply the former." In his use of analogies that illustrate the unique, directive purpose of the common good, Aquinas is always careful to say that the part has an operation that is different from the unified whole.[36] Thus, the primacy of the political common good is rooted in its communication and extension of the human good—not primarily in its embodiment of a unique mode of association into which other goods are incorporated because of its intrinsic perfection.

JUSTICE AS THE CORE POLITICAL VIRTUE

This prompts us, as Finnis is keen to point out, to give particular attention to the unique good that political community contributes to human social flourishing. For the nature of its goodness may simply be found in its necessary relationship to other basic human goods—not in its independent desirability. Such an investigation must begin, of course, with the virtue of justice. As we saw in considering Aristotle, justice would seem to be the first social virtue inasmuch as it enables associations by securing a common good that supports mutual goodwill. Apart from justice, there is no common good and thus no basis for genuine community, that is, common pursuit of a common end. The virtue of justice takes this fundamental condition of equality as its object, being defined by Aquinas as "a habit whereby a man renders to each one his due by a constant and perpetual will."[37] Justice in this sense, as it governs the interaction between individuals, Aquinas follows Aristotle in calling *particular justice*. The nature of political community and law, of course, essentially concerns administering and securing such justice among individuals, and thus the political common good takes shape as the preservation of justice and peace.[38] This puts individuals into relationship not only with other individuals but with others in general—with the community formed for the administration of justice. Thus, justice becomes a general virtue inasmuch as it rightly orients individuals with respect to the community itself. This general justice—called legal justice because this is law's primary aim—considers individuals and subpolitical associations specifically as *parts of a whole*.

The virtue of legal justice is architectonic in an important sense insofar as it directs acts of virtue to its own object, that is, the good of the whole community. Aquinas specifies that the directive function of legal justice applies both to self-regarding and relational virtues. "The good of any virtue whether the virtue directs man in relation to himself, or in relation to certain other individual persons, is referable to the common good, to which justice directs, so that all acts of virtue can pertain to justice, in so far as it directs man to the common good."[39]

As a general virtue, legal justice stands in special relationship to all other virtues as, in a sense, the supreme virtue. "Every virtue strictly speaking directs its act to that virtue's proper end." Directing the act to a further end all or some of the time does not belong to that virtue considered strictly, for it needs some higher virtue to direct it to that end. Consequently, there must be one supreme virtue essentially distinct from every other virtue, which directs all the virtues to the common good. This is legal justice.[40]

Now, as Aquinas understands it, the virtue of justice is a perfection of the will, something he calls the "rational appetite." Being located in the will, it is distinct from other moral virtues by its uniquely rational character. Justice is a rational virtue, Aquinas explains, insofar as the intellect is able to apprehend and respond to *universal good*.[41] There are a couple of important ways that this should be understood. In the first place, the basic desirability of the simple *extension of goodness* that characterizes the preeminence of political community is a rational apprehension of universal good. All things being equal, attaining the good of both A and B is simply better than only attaining the good of A—and so on without limit. More specifically, apprehension of a universal good entails understanding it as a good for everyone who shares my nature. As Finnis puts it, basic human goods do not present themselves to the intellect with "for me" attached. That is, I can understand knowledge and the pursuit of it not simply as a good for Matthew but as a good for each person who shares those characteristics that make the good beneficial for me. Thus, to understand the universal character of goods is to realize that insofar as I have a claim in justice to certain goods as being due me, those similarly situated have the same claim.[42]

Now, of course, we do not tend to experience justice as an abstract cerebral perception. The rational component is accompanied by what are often powerful affections. We do, of course, experience immediate and visceral emotions when personally suffering injustice. But these emotions, too, have much wider extension. In nascent form, the affections of justice are expressed in what Aristotle recognizes as a general goodwill that humans feel for fellow creatures. We wish them well, it would seem, from a basic sympathetic identification with creatures with whom we share a common nature. Goodwill, however, does not necessarily entail action on another's behalf. Rather, love moves us to action. "Part of the love which should exist among men is that a man should preserve the good of even a single human being."[43] Aquinas reasons that political community expresses the virtue of love because of its basic commitment to acting for the good of others—those who by rational principle we understand to deserve the same goods that we ourselves perceive and pursue. Love seeks to extend those goods.

The universal dimensions of our rational apprehension of good, motivated by the active desire to extend that good to kindred human beings, seem to suggest a universality to the human desire for justice. Indeed, in the passage just quoted from Aquinas, he articulates a strongly universalist dimension to the aspirations of political community. This has important limitations that we will return to momentarily, but for now let us mark the movement of love (and justice) in a universal direction. Jacques Maritain calls this the human capacity for "radical generosity," and Yves Simon refers to it as a basic disinterestedness in human sociability.[44] Such radical generosity is importantly distinct from Christian charity, which is even more radical insofar as it requires love even of one's enemies for the sake of God. Radical generosity of this sort seems simply to be an extension of human action according to the universal dimensions of human reason (and benevolence). Thus, we can be motivated to act for the benefit of some fellow human—or creature—a world away simply on the basis of a love of justice and/or a desire for his or her good.

In summary, political community operates as a commitment to justice. Moreover, insofar as it extends the good, it cultivates the human capacity for love and generosity. It is a movement beyond the immediate social conditions and relationships to which one is personally attached and committed, to an extension of good to *the other*. As Mary Keys puts it, political community "raise[s] the sights of humans beyond self and nearest of kin, to establish and secure a more (though far from perfect) universal order of justice, peace, and virtue among humans."[45]

Civic Friendship: Difficulties and Possibilities

The basic nature of civic or political friendship is found first in its object, that is, the formation and maintenance of a community dedicated to securing human needs and goods in a just and equitable manner. Inasmuch as it situates pursuit of one's personal interests within a broader context of common good—substantively including the good for each member of the community—it involves members in consideration of and activity for the good of those outside the scope of immediate personal interest. *Political community, especially as it becomes the locus of a real form of civic friendship, thus serves to expand and strengthen the scope of justice, love, and generosity.* In order to get a clearer picture of the character of civic friendship, let us consider several difficulties that the relationship poses.

UNIVERSALISM

We may well ask, what distinguishes civic friendship from an orientation of the will to a truly universal human community—one unbounded by particular political commitments? Certainly the requirements of justice derived from a universal human nature transcend particular political communities. Why not, as the Stoics recommended, encourage allegiance to cosmopolis rather than polis?[46] If the virtues of justice and generosity are the central virtues of political association, why shouldn't the scope of justice include that which is due to all humankind, not merely one's own political community, or the breadth of generosity extend to even the farthest reaches of the earth? (Here I return to the "superpolitical challenge" to the political common good mentioned in the Introduction.)

Of course, the natural law tradition is essentially defined by a partial, but important, concession of this point. Positive law, the law of the polis, is *not* the highest authority. Rather, human law derives its authority from consonance with the universal norms of the natural law, which themselves derive from the eternal law of the divine lawgiver.[47] Thus, in fundamental respects, natural law directs our allegiance to a wider community and subjects the particular conception of justice within a community to evaluation against a transcendent standard.[48] Moreover, these universal dimensions suggest that the virtue of generosity does not rightly terminate at the borders of one's political community. Indeed, it would seem to require that we move beyond them insofar as the virtue is more perfected the more one's beneficence is removed from potential for personal gain.[49]

There is some truth in this universalist line of thinking, but at the same time it has serious limitations. These constraints do not call into question the universal dimensions of justice, love, and generosity, but they do importantly direct and restrict these virtues according to the limitations of human finitude and the positive goods of particular relationships (recalling the distinction between intensive and extensive goods raised in Chapter 3).

Consider Aquinas's analysis of the appropriate scope of love. Even while recognizing the universal dimensions of justice and love, he does not shy from privileging proximate relationships in a number of ways. We must make distinctions, Aquinas argues, between *benevolence* (willing the good for another), *affection* (how we feel toward another), and *beneficence* (doing the good for another). As to how we feel, it is simply impossible that we will not be more attached to some people more than others, and there is no moral reason to wish this were otherwise. As to what we *will* for others, Aquinas reasons that this is ultimately equal since a good will wishes that everyone come to the enjoyment of God. However, beneficence, the good that we *do* for others, simply cannot be equal because we are contingent, finite beings for whom—in most cases—doing one good prevents us from doing another. Therefore, our ability to *act* in generous love for the extension of good to others must of necessity be unequal.[50]

As a general rule, our responsibilities of beneficence are guided by relationships of nearness, that is, we must first *act* for the good of our closest family and friends, extending outward as resources allow. There are, of course, times when our personal good and our responsibilities to the closest of kin must be sacrificed for the great, "godlike" good of the political community, and even cases where the extreme need of a stranger will outweigh the lesser needs of a family member. Yet, these are the exceptions to the general rule of local beneficence—and priority of the remoter need must be prudentially determined on a case-by-case basis.[51]

Consider, for example, how we might evaluate the responsibility of a polity that acknowledges a universal human community to act in its foreign policy and military decisions to secure justice and prosperity for other nations. Does the natural law require a proactive foreign policy, guided by a commonly shared generosity toward other peoples? As to *benevolence*, absolutely. Every nation has a responsibility to conduct its affairs with a consistent *will* for the good of all nations. This does not mean that it fails to aggressively pursue its own good and national interests, but it must do so according to principles of justice and the law of nations.[52] How about *beneficence*? Perhaps. Certainly there is an obligation to consider what can be done, in concert with other nations, to protect and promote the welfare of the most vulnerable peoples around the world, particularly those abused by their own governments. In some cases, military action consistent with the principles of just war may be necessary to come to the aid of a seriously and immediately endangered people. Nevertheless, responsibilities of justice and generosity primarily reside within one's own community—just as commitment to the good of one's country does not simply supersede (that is, in all cases) a more immediate responsibility for the good of one's family. Even though there is a universal orientation of these virtues, there are immediate and personal applications that one cannot rightly abandon in favor of wider community ties. Thus, a polity concerned with its obligations to other nations, desiring to contribute to a just international order, must order and prioritize these important aims among a range of other political goods, for example, the safety and provision needed within its own borders, the good functioning of its own political system, the flourishing of its subpolitical associations, and so on. If we allow the political virtues to pull us too strongly in a universalist direction, we are liable to overlook the unique goods and possibilities available only in particular political communities.

The genuine potential of civic friendship follows from the creation of a real relational community—most basically characterized by common action for a common end and reciprocated goodwill among members—oriented to these virtues of justice and generosity. Yves Simon highlights the way that a political community's common action *itself* comes to embody what is, he argues, the essence of the common good. "Collective transitive actions" for particular ends, for example, building a railroad or digging a canal, are themselves "social facts" and thus elements of the common good (distinguishable from the product itself). More profound, however, are what he calls "immanent" social actions. These result not only from coordinated action but from mutual awareness of a common knowledge, love, or hate.[53] In the case of political action, the awareness of common intent *as a community* or *on behalf of the community* entails a basic friendliness in the commitment to pursue common needs and goods in a way that includes the good of each member. Thus, Simon's argument here suggests that we should not overlook the real goods inherent in shared, interactive political action for a mutually recognized common purpose. Even allowing for globalization and the communicative possibilities of modern technology, it seems unlikely that this kind of reciprocated political good is possible on the international stage. Moreover, as I shall argue, discreet social actions of this sort are but one aspect of a broader political culture that itself embodies, informs, and grounds these activities.

There is more to say about universalism, but let us consider it as it arises within the context of two more related concerns. As I noted from the outset, the first of these related difficulties concerns the practical issue of *attenuation*; the second concerns the charge of theoretical *incoherence*. Let us consider these in turn.

ATTENUATION

The concern here is this: it would seem that civic friendship is a practical oxymoron given that even in relatively small political communities, citizens are unable to cultivate personal knowledge of each other or spend sufficient time in each other's company to sustain anything like genuine friendship. The idea of civic friendship seems to entail a level of gregariousness that is at best superficial and at worst obsequious. Civic relations are simply too attenuated to be likened to friendship, and, moreover, doing so threatens to eclipse the importance of genuine, personal friendships.

As with our comments on universalism, the first response to the difficulty of attenuation is simply to allow that the criticism has genuine merit. If civic friendship is proffered as a grander or more virtuous version of its lesser cousin, private friendship, it is clearly inadequate. For civic friendship to replace or eclipse personal ties the important differences between intensive and extensive goods discussed in the previous chapter must be ignored.

However, there is more that must be conceded here. Recall that a funda-mental component of political association that suggests that it is inherently friendly—that is, a commitment to the good of each group member inas-much as each one's good is substantively part of the common good—closely approximates Aristotle's account of utility friendships, in which one's com-mitment to the relationship refers directly back to its contribution to one's personal interests. Thus, the attenuation of civic friendship raises the real possibility, perhaps even likelihood, that political association comprises little more than a utilitarian settlement, analogous to business partnerships, not the virtue-oriented friendship of close companions.

Indeed, despite my adherence to Cooper's argument that Aristotle ulti-mately espouses a virtue-based account of civic friendship, he gives ample warning about being too sanguine concerning the development of real civic friendship. His discussion in the *Eudemian Ethics* (Book VII, chapters 9–10) treats civic friendship primarily on its utilitarian footing, arguing that try-ing to treat it as virtue-based or "moral friendship" often leads to greater political conflict than if the self-interest of each party had been forthrightly assumed from the outset. The problem arises, Aristotle explains, when the forms of utility friendship—strict legality and objective value—are replaced with the forms of moral friendship—trust and personal regard. The utili-tarian concerns that activate most interactions between citizens are neces-sary and pressing; still, fellow citizens very often aspire to the good faith that informs "moral friendship," seeking to carry out business and civic inter-action on this basis. When necessity forces the issue, however, the trappings of real friendship are often jettisoned for the objective remedies of law. The ensuing conflict is then fueled by wounded pride and hurt feelings *in addition* to the underlying need to protect personal interests. Thus, political disputes of this sort are much more acrimonious than necessary for having been too optimistic in the aspiration to virtue in the first place (and this is a problem that seems to follow in large part from the basic problem of lack of personal knowledge among fellow citizens).

Aristotle's caution here is insightful, I think, and suggests the following general caveats about the nature and scope of civic friendship. First, because fellow citizens are not generally personal friends, the difficulty of discern-ing the extent of virtue or goodwill—and its reciprocity—makes dispensing with the forms of legality and justice inadvisable. Second, to elaborate Aris-totle's point a bit, we should not expect too much of civic friendship by at-tributing to it a level of personal regard and kindness only nurtured in close relationships. Rather, we should anticipate that the object of civic friendship will be relatively limited to the concerns and affairs of public life. For example, I may have a genuine form of virtuous friendship with a fellow citizen in debating the course of a new public road that must encroach more or less upon both of our tracts of land (i.e., we enjoy, in fact, a mutual desire to see the just interests of each other honored in the final settlement). At the same time, neither of us anticipates—aside from further interaction that develops a more personal regard—meeting weekly for drinks, or that we can assume the proactive kindness from each other that we receive from personal friends. Of course, the greater the degree of sacrifice on either side required to reach a mutually beneficial arrangement, greater will be the degree of personal regard fostered in other domains of life. Thus, civic friendship may serve effectively as a catalyst to personal friendships, but it is a mistake to conflate them, thereby expecting more than civic friendship is able to provide. (Aristotle's critique of Socratic communism gives evidence of his sensitivity to this point as well.)[54]

Third, and perhaps most important, Aristotle's caution with respect to civic friendship suggests that political authority in particular should not be too cavalier in its attempt to promote civic friendship. This is a temptation, for as Aristotle observes, most rulers are aware of the usefulness of civic friendship to the regime.[55] Moreover, although political authorities cannot manufacture genuine feelings of friendship, they *do* set the requirements and expectations of citizenship. Insofar as citizenship creates the form or structure of political association, the authoritarian temptation is to attempt to superintend civic friendship via the requirements of citizenship. This is an undoubtedly complicated issue, for it seems clear that a regime does have a responsibility to articulate a form of citizenship that conduces to civic friendship inasmuch as a real regard for justice and the common good serve as the soil in which civic friendship grows. At the same time, insofar as civic friendship represents a political purpose simply beyond the control of governance and law, overeager pursuit of it by imposing forms of citizenship more fitting to friendship are not only likely to fail, but worse, backfire. Better for government to recognize that even within the public realm what it can achieve is significantly limited and subject to profound exogenous influences.

Notwithstanding these important caveats, there is a solid foundation in political association for a limited, but particular, form of friendship. Better seeing what this is will be aided by considering the second challenge, incoherence.

INCOHERENCE

The charge of theoretical incoherence pushes the attenuation critique a few steps further by arguing that, in fact, the qualities essential to friendship (personal connection and commitment) are simply logically opposed to essential components of political virtue. In order to maintain basic fairness, justice must be impartial, and thus impersonal. The administration of justice requires that citizens not be considered on the basis of particular ties and affections but according to an impersonal assessment of just deserts. Thus, as Gilbert Meilaender argues, "The fellow-citizen bond, precisely because it must concern itself with justice, is not a *personal* bond."[56] This basic difficulty, Meilaender contends, becomes evident in a common political problem, namely, distribution of limited resources. Consider, for example, the case of parents who seek to secure scarce and costly, but necessary, medical care for their young daughter. Their success may entail that others do not receive similar medical care, yet clearly they are under a moral obligation to actively try to get their daughter the care she needs. How is their plight to be assessed in view of the needs of other people similarly situated who seek the same scarce resource for equally justifiable ends? Adjudicating dilemmas such as this in an equitable manner requires the establishment of impersonal political authority, someone to assess the various claims and needs—apart from personal ties and loyalties that rightly motivate each party individually—in an effort to determine what is just for each and to the common good. Because individuals so situated rightly seek their interests based on personal bonds, and public authority is instituted precisely to abstract from them, Meilaender concludes that political relationships are essentially impersonal and necessarily so if justice is to be realized (however imperfectly). Friendship, then, inasmuch as it is rooted in personal affections and loyalties, is logically dissonant with political ties. Moreover, Meilaender suggests, the upshot is that even in mundane political situations such as the one described, the common good is sought *only* by public persons; the justified pursuit of private goods seems to preclude a positive orientation toward others' goods when a conflict emerges.[57] Thus, in addition to being rare on any account, civic friendship is an incoherent ideal.

Meilaender is advancing two related, but distinct, ideas here. The first is a claim about impartiality in rendering political judgment, that is, the just adjudication of even mundane conflicts necessarily makes politics an impersonal, objective affair. The second claim is that the reasonable and laudable commitment of individuals to securing real needs for themselves and their loved ones precludes their acting with positive intention for the common good (at least in times of conflict). Public authority is, in fact, instituted in large part precisely to redress this deficiency. Whereas there are substantial truths in Meilaender's claims, I think there are also important oversights that skew his conclusion.

It is right, of course, that political authority must be impersonal in essential part. *Nemo iudex in causa sua*, the legal maxim runs. More broadly speaking, the legitimate *purposes* of political community require a fair and equitable orientation to the good of all, which in turn requires that special attention be given to the common good. To this premise (which I take to be correct), Meilaender adds another (to which I object in part): justice and law comprise the link between citizens. From this, it follows that the link between citizens is fundamentally an impartial, impersonal one.

Now, this conclusion is valid, but it is not sound because it unjustifiably assumes that justice and law comprise the *only* link between citizens, and thus citizenship is solely a relationship of impersonal impartiality (and thus incoherently wed to the intrinsic partiality of friendship). To begin, I think it's clear that this conclusion suffers the immediate liability of producing the counterintuitive result that fellow citizens abroad, for example, would have no reason to show partiality or preference for each other over any stranger they might chance upon. Yet it seems perfectly consistent with the bonds of citizenship—even reasonably desirable—that fellow citizens show just such an affinity. (This is not, of course, to say that such a preferential stance may not be overridden, even as other personal bonds may be superseded in certain circumstances.)

This suggests that the ties of citizenship extend well beyond the administration of justice and impartiality before the law. And upon consideration, we can see that justice and law are not themselves primarily *ends* so much as *means*—a way of pursuing common aims that their existence presupposes. To stick with Meilaender's example, a commitment to an impartial, rule-governed distribution of health care presupposes a community formed for the purpose of better and justly securing basic human needs. Justice represents a common commitment to pursue that end in a particular way (i.e., one that respects the worth of each member), and government and law emerge as instruments necessary to a consistently just form of community. Thus, justice and law denote a form of interaction; they govern a relationship. Yet, they do not explain why the relationship exists in the first place, and thus—though necessary—are insufficient in themselves to explain political bonds.

Fair enough, Meilaender may respond, but still, I have conceded precisely his point: justice *governs* the political relationship, whatever its aims might be. So fellow citizens still relate on an impartial basis that is at odds with real friendship. To this I rejoin that we must be more precise about the relationship of impartiality to justice. It is specifically the equitable administration of justice that requires an impartial arbiter, not the existence of a just relationship between parties per se or a mutual desire that the good of both be pursued justly. Thus, if I am a just man, I will be habitually disposed to extend the consideration and respect to my fellow citizens that giving them their just due requires. Moreover, I may be more personally inclined to extend such consideration to a fellow citizen rather than a foreigner precisely because we as citizens are engaged in the common project of achieving political aims in a just manner. Thus, even if I concede that we will frequently have recourse to impartial arbitration of our conflicting interests or practical judgments, this does not exclude the possibility of a personally embraced and mutually shared commitment to securing a common good. Therefore, the appropriate dividing line between personal engagement and dispassionate analysis is not rightly drawn between the private or personal, on the one hand, and the political, on the other, but rather between the *political* and the *governmental* or *public*. Meilaender mistakenly attributes the impartiality of public officials to the relationship between citizens because he is insensitive to the important difference between the institutions of government and the interactions of political society.

What should we say about Meilaender's second claim, that the praiseworthy pursuit of a private good precludes intention for the common good? Here again, the point conveys an important truth. The necessity of objective, third-party judgment follows not only from a disposition to give self-interest absolute priority but also from the difficulty one has in abstracting from personal desires and attachments even to perceive the common good. And surely personal attachments often command a much greater fervor than a rational commitment to more abstract, general goods can incite.[58] So we may well ask, if we rightly and ardently desire these private goods, is it possible to maintain an intention toward the common good when doing so may well jeopardize securing our private good? Meilaender apparently thinks not, but perhaps the issue of intention is more complicated.

Aquinas suggests that it is. In situations of conflict like those we have been discussing, Aquinas reasons that good intention is not maintained simply by *subjecting* private goods to a more virtuous commitment to the common good. No, he maintains, we should rather view our pursuit of private goods *in a particular light*, namely, as part of a wider common good. Or, in the Aristotelian argot he employs, a good will intends the private good *materially*, and the common good *formally.*[59] What this means is that we act to bring the particular state of affairs comprising our private good into existence, but we do so *as being part of* the common good. But is this simply a prime example of what critics dismiss as scholastic verbal legerdemain—an effort to explain away a real moral and political problem? What real difference does my "formal intention" for the common good matter if the immediate purpose of my actions, that is, the state of affairs I want to bring into existence, remains unchanged? Wouldn't a *real* intention toward the common good require that I actually give up on my aims so that the common stock is increased for the good of the community?

We should first recall that any adequate account of the common good (as I argued in the previous chapter) must be, in part, conceived as the aggregative (or additive) good of all persons and intrinsically good associations within the political community. Thus, no essential violence is done to the notion of the common good by saying that I am promoting it by realizing my own private or personal goods. Personal goods are partially constitutive of the common good. In addition, there does appear to be a substantive difference between saying (a) I will or intend state of affairs X (comprising my personal good) tout court, and (b) I will X as part of or as ordered to the common good. The primary way this difference is seen, I would submit, is in how it informs the means whereby I pursue X.[60] An orientation to the common good requires that I give credence to the similar needs and interests of others that may come into conflict with my own. It is guided by the rational insight of justice that enables me to understand the goods I seek not simply as *goods for me* but as human goods to which others may and often do have equally legitimate and conflicting claims. Thus, it is a reasoned commitment to pursue goods in an equitable manner by submitting to the procedure and, ultimately, dispositions of impartial political authorities who have been given particular care for the common good.

Of course, if we take the human commitment to justice fundamentally to be only a love of what is one's own (issuing in demands that I get my just due), the processes of political debate and legal adjudication appear more as necessary means to maximizing self-interest. And certainly a great bulk of political activity transpires at this level. From Meilaender's perspective this is the result of a corrupt human will and unruly passions that demand the impartial enforcement of order and justice by law.

This is true enough, but it is not, in my view, the whole story. Aquinas is right to describe justice as a *rational* appetite insofar as it apprehends universal goods and norms. Such norms not only underwrite self-interest by grounding *my claim*; they also impose obligations on me insofar as they require that I recognize and respond appropriately to the claims of others. This essential aspect of justice orients the will to the common good of political community not simply as the best available means of my securing personal goods but to the personal goods of fellow citizens for their own sakes, in recognition of their basic human status and personhood. Thus, justice, insofar as it is rightly understood and cultivated within a polity, will draw citizens into a friendly stance toward one another—in which the goods of fellow citizens are pursued *for their own sakes* in the common commitment to justice—which, in turn, may serve as the basis for personal interaction and regard.

This is, of course, not to say that civic friendship easily takes root in any political soil where a commitment to justice is professed. As was noted, a good deal of caution and realism about the character of a people is required. However, at the same time the commitment to justice instantiates a basic friendliness among community members that, to the degree that it forms the basis of a political society, provides the basis for a real form of friendship.

SUPERVENIENCE

A range of characteristics has been discussed thus far that serve to focus attention on what is an essential feature of civic friendship, namely, its *supervenience*. That is to say, civic friendship is not a relationship that can be simply posited by law, as a business partnership creates a particular relationship between entrepreneurs or even as a constitution codifies a relationship between citizens. Civic friendship is a relationship for which prerequisite conditions may be created, even particular civic activities fostered, but that fundamentally requires the free exercise of goodwill among persons within a political community. This has been evident first, of course, in the distinction between formal legal requirements of justice and intentional criteria defining virtues and relationships between friends. (This distinction informs Aristotle's caveat about civic friendship in the *Eudemian Ethics*.) Second, there would seem to be a fundamental difference, entailing supervenience, between the virtues of justice and love or generosity. Justice, inasmuch as it denotes giving what is due, lends itself to being ensconced in law—this is indeed its central case—whereas the further virtues of love and generosity appear to be at odds with legal enactment. The essential liberality of these virtues would seem to be substantially undermined by codification. Finally, the distinction between the formalized requirements of law and governmental procedure, on the one hand, and political association more generally, on the other—which we had to employ even to describe adequately the relationship between citizens—applies even more so to civic friendship. When civic friendship arises among citizens and becomes in the best circumstances characteristic of a political culture, it does so not as the *product* of legal enactment. Of course, for reasons we have discussed, good law importantly establishes preconditions for friendship (a friendly stance toward fellow citizens), but this connection is best described as indirect. The virtues and attitudes that define friendship itself *supervene* on formalized political relationships. Thus, it is of great importance not to locate civic friendship directly in the operation of government and law. To do so is to collapse an important distinction and to run the risk, if Aristotle is right, of aggravating, or worse, generating, political problems rather than solving them.

Insufficient attention to this supervenience, I would argue, is a significant problem with Sibyl Schwarzenbach's account of civic friendship. Wishing to ground political friendship in the relationally "reproductive praxis" that she argues women exemplify in private relationships, Schwarzenbach recommends structuring legal norms around an "ethic of care" that will express the political society's commitment to civic friendship. In so doing she gives short shrift to the very limited ability the state has to engender and sustain high levels of care and concern apart from the particular personal relationships in which such care originates. Of course, this points to the deeper problem (aside from the state's limited capacity to affect the kind of civic friendship Schwarzenbach envisions) that she simply practically elides an important difference between familial and political relationships.[61]

PATRIOTISM: COMMUNITY AS THE LOCUS OF CIVIC FRIENDSHIP

If civic friendship is an ideal not only consistent with, but complementary of, political virtues, it still seems subject to the criticism that, save for small participatory polities, it lacks the reciprocity that any true friendship requires.[62] For there to be real friendship, goodwill must be mutually felt and known, but such mutual commitment is only communicated haphazardly in large modern nation-states. So for life beyond Sparta or the long-disintegrated New England townships that Alexis de Tocqueville praised so highly, there is little to say about civic friendship. Better to speak simply of patriotism or the personal bonds cultivated in intimate, private associations.

Such criticism, once again, has a lot of force. Indeed, there is much to be said for a political arrangement that vests political power and responsibility in localized communities in order to facilitate not simply political activity, but the greater occasion for common action and community relations that heightened political importance is likely to stimulate. Such a localized structure, as Tocqueville argued, while not strictly necessary, is a primary catalyst to the cultivation of a vibrant patriotism.[63]

Nevertheless, I think that there is also something important to be said about the potential for civic friendship that exists in even large, relatively diffused polities. For there is, I think it is clear, a vital symbiotic relationship between patriotism and civic friendship that ought to be given due consideration. By "patriotism," I do not mean to invoke the preferential loyalty that the term usually denotes. For the purposes of this chapter, I simply mean a commitment to one's political community *as such*—the traditions, mores, culture, history, constitution and laws, and so on—that together comprise what is meant by referring to this particular community. Patriotism in this sense (or in any other, really) does not amount to civic friendship since it describes a relationship between citizens and their country—one of commitment to the good of a particular political community. It does not strictly describe the relationship *between citizens*, and insofar as it refers to the civic bond, it would seem to describe a rather general, impersonal relationship mediated by a social entity (in other words, the relationship of parts as they see themselves related by the whole). Despite this difference, there are a couple of important points of contact between the two.

In one sense, of course, insofar as friendship is characterized by common action for a shared purpose, actions and expressions of patriotism strengthen the general awareness and commitment to act as fellow citizens in a common cause. The ends of politics do not terminate in preservation of the state or its political culture, yet this must be a very large part of what politics is about. Thus, civic friendship is in significant part directed to patriotism's object, that is, the community as such.

But what might we say of civic friendship in a more robust sense, not simply common cause in preservation of the political community and execution of political projects but civic friendship as a mutually recognized commitment of goodwill among citizens? If it is true that a right understanding of justice ensconces a friendly stance among citizens in a community's constitutional structure, it follows that—at least formally speaking—a commitment to the good of one's community entails a commitment to the good of each of its members. Moreover, such a connection is not necessarily always that far from individual consciousness. Consider, for example, the common affirmation in the Pledge of Allegiance that commitment to the *indivisible republic* entails liberty and justice *for all*. Commitment to the whole is essentially linked to its inclusion of all persons and protection of their good according to fair and just principles. Thus, in an important sense, commitments of patriotism are commitments to the good of one's fellow citizens. Of course, they are at best indirect commitments—both insofar as patriotism is immediately directed to the good of a social entity and, practically speaking, insofar as expressions and actions of patriotism are often simply left to be observed or are indiscriminately broadcast to the general public or in common assemblage.

At the same time, I think it is not difficult to see that a vibrant life of patriotism within a political community creates a social reservoir, so to speak, upon which citizens draw in their direct, personal interactions. The engagement of citizens does not occur like that of two strangers who meet by happenstance of a mutually advantageous end. It occurs within the context of a political culture that informs what the relationship is about. This is, of course, not simply comprised of the formalized constitutional and legal structures of the polity but, just as important, by the shared understanding of and attitude toward these things embodied in the customs, virtues, and history of the broader political culture. The personal connection that a citizen has with these things may run very deep, particularly insofar as they inform her life on a regular basis or, perhaps, have deeply affected friends and family near to her (as when a family member has been lost in a war). These attachments to a political community can be brought to the fore or, in a sense, activated, by connection with a fellow citizen. Such interactions may be sporadic and may rotate among a group of citizens. Yet, within the context of the political culture that grounds and informs them, as well as the personal attachments of patriotism that each citizen has to the community, they create the possibility of vibrantly experienced relations of friendship among citizens.

My point in drawing attention to this somewhat pedestrian connection between patriotism and civic friendship is twofold (and is not as pedestrian as the connection itself). In the first place, it is to bolster the possibility of civic friendship as a form of association that may be realized in important ways even in societies that do not emphasize or give primacy to life at the political level. Civic friendship in the sense I intend here does not entail the supremacy of political activity, in which—as for Aristotle—all social forms are directed toward contribution to or participation in political life. (Of course, all forms of association have something important to contribute to the common good, but with Aquinas I would affirm that in ordered entities the function of constitutive parts is not *primarily* that of the whole.[64]) I take the view of civic friendship I am advocating here to be quasi-Aristotelian.

It does importantly follow an Aristotelian line by tying the purpose of political community to human virtue and recognizing the way in which substantial political cultures and particular friendships may foster the human good in unique and irreplaceable ways. It is less Aristotelian in its emphasis on the way civic friendship draws upon a *repository of goodwill* instantiated in the political culture rather than a *mode of life* in which political activity and virtues come to predominate. Finally, it is counter-Aristotelian in its affirmation of the intrinsic and independent goodness of life beyond the elevated domain of politics and philosophy. In this way it is more compatible with viewing political society as a community of communities—a proposition that I argued in the previous chapter is necessary if the political common good is to possess real normative priority.

Second, this connection between patriotism and civic friendship is an important one because it draws attention to the significance of the community *as such* in fully realizing the goods of political association. I argued in Chapter 3 that if we take real community to be a basic human good, and if we recognize that it makes good sense to speak of the good or flourishing of communities as such, then perforce we must give the good of communities as such fundamental consideration in our practical deliberations about human flourishing. The argument here adds to that this further point: it is often precisely the community as such that not only serves as the common object of action among associating members but *also* embodies the ideals, virtues, and practices they share. The significance of this point is that the goods of political association cannot be fully realized apart from a firm commitment to the polity as such. Contrary to this view, in a vein similar to that of Mark Murphy discussed in the previous chapter, John Finnis suggests that it is best to think of "community or association not as *a* community or *an* association (an 'entity' or 'substance' or 'thing' which 'exists,' acts, etc.) but rather as community or association, an ongoing state of affairs, a sharing of life or an action or of interests, an associating or coming-together."[65] The merit of this formulation is that it encourages us not to abstract associational goods from the concrete benefit and flourishing that they contribute to their members, namely, individual human persons. However, if my argument here is correct, both Finnis and Murphy are wrong to conceive of the political common good apart from its instantiation as *the* common good, the flourishing of this particular community. Thus, to use Murphy's terminology, we must employ as part of an adequate description of the common good not only the aggregative (or additive) goods of all individuals and basic associations within the community but also the *distinctive* good of the political community itself. The essential flaw of Murphy's account, I would submit, is that he fails to include this distinctive good as part of the overall range of goods that comprises the political common good. Instead, he posits a dichotomy between the aggregative and distinctive views of the common good that fails—as we must—to take them both in hand. As it touches civic friendship, this error overlooks the vital role that the community as such plays in contextualizing and facilitating friendships among citizens—as a reservoir of goodwill—embodying essential political virtues of justice, love, and generosity.

This reservoir of goodwill is a vital part of a larger political culture, and understanding the full range of goods intrinsic to political life requires that we take up that concept directly. This is the subject of the next chapter.

5

Political Culture as an Intrinsic Good

I have argued that civic friendship is a core part of what it is that makes politics an intrinsic good. It provides a real form of friendship that is unique from those forms experienced at other levels of association—personal, familial, and so forth. And it is uniquely focused on the virtue of justice, directing all other virtues to the common good. This is essentially the Aristotelian form: citizens being ruled and ruling in turn, carrying on the pursuit of questions of goodness and justice in community together.[1] Although Aristotle envisioned a community focused on the political sphere—and one in which subpolitical associations become directed toward the good of the polis—I argued that (a) the Thomistic model views political association as an intrinsic good, but not *the most important good*, and (b) a real form of civic friendship can exist even in extended democracies because of a "repository of goodwill" that informs citizens' actions in specific instances of political partnership. Constant and close political involvement is not required for citizens' actions to be guided by a mutual commitment to each other and the common good.

To say that a "repository of goodwill" informs citizens' activities is simply to say that they take place within a particular political culture. Political culture is a broad and slippery concept, denoting everything from widely held philosophical views (e.g., Enlightenment individualism, human equality) to practices, customs, and mores of citizens and public officials (e.g., rules of decorum in the US Senate, law-abidingness) to shared political history, celebrations, and symbols (e.g., the American Revolution, Independence Day, the United States flag, etc.). I intend all of these things to some degree: everything that makes up a political tradition and characterizes a people's shared identity and life together.[2] Some philosophical ideas are more political than others, of course. Affirmation of human equality is more directly political than a general cultural tendency toward individualism. Likewise, a custom of law-abidingness is more political than a cultural habit of hospitality. I will focus on those dimensions of culture that are more directly political, but as the argument progresses the line between the specifically political and more broadly social will necessarily blur.

We must wade into the ambiguity, however, because profound political goods are to be discovered there. My argument will be that it is most of all in understanding and participating in the goods of a healthy and dynamic political culture that the *intrinsic value* of politics resides. This moves us beyond civic friendship, which is (especially in its classic Aristotelian form) centered on the *activity* of citizens in shared governance. The vantage point of political culture takes another step back and considers the customs, institutions, history, and traditions of a political community. It considers the citizen not only as a present actor but as a participant in a community extended through time.

The argument I advance draws heavily on the work of Edmund Burke, particularly his *Reflections on the Revolution in France* and *A Philosophical Enquiry into the Origin of Our Ideas of the Sublime and the Beautiful*. In a book like this one, it is worth asking, why Burke? He is often thought to be not only outside the Thomistic-Aristotelian natural law tradition but also deeply opposed to it. Where the natural law recognizes transcendent moral norms, Burke eschews abstract principle in favor of custom and convention. Indeed, Alasdair MacIntyre has offhandedly dismissed Burke as a defender of irrational tradition, since in the *Reflections* he describes nature as "wisdom without reason."[3] However, in my view MacIntyre's dismissal is badly mistaken. In this, I follow many Burke scholars of the past fifty years who recognize the importance of nature and transcendent moral norms to Burke's thought. These scholars reject the old view that Burke was essentially a pragmatic utilitarian who privileged convention and custom above any idea of natural law.[4] There are some prominent outliers like MacIntyre, but the scholarly consensus now seems to be that this gets Burke significantly wrong.[5] Although Burke may not qualify as a natural law theorist per se, he grounded his political thought and action in a notion of real human nature.[6] Burke was certainly a theorist of tradition, but his defense of particular traditions is situated within the larger framework of universal moral norms. Thus, I agree with Jesse Norman's observation that MacIntyre's own brand of Thomism owes much more to Burke than he allows with his dismissal.[7] Indeed, when Burke is understood to be defending traditions of *rationality*, in important respects his ethical and political theory begins to resemble MacIntyre's.

It will be helpful to begin by limning the contours of my argument. My first task will be to reconstruct Burke's account of the goodness of political culture. In my view this rests on two related goods, both of which spring from his doctrine of politics as an "entailed inheritance": a tradition of rationality and a tradition of the moral imagination. Grasping the full import of his view of the moral imagination requires that we move from the *Reflections* to the *Enquiry* to explore his ideas of the sublime and the beautiful. This move is necessary for two reasons. First, it explains the centrality of the imagination to Burke's view of political culture, and second, it illuminates the meaning of the "noble equality" embodied in the "idea of the gentleman"—something Burke takes to be an essential goodness of Western political culture. I then pause to consider two worries about Burke's view, that is, the sacralization of politics and the aristocratic sociopolitical structure that provides the context of his argument. My second major task is to argue that the Burkean picture I have painted indeed constitutes a good intrinsic to human sociability. The main task here is to demonstrate that the goods of political culture hold out *unique* opportunities for flourishing not available in other forms of association. By way of illustration, I look to Abraham Lincoln's reliance on the Declaration of Independence to challenge nineteenth-century proslavery arguments. This pivotal American contest demonstrates the general applicability of the Burkean notions of traditions of reason and the moral imagination. Finally, before addressing the most salient objections to my argument, I elaborate the way in which a tradition of the moral imagination ennobles citizens by drawing them into a particular kind of community membership.

Edmund Burke and the Good of Political Culture

Reflections on the Revolution in France is a sprawling letter written to an associate of Burke who was intrigued by the very visible support of the French Revolution in England.[8] Burke responded to his query with roughly two hundred fifty pages of sometimes circuitous, often impassioned, and consistently brilliant argument for the superiority of the English constitution over the Enlightenment pretentions of the French Revolution. Although the work is ad hoc, it contains the mature philosophical and political reflections of one of the great minds of Western civilization. For all its complexity, however, the *Reflections* evinces a thorough consistency and argumentative focus. In my view, the essence of its argument may be helpfully expressed in this basic idea: the English constitution of "entailed inheritance" creates a politics of "rational and manly freedom."

There are three key components here, all of which are necessary to understanding Burke's view of political culture. First, "entailed inheritance" refers to the particular way that traditions develop within the English constitutional mind.[9] From the connection between generations emerges two closely related forms of tradition—a tradition of rationality and a tradition of the moral imagination—that embody the great Burkean political desideratum: "a rational and manly freedom."[10] Understanding the real meaning and import of the entailed inheritance is necessary to see why Burke takes tradition to be a distinctly *rational* thing, so let us begin there.

ENTAILED INHERITANCE AND A TRADITION OF RATIONALITY

Early on in the *Reflections* Burke establishes the idea of entailed inheritance as the cornerstone of English constitutionalism. "You will observe," he argues, "that from Magna Charta to the Declaration of Right, it has been the uniform policy of our constitution to claim and assert our liberties, as an *entailed inheritance* derived to us from our forefathers, and to be transmitted to our posterity."[11] This use of "entailed inheritance" is a legal analogy that conveys the idea of *a tradition animated by moral responsibility*. At common law, an estate passed on with an entailment could not be later disposed of at the inheritor's discretion, but was rather marked for bequest to specified descendants. It involves not simply bequest according to the normal course of the common law but particular intentionality on the part of the grantor.[12] It is a form of inheritance that reaches across multiple generations and places limitations and responsibilities on those in the middle, so to speak. The bequest does not belong to any one generation; it is the joint possession of generations united in community.

Significantly, Burke argues that this way of looking at traditional liberties is not merely a fortuitous idiosyncrasy of the English. Rather, it follows the "pattern of nature."

> Our political system is placed in a just correspondence and symmetry
> with the order of the world . . . wherein, by the disposition of a
> stupenduous wisdom, moulding together the great mysterious
> incorporation of the human race, the whole, at one time, is never old, or
> middle-aged, or young, but in a condition of unchangeable constancy,
> moves on through the varied tenour of perpetual decay, fall, renovation,
> and progression.[13]

Thus, recognizing the social and political bonds that unite generations is
not a pious contrivance peculiar to English constitutionalism; it is a recognition of the basic connection *in all of nature* among generations. And because
we are connected by nature, so we are bound by the moral responsibilities
that define our communities.

Burke's approbation of the "entailed inheritance" begins to take shape,
not as a jingoistic sneer at the French but as an account of social realities.
"This sort of people are so taken up with their theories about the rights of
man, that they have totally forgot his nature," Burke argues.[14] The French
revolutionaries were emboldened by the Enlightenment project of articulating the fundamental rights of man on the basis of a universal rationality:
"Liberté, Égalité, Fraternité." Theorizing a Rousseauean "state of nature,"
one could describe the essential nature of man and define his rights accordingly. Burke makes what is now a familiar critique of this abstract state-
of-nature speculation: it does not account for the deeply *social dimension* of
human nature. One cannot adequately describe human nature apart from
embeddedness within a community, and if that's the case, *human* rights are
fundamentally *social* rights.[15] That is, they must be experienced, given context, and finally understood within communities. The Jacobins snatched up
the axe of absolute, abstract human rights and used it to hack down the tree
of state. Yet, they had already carved up human nature itself.

Burke is not an opponent of rights, but "real rights" are those possessed
by real human persons, that is, men and women in community: "Far am I
from denying in theory . . . the real rights of men. In denying their false
claims of right, I do not mean to injure those which are real, and are such as
their pretended rights would totally destroy. If civil society be made for the
advantage of man, all the advantages for which it is made become his right.[16]
This may sound like Burke is saying that people have rights to whatever it is
that the social contract specifies. Thus, *human rights* do not exist, only *positive rights* invented by convention. Yet, this misses his point because society
is *not* created by the social contract. Because society is mankind's natural

state, human rights are the rights of men and women in society, which in significant part consist of the rights *to the goods of society itself.* These include, Burke goes on to say, a right to the administration of justice, a right to inheritance, and a right to "instruction in life and consolation in death."[17] Therefore, any vindication of human rights that explodes rights connected to the goods of society itself is a travesty of moral and political reasoning.

In addition to missing the natural *social content* of rights, Burke contends that the French revolutionaries mistake the true *process* of identifying rights. "The rights of men are in a sort of middle, incapable of definition, but not impossible to be discerned. The rights of men in governments are their advantages; and these are often in balances between differences of good."[18] While Burke agrees that we can know by reason that human rights exist, saying what they are precisely is not something we simply reason our way to via a process of abstract deduction. Defining the content of rights happens in the lived experience of communities. Abstract theorizing yields extremes that appear to be metaphysically certain (for example, all people have a right to access the basic essentials of existence) but wind up being morally and politically more ambiguous. What happens when our legitimate uses of the river water exhaust all available supply before everyone's needs are met? What happens when my freedom of speech or right to be heard encroaches on your right not to be slandered? Or again, when putative rights of individual autonomy come into conflict with community standards, and thus other people's rights to engage in meaningful association. The real content of rights must be worked out in specific situations.[19]

This is not to say that Burke did not believe in absolute human rights and that everything is determined purely by context. As Peter Stanlis argues, his early defense of the religious liberty of the Irish demonstrates a clear commitment to the laws of nature that grant basic rights of justice, as did his vigorous and harsh condemnation of the administrative abuses by the East India Company.[20] Still, the rights of social beings are specified within the life of the communities they inhabit.[21]

Furthermore, the discerning process has a generational component. Where the pride and self-confidence of the French inclined them to "despise experience as the wisdom of unlettered men," Burke argues that we are bound by the "solid test of long experience."[22] The complexities of human life and society are such that we should not expect to be able to arrive at reliable conclusions in isolation. Society is a partnership, and "As the ends of such a partnership cannot be obtained in many generations, it becomes a partnership not only between those who are living, but between those who are living, those who are dead, and those who are to be born."[23] Applying this idea specifically to politics, he argues, "The science of government [is] a matter which requires experience, and even more experience than any person can gain in his whole life, however sagacious and observing he may be."[24] This generational character of our search for truth ultimately underwrites Burke's doctrine of prescription, according to which long-accepted usage and custom are morally and legally binding—at least presumptively. The longer the usage, the stronger the prescription in its favor. Burke goes so far as to say that prescription is part of the law of nature.[25]

So, what do we say about MacIntyre's proof text against Burke's commitment to the rationality of tradition? Nature is "wisdom without reflection, and above it."[26] First, one notices that the claim is *not* that wisdom does not involve reflection. Rather, it is nature that operates above the reflection of wisdom. In this passage Burke is not making a claim about human nature but rather about the pattern of the cosmos in general. The idea, in fact, appears within the context of Burke's argument that the generational continuity of English constitutionalism follows the pattern of nature. The policy of entailed inheritance, Burke maintains, is the result of "profound reflection," and thus it ends up corresponding to the pattern of nature. Nature itself operates above *our own reflection*, but we achieve the wisdom of nature precisely through reflection carried out across generations.

For Burke, the point is not simply to resist change. He is not a reactionary. "The idea of inheritance furnishes a sure principle of conservation, and a sure principle of transmission; without at all excluding a *principle of improvement*."[27] Society is, in fact, a partnership in "all perfection," and he readily allows that the French government was "full of abuses."[28] The Jacobin folly was not a desire for reform; it was "to consider his country as nothing but carte blanche, upon which he may scribble whatever he pleases"—and so to discard the distilled wisdom of past generations.[29]

The rationality of tradition, therefore, is evident in Burke's understanding of both the *means* and *end* of political society. On the one hand, reason is distilled and expressed in generations of social practice because the complexity of life requires extended reflection. On the other, the *goal* of society is continued improvement, rooted in a humble acknowledgment of faults, not a smug satisfaction with the status quo. Yet, on that very same principle of humility, a prudent reformer will adopt a posture of deference to past generations earnestly engaged in the very same pursuit of a good society.

ATTACHMENT, SENTIMENT, AND A TRADITION
OF THE MORAL IMAGINATION

From Attachment to Just Moral Sentiment

If Burke's object in the *Reflections* is to demonstrate that the French revolutionaries have misconstrued human nature by trading on a specious brand of Enlightenment rationality, he is equally concerned to show how employing *any form of reason* devoid of real feeling and moral sentiment is bound to deform human nature as well. "Without opening one new avenue to the understanding," Burke charges, "they have succeeded in stopping up those that lead to the heart."[30] Here again, where French innovations will fail, the English tradition of "entailed inheritance" succeeds because it gets human nature right. Just as the "private stock of reason" cannot achieve the wisdom of a tradition of rationality, human nature without engaged affections is vulnerable to "the fallible and feeble contrivances of . . . reason."[31] The goal of political community is a "rational and *manly* freedom" because reason alone is insufficient to restrain the passions. As the ancients taught, the head rules the gut through the chest.[32] Burke stands against Enlightenment rationality here again by highlighting the necessity of rightly ordered affections to the moral and political life. As Jesse Norman explains Burke's stance, "People cannot reason themselves into a good society, for a good society is rooted not merely in reason but in the sentiments and emotions."[33]

The tradition of entailed inheritance engages the affections in several ways, most immediately by "binding up the constitution of our country with our dearest domestic ties; adopting our fundamental laws into the bosom of our family affections."[34] This is the nature of an inheritance: something passed down from your parents and forebears and—especially because entailed—bequeathed to your children and grandchildren. Because the English constitution is the family inheritance of every citizen ("a sort of family settlement"[35]), the natural affections of the human heart are enlisted in its service.

Burke, however, is making a much larger point than this about the affections. It is this: just as human rationality is developed and matured over time, natural human affections should become part of a broader system of cultivated moral sentiment that flourishes in a society's shared customs, manners, institutions, and history. Famously, Burke calls this system "the wardrobe of a moral imagination."[36] At first we are attached to those things we are intimately related to—friends, family, our home, and so on. These affections are immediate, untutored, and visceral. As we mature, however, without being replaced, our affections develop into a deeper and broader array of just moral sentiment. Even as virtues are cultivated, indeed, in the very process of cultivating virtue, we should begin to acquire feelings and sentiments—one might think of them as postures of the soul—that are not necessarily instinctive but are nevertheless fitting and perfective of human nature.

Consider, for example, the moral development of a young boy. He begins with a simple and visceral attachment to his parents. Over time, if all goes well, these will mature into sentiments of respect, gratitude, duty, and a deeper love borne of fuller understanding and appreciation. Even within the home, this is part of a fuller moral development. He will be taught that certain sentiments—whether he naturally feels them or not—are good and suitable: sympathy for an injured friend, care for the beauty and fragility of nature, gentle deference to an aging grandparent. These are sentiments he should foster in his heart and with his actions so that in time they will define his character. Likewise, as his activity reaches beyond the domestic realm, he will see that the virtues and sentiments he has cultivated at home apply in the broader community. His parents' rules are not the only laws he must respect and obey. His immediate relations are not the only ones to whom he is bound in relationships of duty and accountability. Finally, he will encounter (in some ways) a wider scope of appropriate sentiment—greater crimes that demand fiercer indignation, more majestic sublimities that invoke awe, and a vast array of human excellences that should elicit delight and emulation. In matters of the heart, such sentiments are the stuff of a well-cultivated human soul.

The Moral Imagination: Beauty, Sublimity, and the Spirit of a Gentleman

One of Burke's greatest indictments against the French revolutionaries is that they have assaulted their countrymen's capacities of just this sort of right moral sentiment. In a reckless enthusiasm to establish a new "empire of light and reason" and to vindicate its supposed rights, they have denuded social relations of all their humanizing feeling.[37] By severing the ties of inherited tradition, they lost their hearts as well as their heads. In a celebrated passage, Burke describes the spiritual poverty into which the revolutionary fervor dragged France:

> All the decent drapery of life is to be rudely torn off. All the superadded
> ideas, furnished from the wardrobe of a moral imagination, which
> the heart owns, and the understanding ratifies, as necessary to cover

the defects of our naked shivering nature, and to raise it to dignity in our own estimation, are to be exploded as a ridiculous, absurd, and antiquated fashion.[38]

The term "moral imagination" is Burke's neologism,[39] and by it he intends an elaboration on the idea of just moral sentiment. By a "wardrobe of the moral imagination" he intends not only the spiritual condition of an individual soul—but just as important, the cultural storehouse of feeling and sentiment that informs social relationships. These inherited resources comprise a tradition of the moral imagination.

There are two main features of Burke's idea of the moral imagination to highlight in this discussion. I alluded to the first with the example of the boy, that is, the moral imagination is a faculty of real moral perception, not mere subjective feeling. The second is a more complicated point about why Burke draws on the human capacity of *imagination* when talking about the moral sentiments. Answering this question requires that we consider his ideas of beauty and sublimity (however briefly) and the way they are expressed in what Burke calls "the spirit of a gentleman."[40] This, in turn, is necessary to grasping the full force of Burke's idea of political culture.

Concerning the first point, notice first the provenance of the moral imagination: it is something "the heart owns and the understanding ratifies." Cultivated moral sentiment is not *only* a matter of feeling but also a posture of the soul that commands rational assent. It is, therefore, as Russell Kirk observes, primarily a matter of perceiving moral realities in the world around us: "Burke signifies that power of ethical perception which strides beyond the barriers of private experience and momentary events."[41] Moreover, Burke immediately follows the "wardrobe" passage with examples that indicate the objectivity of the moral imagination: "On [the French] scheme of things, a king is but a man; a queen is but a woman; a woman is but an animal; and an animal not of the highest order."[42] The moral imagination concerns not simply the unique dignity of kings but the dignity of humanity itself. So we should rule out the possibility that Burke only has cultural convention in mind. Moreover, in a later passage he argues that various sentiments like awe to kings, duty to magistrates, and reverence to priests are "natural . . . because all other feelings are false and spurious . . . and render us unfit for rational liberty."[43] In other words, these moral sentiments are natural to human relationships, and apart from them we do not achieve full, rational human flourishing. The moral imagination perceives that a regicide is no mere homicide because to kill a king is an affront to the high honor—even awe—

due one given the august charge of representing and caring for the common good.[44] It understands the respect owed to human dignity and that to dehumanize always leads to exploitation. Not to perceive these things, as well as not to *feel* them, is a failure of the moral imagination. Thus, Burke describes a capacity of objective ethical understanding.

Given this, it may seem odd that Burke chooses to connect the moral sentiments to the imagination. It is, after all, the realm of "wit, fancy, invention, and the like."[45] However, he does so for important reasons. In the first place, the imagination is that power of the soul most affected by the passions we experience when encountering the beautiful and the sublime.[46] And in turn, a kind of dialogue or harmonization between beauty and sublimity is at the heart of what Burke takes to be the great genius of the Western ideal of the gentleman. Although the *Reflections* is more than three decades removed from Burke's *Enquiry* and a life of politics filled that interim, the imprint of Burke's aesthetics is evident in his account of the moral imagination and political culture. A full account of that work is impossible here, but it is necessary to highlight those key ideas that shape Burke's later thought.[47]

On Beauty and Sublimity

As Richard Bourke reports, Burke began the *Enquiry* as a result of being captivated by the "great tho' terrible Scenes" of a river overwhelming its banks.[48] He was awestruck by the greatness and terrifying force of nature, next to the smallness and fragility of man. This, he noted, is a markedly different kind of passion than is commonly induced by the beauty and serenity of nature. Thus, by "beautiful" Burke means the wide range of things we find pleasant and attractive, and thus are instinctively drawn to love (albeit in different ways): a rose, a small child, a quiet meadow, the soft grace of physical form, and so forth. The sublime, in contrast, picks out those things that stimulate passions connected to terror or fear. It gives us the feeling of being imperiled or overwhelmed. Just as there are different kinds of beauty, there are a range of feelings associated with the sublime: from "terror" and "astonishment" to less intense experiences of "admiration, reverence, and respect."[49] So it encompasses, on the one hand, the sense of foreboding or dread we might get standing at the edge of a dark, vast forest, and on the other, the respect we would feel in the presence of a great statesman or a world-class musician. These feelings are very different, of course, but they are connected by a thread of greatness that is in some sense truly awesome. As Richard Bourke explains, "The admiration of the sublime takes us beyond ourselves . . . as the soul expands to embrace objects at the limit of its comprehension, or to exercise self-control beyond the natural human capacity. . . . Awareness of surpassing greatness ennobles the mind."[50]

Burke realizes that, as with beauty, the sublime has a kind of attraction for us too. He calls this feeling "delight," as distinct from the "love" that beauty engenders.[51] Even things that strike terror in our hearts can delight us with a sort of negative pleasure at not being destroyed. And we are, as well, attracted to milder expressions of the sublime, even though admiration is still a notably different attraction than love.

The *Enquiry* is a treatise on aesthetics, but one begins to see potential connections to the moral virtues that, indeed, Burke incorporates into his analysis. The "sublimer" virtues, he reasons, are those such as justice, wisdom, and courage—virtues that evince a sternness, self-discipline, and greatness of soul. The "softer" virtues are those such as patience, kindness, and compassion. They're not characteristics that command respect exactly, but they are lovely and wonderfully attractive. Give us an august and commanding general for the battlefield, but in our private lives we prefer amiable companions and "the soft green of the soul."[52]

Now, Burke does not take these qualities of sublimity and beauty to be mutually exclusive. They overlap and blend sometimes. (He might have said often.) But they do tend to characterize different spheres of life, different passions, virtues, and dispositions that attract us in distinct ways. We will see shortly that as Burke conceives of them in the social sphere, they broadly describe different modes of life experienced in the private and public spheres, respectively.

We can now begin to understand why Burke speaks of a moral *imagination*. The imagination is the capacity of the soul in which the passions associated with beauty and sublimity can most profoundly take root. Unlike our powers of sense and judgment, the imagination is "a sort of creative power" that encompasses "whatever is called wit, fancy, invention, and the like." Even more than the senses, Burke argues, it is "the most extensive province of pleasure and pain, as it is the region of our fears and our hopes, and of all our passions that are connected with them."[53] Consequently, whatever captures the imagination becomes a "commanding idea" in the mind and heart—ultimately defining what we love, what we fear, and what we aspire to. A very great power of the soul indeed.

The Spirit of a Gentleman

All of this establishes the connection between beauty, sublimity, and the imagination, but it does not yet make plain why beauty and sublimity are central to Burke's account of political culture. For this, we need to consider what Burke calls one of the two fundamental principles of Western civilization, namely, the "spirit of a gentleman."[54] This spirit derives from the "antient chivalry" of Europe, which Richard Bourke describes in this way: "The mutual allegiance between vassal and lord was a reciprocal tie of loyalty based, as Burke presented it, on disinterested attachment. Pledged to fidelity, the medieval knight was at the same time typically animated by chivalry and piety. His code of honor thus bound him to God, women, the vulnerable, and his superiors."[55]

From this root, Burke understood the modern spirit of a gentleman to animate social and political relationships with sentiments of mutual regard. In particular, it embraces sentiments that bring the great and powerful together in a kind of friendship with the common and vulnerable. "It was this," Burke explains, "which, without confounding ranks, had produced a *noble equality*, and handed it down through all the gradations of social life. It was this opinion which mitigated kings into companions, and raised private men to be fellows with kings. . . . The fierceness of pride and power [was obliged] to submit to the soft collar of social esteem."[56] Power was made "gentle" and obedience "liberal" in a system of relationships that imposed moral obligations in both directions: kindness and deference. All of this represents an "incorprat[ion] into politics [of] the sentiments which beautify and soften private society."[57] Thus, on the one hand, the moral imagination of the gentleman beautifies and softens the august sublimity of authority, and on the other, it elevates and ennobles the loveliness of private life. King and citizen are brought together in a sort of "noble equality."[58]

We can now see the full significance of Burke's use of the term "moral imagination." On the one hand, it is a faculty of real ethical perception that recognizes appropriate sentiments and real moral duties. On the other, it is an *imaginative* capacity that may become impassioned and captivated by the beauty and sublimity of life. Thus, a principle of gentle power may really become a "commanding idea" in a king's mind because its beauty stirs the heart and captures the imagination.[59] It may be a moral sentiment that most naturally grows in the soft loam of family life, but a mature mind will imagine its beauty in other soils as well. Likewise, things that are noble really deserve respect and admiration, but these are freely given when the imagination is inspired by greatness.

Moreover, it is an imaginative capacity in the sense that it is *creative*. It admits of cultivation and elaboration as the realm of wit, fancy, and invention. The images of the imagination can build upon themselves (for good or ill) and ultimately dominate: "When men have suffered their imaginations to be long affected with any idea, it so wholly engrosses them as to shut out by degrees almost every other."[60] Thus, in shaping the moral sentiments, Burke recognizes the pivotal importance of the imagination. In a healthy soul, reasoned judgment will direct the imagination and oversee its creations. But what captures the imagination captures the soul.

The Moral Imagination and Political Culture

The goal of political culture, therefore, should be twofold: first, to cultivate manners, customs, and institutions that habituate citizens and statesmen to rightly formed moral sentiments. This is a crucial part of the picture because human nature is, in a sense, open. We may cultivate it in a way that is perfective of our nature, or in a way that is destructive. The imagination, like human reason, is susceptible to being carried away by base passions. Love may be corrupted to lust and nobility to pride. Thus, Burke argues that the "wardrobe of the moral imagination" should be stocked with "coat[s] of prejudice" that inform our opinions, establish just sentiments, and specify duty. "Prejudice renders a man's virtue his habit; and not a series of unconnected acts. Through just prejudice, his duty becomes a part of his nature."[61] Furthermore, the forms of public life should mirror and instruct our attraction to beauty and nobility. "There ought to be a system of manners in every nation which a well-formed mind would be disposed to relish. To make us love our country, our country ought to be lovely."[62]

Second, and very closely related, a healthy political culture will stock the moral imagination with captivating images of beauty and nobility. In significant part, this is not something that is *done* but is simply something that *happens* when continuity in the life of a people is maintained. Over time, the "gallery of portraits" of "canonized forefathers" and "illustrating ancestors" grows larger. "Records, evidences, and titles" build up over time. Institutions are strengthened as they become identified with particular beloved and august persons who have held them.[63]

Nevertheless, such images must be *cultivated* as well. "*Always acting as if in the presence of canonized forefathers*" denotes the intentional embrace of the generational community.[64] And because of such *participation*, a "habitual native dignity" is instilled in citizens who consciously understand the gravity of the "liberal descent" of their constitution.[65] In a sense suggested by cultural historian David Hackett Fischer, by the imagination of citizens acting as members of a generational community, images are transformed into "icons"—"regarded with reverence and protected from pollution."[66]

Moreover, Burke admonishes public authorities themselves to cultivate the nobility and greatness of their positions. They ought to be inspired in their duty by the "sublime principles" of a "permanent fame and glory, in the example [you] leave as a rich inheritance to the world."[67] It is the *responsibility* of subjects to show awe and respect to public authority, but at the same time, the authorities themselves bear a responsibility to live up to the dignity and nobility of their offices. They ought to embody the "sublimer virtues" of courage, wisdom, self-sacrifice, determination, and so forth, necessary to establish and sustain the great good of the state as a partnership in the common good of life.[68]

It is of the essence to understand that *both* of these functions of political culture—creating institutions and icons—require concerted action across generations to attain the goods they offer. The great folly of the French revolutionaries was to suppose that they could attain the goods of society on the basis of human nature, when such goods are, in fact, the product of a long-habituated second nature.[69] Social institutions are not pulled out of thin air. The revolutionaries boasted of being able to create customs and institutions on the basis of a new, imposed "geometrical policy." Their conceit, however, misdiagnosed the source of social forms and thus was bound to fail. Not perceiving human nature correctly, they failed to understand the nature of humankind's social inventions, and thus the value of what they had: "You had all these advantages in your antient states; but you chose to act as if you had never been moulded into civil society, and had everything to begin anew. You began ill, because you began by despising everything that belonged to you."[70]

To summarize, Burke views political society as a tradition of the moral imagination as well as a tradition of reason—a community fostering "a rational and *manly* freedom." Human nature dictates that this *must be* the case, simply because people do not act virtuously simply by dent of reason's command. Social order depends upon an engagement of the heart as well as the head. The entailed inheritance accomplishes this according to the "pattern of nature" because—on the basis of the "spirit of philosophical analogy"— it attaches political loyalties to the familial bonds that unite generations.[71] Whereas natural affections are a beginning, a seedbed, human nature matures in a system of moral sentiments ignited by the heart's passion for beauty and greatness. The manners, customs, and institutions of society should all be ordered to create a kind of resonance in the soul with all that beautifies and ennobles.[72] A "generous sense of glory and emulation,"[73] in addition, is fostered by giving citizens and statesmen something to emulate, that is, consciously drawing on the country's history and heroes to transform images of the past into venerable icons of moral and political aspiration. Those who will join the generational partnership that precedes and looks beyond them will attain the riches of a well-furnished moral imagination.

In Burke's view, the political society that emerges from this is marked by a kind of conversation between beauty and sublimity, love and awe, the familiar and the noble. Power is made gentle, and the amiability of private life is ennobled by the greatness of political society—each without losing its own unique contribution to human flourishing. Burke's "little platoon" passage is perhaps his most famous expression of this idea,[74] but a related passage from the *Reflections* makes the point better:

> We begin our public affections in our families. No cold relation is a
> zealous citizen. We pass on to our neighborhoods and our habitual
> provincial connections. These are inns and resting places. Such
> divisions of our country as have been formed by habit, and not by a
> sudden jerk of authority, were *so many little images of the great country in*
> *which the heart found something which it could fill.* The love to the whole is
> not extinguished by this subordinate partiality.[75]

The politics of the French revolutionaries was marked by a self-importance that ran roughshod over the seemingly insignificant patterns of private life. The greatness of the state consumed the small joys of mundane associations. And as we have seen, this is not a vice unique to Jacobin France. Aristotle's polis ultimately subordinates the rest of life to its own ends. Instrumentalizing civil society to the state is a ubiquitous sin in the history of political thought. In my view, however, it is not a mistake that Burke makes. "So many little images of the great country": the proximate connections of everyday life—family, neighborhood, community—are not goods in competition with the overarching political good. *They are images of the country itself.* The greatness of the country is realized in large part in the day-to-day lives of its citizens who, in their local communities, find scope for meaningful connection and action—"*in which the heart found something which it could fill.*" As society is a partnership in "all perfection," it must necessarily include those intimate associations that provide so much of the meaning and joy of life. And as the locus of so much human flourishing, they are themselves "little images of a great country."[76]

Moreover, on the basis of Burkean categories, one may acknowledge the intrinsic dignity of private life itself. Although there is a good deal to be said for the greatness and nobility of political life, it is not the exclusive domain of sublimity and greatness of soul. For the courage, self-sacrifice, and spiritual strength that Burke identifies with the "sublimer" virtues sometimes achieve their most glorious expression precisely in the grueling self-denial and fortitude of everyday life. Alasdair MacIntyre observes that perhaps the greatest model of the moral life is the mother of a seriously disabled child.[77] Such a parent simultaneously embodies the beautiful tenderness and affection of personal intimacy as well as the awesome self-command required to face human frailty, suffering, and uncertainty day after day with compassion and determination. And surely the bravery and self-sacrifice of a soldier on the battlefield is no more sublime than that of Tom VanderWoude, a father who drowned submerged in a septic tank while rescuing his twenty-year-old Down syndrome son.[78] VanderWoude confronted the terror and darkness of death with a profound courage that demands respect, even awe, and inspires emulation.

Therefore, it would be a grave mistake to see political life as the exclusive domain of ennobling virtue. Nevertheless, it is uniquely ennobling in its *extensive* concern for the common good of the whole community and in the way that it fosters traditions of reason and the moral imagination. The political common good involves us in a generational partnership that raises our sights above present concerns and ennobles the mind and heart with permanent things.

Two Clarifications: Sacralization and Nobility

Before proceeding further, it will be helpful to consider a couple of roadblocks to accepting Burke's thought as a viable way to think about the goods of political society: first, the sacralization of politics, and, second, his identification of nobility with *the* nobility, that is, with social rank and class. The *Reflections* is a defense of the English constitution, and a central part of that constitutional tradition, of course, is an established church. Burke defends church establishment. Moreover, his political language is replete with discomfiting religious overtones: "sacred rights," "canonized forefathers," the "consecration" of the English commonwealth and laws, and so on.[79] David Hackett Fischer's use of the term *icon* connotes not merely persuasive or transforming ideas but "sanctif[ied] thought."[80] This kind of language raises multiple concerns: for religious believers, the instrumentalization and subordination of authentic belief to the ends of state by means of civil religion; for Americans, First Amendment concerns about the establishment of religion; for survivors of the twentieth century, the ugly specter of militant nationalism fueled by a sacralized state. Does Burke's account of the reverence and solemnity that should be attached to political institutions poison his thought with political dominance and idolatry? For the following reasons, I think not.

From an American constitutional perspective, of course, Burke's defense of an established church is simply unacceptable. It is important to realize, though, that Burke doesn't argue this as a normative constitutional feature, only as a good for British constitutionalism. What is more important is the underlying message of an established church, that is, that political power of all stripes, from that held by the king to that enjoyed by the citizen, is subject to and constrained by a divine power. "All persons possessing any portion of power ought to be strongly and awefully impressed . . . that they are to account for their conduct . . . to the one great master, author and founder of society."[81] Burke does not suggest the deification of the state; far from it. He embraces the Augustinian principle that the church stands against the abuse of earthly power out of allegiance to a higher kingdom. Genuine faith is the greatest threat despotism faces because "he who fears God fears nothing else."[82] Thus, for Burke, religion is not subordinated to aims of politics.

In light of this, Burke's consecration of the laws and institutions of the state should be understood in a diminished sense. They are sacred in a sense analogous to the ultimate one, that is, set apart for a high and special purpose—not for common use. The consecration of the state is based upon its vital connection to the human good and the extreme harm that can result from pulling it down except in cases of strict necessity.[83] This is another place where Burke mirrors the views of Aquinas, not a thinker questionable in his devotion to the primacy of religion over politics.[84]

In a similar fashion, on the question of nobility Burke's embrace of the aristocratic class structure of England may seem to discredit his ideas in a democratic republic. The US Constitution explicitly bars such positions of rank (Article I, Sections 9, 10), and as Tocqueville explored at length in *Democracy in America*, the spirit of democracy chafes against the pretentions of greatness—whether embodied in systems of rank and preferment or not. Democratic peoples love equality above all else, and the very ideas of nobility and greatness militate against that egalitarian passion.[85] Although he thought democracy unavoidable, Tocqueville was not himself willing to give up on greatness, and he thought he saw some potential for it in a new "American aristocracy," namely, the legal profession. Where democracies hate forms, structure, and tradition, Tocqueville discerned an attachment to all these among lawyers. Thus, the legal class could supply, at least in part, what society lost with the destruction of the *ancien régime*.[86] Yet, his prediction proved false.[87] Burke seems more irrelevant than ever to a democracy two hundred forty years on; Thomas Paine won and Edmund Burke lost.

To a certain degree, this is undeniable. The spirit of modern democracy is not only hostile to the political and social institutions of nobility; it is in many respects opposed to the spirit of nobility and greatness insofar as it is opposed to distinction. Nevertheless, just as the elaborations of the moral imagination are rooted in deeper truths of moral perception, the social accoutrements of nobility are imperfectly reflective of deeper features of human nature not easily expunged by democratic egalitarianism. The task of recognition may be harder and its characteristics obscured, but even in democracies we recognize greatness. We recognize it because it is an inescapable quality of human nature that demands respect. The sacrifice of a soldier, the dignity of a true statesman, the excellence of an Olympic athlete, feats of engineering genius, magnanimous projects undertaken by a whole community: all ways in which human virtue reflects the sublime and fires the imagination. Nobility will mark the citizens and common life of decent societies in inescapable ways, and thus, Burke's insight into the nature of human community can serve to ennoble even democratic republics like ours.

An Intrinsic Political Good?

The burden of my argument is to demonstrate that the good of political association is a unique and intrinsic good, that is, its essential features are not present in other associations and it holds out a good that we seek for its own sake. So, how does Burke's picture of the political common good measure up to this task? The Burkean political desideratum is a "rational and manly freedom," but does politics itself intrinsically produce this—or merely provide the context in which it can be produced by other virtue-oriented associations?

If Burke is right, and I think that he is, that the traditions of a political community represent the distilled practical reflection of generations over time, then clearly this represents an intrinsic good. Wisdom fulfills an essential human desire and capacity not merely to live, but to live well. The difficulty, however, is that this is not a good limited to the traditions of political communities. Indeed, Alasdair MacIntyre's extensive account of tradition as rational inquiry transcends particular polities. Although embodied in real communities, for MacIntyre, traditions are systems of *thought and social practice* that extend across centuries and often exist as competing traditions within political communities.[88] Moreover, Burke himself argues that the spirit of the gentleman and the spirit of religion have been the pillars of *European* civilization, not only English constitutionalism.[89] So then, do traditions of reason represent a superpolitical good that political communities participate in but do not uniquely embody?

Now, clearly traditions of both theoretical and practical reason do transcend political sovereignties. Although expressed in discrete communities at particular times and places, rational thought engages universals.[90] Nevertheless, real resolution of this issue turns on a further question: do political communities *uniquely embody* traditions of rationality—just as the family uniquely fosters the cultivation of virtues that also may be learned in public institutions? As I argue in Chapter 2, there are unique and intrinsic goods in the particular way the family educates in virtue, even though that function can be carried out at the political level as well. This uniqueness invests parents with a primary responsibility and right (in normal cases) to oversee their children's education. Thus, we must look to the particular way that an association practices a good. There may be unique values in a tradition of reason pursued at the political level that do not obtain at the universal level.

This further question directs our attention to a deficiency in MacIntyre's account of politics. He defines politics as a practice-ordering practice and understands it as a form of association essential to traditions of reason.[91] Because we are social beings, reason develops within a community as the common life is ordered for the common good (by now, a familiar argument). I noted before that this defines politics too broadly because it turns the family into a political institution. Families, too, are groups that order a wide array of goods and practices toward a common good. Thomas Hibbs has criticized MacIntyre for much the same reason, but his criticism comes from the opposite direction. He contends that MacIntyre's account of politics does not, in fact, rise to the level of political association due to its lack of a regime theory necessary to ground political sovereignty. The polis, for Aristotle, is not only a community of reason that self-orders toward a common good; it is a *sovereign* community that governs and protects itself according to the rule of law.[92] MacIntyre is insufficiently attentive to the *institutional* requirements of politics, and thus political life takes on an amorphous role in his account of traditions. On the one hand, traditions transcend political communities, and on the other, the practice of politics does not rise to the level of real political society.

This is significant because it causes MacIntyre to undervalue something Burke sees, namely, the importance and good of the state as a political institution.[93] The implications of this are numerous, but there are two that I want to emphasize here. In the first place, the state provides the continuity political communities rely upon to develop unified traditions of rational inquiry. When the state is destroyed, "the whole chain and continuity of the commonwealth [is] broken. No one generation [can] link with the other. Men . . . become little better than the flies of a summer."[94] In Burke's view, the basic legitimacy of the Glorious Revolution of 1688 and the claims of the American colonists against the British is that they were both rooted in an identifiable tradition of liberty. Magna Charta, the Petition of Right, the Declaration of Rights, and so on, marked a continuous political tradition of liberty that then became a standard of evaluation.[95] Without a generational connection provided by the institutions of government, political disputes are cut off by ad hoc philosophical abstractions from engaging and building upon past reflection.

The second point is closely related but moves from the domain of rationality to that of the moral imagination. The state provides a critical means of attachment to the history, ideals, and aspirations of the political community (though not the only one). It provides a means of engaging affection and sentiment as well as reason. In order to illustrate and elaborate both of these points—and to think further about the applicability of Burke's ideas outside his particular political context—we will turn now to consider the US Declaration of Independence as an anchor of rational discourse and national affection in the American experience of slavery.

ABRAHAM LINCOLN AND THE DECLARATION OF INDEPENDENCE

In the American mind and heart the Declaration of Independence quickly became the equivalent of the Magna Charta for the British. John Adams famously predicted that July 2, 1776, the day the Continental Congress passed a resolution of independence, would become the national day of celebrating independence. In retrospect, it is unsurprising that July 4, the day the Declaration of Independence was signed, actually became the point of celebration. Adams underestimated the power of political icons to capture the imagination. And from the start, David Hackett Fischer notes, Americans made the Declaration a national icon. Celebrations quickly sprang up throughout the colonies employing festivities once used to mark the King's Birthday to hail the new emblem of national unity: fireworks, cannonades, parades, dinners, toasts, and so forth. "George rejected and Liberty protected!," ran one Massachusetts salute to the document. In New York City, John Holt included a special print of the Declaration in his newspaper, suggesting that readers display it in their homes. Many did so, as evidenced by markings on extant copies.[96]

The Declaration was a symbol of national unity insofar as it forcefully severed ties with Great Britain, but it was less clear what unified commitments the document bound the states to. Infamously, Thomas Jefferson's ringing condemnation of slavery was cut from the final draft at the insistence of the Southern states. Fischer suggests that other changes, as well, indicated deep differences in the ethical and political understanding of various regions. For example, Jefferson's original "all men are created equal *and independent*" was trimmed in the final draft to "all men are created equal." Equality of creation may necessarily imply independence, as some thought, but Fischer argues that the change reflected "New England's tradition of ordered freedom and its institutions of collective belonging such as the town meeting."[97] This suggests a communal dimension of American ideals that moderates the individualistic strain. Be that as it may, the point here is that the Declaration was from the beginning an icon of American liberty but also an icon of unclear meaning and contested application. In one sense it was a clear, definitive declaration, and in another, the beginning of a national conversation.[98]

And, of course, the application of the Declaration of Independence to enslaved African Americans was the first among those real definitions that had to be worked out. As Prentice Hall, a leader of the free black community in Boston, expressed it, it was an "Astonishment" that "It has Never Bin Considered that Every Principle from which Amarica has Acted in the Cours Of their unhappy Deficultes with Great Briton Pleads Stronger than A thousand arguments" in favor of abolition.[99] Yet, as Mr. Hall no doubt knew, many had indeed considered the Declaration's implications for slavery, and most were very clear about the inconsistency—the slaveholding Jefferson chief among them.

It was, however, left to subsequent generations to face the problem squarely—to take up the argument directly. "The Great Compromiser," Henry Clay, managed to stave off disaster for his generation, but Abraham Lincoln was convinced that if the founding generation's policy of "hedg[ing]" and "hemm[ing]" in slavery "to the narrowest limits of necessity" was to be maintained, a line in the sand would have to be drawn.[100] Compromise with the expansion of slavery was no longer possible because ultimately the country would "become *all* one thing or *all* the other." Lincoln applied the biblical proverb to the country: "A house divided against itself cannot stand."[101]

Therefore, it was necessary to take up the argument of the Declaration once again and advance its "axioms of free society" beyond what had hith-erto been accomplished.[102] Lincoln argued in Peoria, Illinois:

> Little by little, but steadily as man's march to the grave, we have been giving up the OLD for the NEW faith. Near eighty years ago we began by declaring that all men are created equal; but now from that beginning we have run down to the other declaration, that for SOME men to enslave OTHERS is a "sacred right of self-government." These principles can not stand together.[103]

Of course, Lincoln is being rhetorically savvy here. The *old declaration*, while not making slavery a positive right, had existed side-by-side with it—implicitly lending weight to the proslavery suggestions that "all men" had a limited racial and political meaning, that is, all white citizens. Yet, Lincoln doggedly defends the plain meaning of the text. Richard Brookhiser explains that "Lincoln dismissed such talk. Jefferson had been writing about men, and he meant all men. . . . Whatever their stray opinions or their stubborn practice, at the moment of America's creation Jefferson had proposed that all men are created equal, and in Congress assembled all the United States had agreed."[104] Therefore, Lincoln went back to the founding text and insisted on the minor premise: The slave is a man. "If the negro is a man," he argued, "why then my ancient faith teaches me that 'all men are created equal'; and that there can be no moral right in connection with one man's making a slave of another."[105] The conclusion inescapably follows: slaves, too, are created equal, and thus are not justly enslaved.

Lincoln, then, calls his countrymen to a reaffirmation of the basic prin-ciples enshrined in the Declaration of Independence—to improve their polity by bringing its practice into conformity with their basic moral and political commitments. "Let us re-adopt the Declaration of Independence, and with it, the practices, and policy, which harmonize with it. . . . If we do this, we shall not only have saved the Union; but we shall have so saved it, as to make, and to keep it, forever worthy of the saving."[106]

So, what features of the political good does this necessarily brief sketch illustrate? First, the Declaration *anchored basic moral truths* in the American constitutional order that worked on the conscience of the nation over time. The point is not to demonstrate the efficacy of reason and logic to bring about political change. Indeed, the American experience with slavery proves Burke's point that pure rationality cannot take the place of rightly ordered affections.[107] The logic of the Declaration was insufficient in itself to bring an end to slavery. To be bound by the logic of Lincoln's argument, one had to accept the truth of his minor premise—the slave is a man—but an ill-furnished moral imagination is easily able to distort the humanity of those it wishes to marginalize and exploit, or simply deny what is plain fact.[108] As Burke noted, when the moral imagination is ransacked, it is not just social and political distinctions that are lost. A king becomes a man, but a woman, also, becomes an animal. Humanity itself is obscured. This is the case with the moral development of an individual and the political change of a nation.

At the same time, the significance of the Declaration was profound. It was an expression of the American mind that was an indictment of the American heart. The establishment of a political order explicitly grounded in the truths of the Declaration kept that indictment before the American people and served as the basis for further argument about the nature of liberty and equality. Moreover, Lincoln argues that the Constitution extended the logical meaning of the Declaration in an implicit indictment of slavery. By refusing to directly mention slavery, "the thing is hid away, in the constitution, just as an afflicted man hides away a wen or a cancer, which he dares not cut out at once, lest he bleed to death."[109] Likewise, constitutional adjudication in cases such as *The Antelope* and *La Amistad* highlighted the "constitutional disharmony" of a political order that at once embraced the moral law in the Declaration and allowed for the violation of that law in the Constitution.

Yet, there was a real danger. Justin Dyer argues that nineteenth-century abolitionists like John Quincy Adams faced a new challenge in

> the rising defense of slavery as something good to be preserved and protected rather than a necessary evil to be tolerated; the cornerstone of American democracy rather than the rock on which it must break. Because of this new challenge, American constitutional disharmony might have found its resolution in *favor* of slavery as a perpetual and fundamental institution, and the Declaration of Independence was the final obstacle, the last stumbling block, to those forces working toward such a resolution.[110]

As Dyer goes on to argue, Lincoln understood the proslavery arguments of Stephen Douglas and Justice Taney in *Dred Scott* to resolve the constitutional disharmony by expunging the Declaration's real meaning from the public mind.[111] Douglas sought to replace it with the idea that "there is no right principle of action but self-interest."[112] And in effectively erasing the Declaration from the American mind, the country's anchor in the moral law would be lost and further political debate would be set adrift, if not quieted altogether. The essential point, therefore, is that an instrument of the state—a founding political document—anchored the country's public argument about the moral requirements of liberty, equality, and the American common good. Lincoln doggedly reasserted the fundamental principles of the regime articulated some eighty years before and challenged his countrymen to come to terms with their inescapable logic.

The next point is that the Declaration also demonstrates the *affective force* of political institutions and instruments. In a very real sense, it represents an integration of the head and the heart, reason and the affections. It immediately became an object of love and veneration and thus a powerful means of attachment to the political commitments it expressed. Its sublime truths and ringing denunciations were not simply statements of universal principle; they were *America's* articulation of those principles and commitment to them. They were universal but also deeply rooted in the experience of the colonies. They were combined with specific historical grievances and violations of the colonists' rights as Englishmen that justified resort to revolution.[113] Americans loved the Declaration for its sublimity, certainly, but they also loved it because it was *their* Declaration.

This represents a political application of a critical point made before, that is, human rationality does not function effectively isolated from rightly ordered affections. Thus, understanding political society as a unique tradition of rational inquiry requires an appreciation of its affective goods as well. The de facto *rational force* of the Declaration in no small part depended upon the country's *affective attachment* to it as the embodiment of American ideals. Lincoln essentially expressed this Burkean argument in an address delivered at the Young Men's Lyceum of Springfield, Illinois, entitled, "The Perpetuation of Our Political Institutions." The attachment of the people to their political institutions, Lincoln argued, is the "strongest bulwark of any government."[114] Apart from a love and veneration of the law, citizens become alienated from their government and civilized society breaks down. Moreover, this underscores the vital significance of political icons, to return to David Hackett Fischer's distinction. Images may communicate a vision and persuade, but icons come to be revered and protected.[115] Such attachment is essential to the health and longevity of the political order.

C. S. Lewis gives a characteristically pithy and cogent illustration of this point in his classic essay *The Abolition of Man*: "Without the aid of trained emotions, the intellect is powerless against the animal organism. I had sooner play cards against a man who was quite sceptical about ethics, but bred to believe that 'a gentleman does not cheat,' than against an irreproach-able moral philosopher who had been brought up among sharpers."[116]

Lewis's primary point is about the necessity of "trained emotions," but notice the means by which those sentiments are cultivated: a captivating and ennobling ideal. Even as intellectual assent relies upon precise argumenta-tion, well-formed sentiment depends upon images, stories, and ideals that fire the imagination. Lewis's preferred opponent has not been merely ha-bituated against cheating; he has embraced a model of integrity, decorum, and sportsmanship. It is a code that includes him in a community of honor and gives him an ideal for which to aspire. The idea of the gentleman not only represents a standard of behavior in the man's mind but is an icon of his moral imagination.

In summary, therefore, the role of the Declaration of Independence in the American experience of slavery fulfilled two vital functions. In the first place, as an anchor of moral and political commitment in the American tradition of reason, it provided the continuity necessary to sustain reflection and im-provement over generations. Lincoln persistently deployed its logic to fore-stall the proslavery attempt to recast slavery as an indifferent issue in the American tradition, about which citizens were free to make up their minds as they wished. The Declaration stood as the official repudiation of that con-ceit. Second, as an object of affection and veneration—ultimately an icon of the American moral imagination—the Declaration became a powerful means of attachment to the American political project and to the realization of its inchoate ideals. It embodied not an abstract intellectual position but the historic and venerable commitment of the Founding generation—those who had "pledge[d] . . . our Lives, our Fortunes and our Sacred Honor" for the sake of the common good.

This forcefully demonstrates, I would argue, the intrinsic and unique goodness of political society as a tradition both of reason and the moral imagination. There is more to be said, however, about the way that political culture embodies and nourishes the moral imagination specifically. To that we now turn.

ENNOBLING THE MORAL IMAGINATION

What about Burke's idea that there is an ennobling quality to political life—what I have been calling a tradition of the moral imagination? Is there a unique and intrinsically good way that being a part of political society con-tributes to a greatness of soul and well-formed moral sentiments? For those not skittish about the value of patriotism, the intuitive answer to this question is likely affirmative. To be without a country and a people is to embrace the myopic isolation of Polyphemus, "deaf to justice, blind to law."[117] Moreover, Burke's vision of a moral imagination furnished with the heroes, hardships, triumphs, icons, and sentiments of a shared history is the beating heart of patriotism. The patriot's aspirations for the future are informed by the lessons and glories of the past—and the real connection one has to them. In Burke's aphoristic words, "People will not look forward to posterity, who never look backward to their ancestors."[118]

But are the intuitions of the patriot right? How do we flesh out the intrinsic goods characteristic of a "tradition of the moral imagination"? We need first to consider the great aims or purpose of political life, and second, the uniquely ennobling character of political traditions. As we have seen, for Aristotle the nobility of politics resided in the completeness of the political art. The polis takes all of life within its purview and orders the entire community toward a common good. Although Aquinas recognizes a similar completeness of the political common good, he lays stress on the *extension of the political good*. Political community is great because it secures the good of a multitude. Indeed, as Patrick Gardner shows, for Aquinas this good has universal extension—ultimately the good of the entire human species.[119] The greatness of politics is found not only in its (qualitative and quantitative) scope but also in its aim, that is, seeking to order a common life according to the requirements of justice and the common good, not for the personal advantage of the powerful and well-positioned. This very aim expresses a largeness and liberality of soul inasmuch as it tempers the human desire for self-determination with the shared need for order and the extension of justice throughout the community. The unruly passions of a tyrannical soul render it incapable of true political participation—unable to live according to a "rational and manly freedom." Thus, politics embodies a form of self-mastery in a broad extension of the human good. As James Stoner has aptly observed, "'Self-government' is not quite a synonym for 'virtue,' but it is pretty close."[120]

Burke expresses these ideas in aesthetic terms, as a type of experience of the sublime. In political community we join with our neighbors and fellow citizens in the broad extension of principles of ordered liberty and the common good. The greatness of these aims, of *our community*, in turn, points beyond itself to the universal dimensions of human community. "Each contract of each particular state," Burke writes, "is but a clause in the great primaeval contract of eternal society, linking the lower with the higher natures, connecting the visible and invisible world."[121] Now, as I will argue further in the Conclusion, this does not mean that the political realm is the only domain of greatness and nobility. Moreover, Burke's notion of the sublime constrains the significance and authority of particular states insofar as it situates them within a broader moral community. Nevertheless, the politics of particular communities embodies a proximate and personal connection to the highest aspirations of individual and social flourishing.

Second, the mind and heart are elevated by placing one within a community extended through time. An essential feature of this intergenerational membership, as Burke is wont to stress, is that our political patrimony *creates a duty* to generations past, present, and future. This feature, I would argue, importantly distinguishes it from other sources of the moral imagination. Here is an example of what I have in mind. My own moral imagination has been elevated to some extent by the lives of both Sir Thomas More and George Washington. More's example of prodigious talent and ambition submitted to Christian devotion and principled integrity makes him one of the great heroes of Western civilization. Likewise, George Washington's dignity, indomitable courage, and disinterested service to his country distinguish him as an exemplar of the republican virtue he so admired. Lord Byron rightly called him "The Cincinnatus of the West."[122] Both are icons of a well-formed moral imagination (More and Washington, that is, not Byron), and I would do well to cultivate them both. Yet, there is an essential difference between them, at least for me, as an American. It is not only, not even primarily, that I may feel more attached to Washington as a fellow American (though this is significant). The essential difference is that, as Americans, Washington and I are joined by bonds of common membership. This is not merely an "antiquarian superstition," a mystical communion of the living with the dead. It is, at root, a matter-of-fact feature of human institutions that Burke pedestrianly calls a "partnership."[123]

What is the impact of this shared membership? Simply that I owe a duty to Washington that I do not owe to Thomas More.[124] As the present beneficiary of institutions of social order established and maintained by previous generations, I bear a moral obligation to those generations to pass down those institutions and liberties to the next generation. The intent of every responsible generation is, as the Preamble of US Constitution puts it, to "secure the Blessings of Liberty to ourselves and our Posterity." The meaning of *posterity*, of course, is indefinite in extension; it does not conveniently end with my generation. Thus, as a natural-born citizen of the United States, I find myself at the point of earliest political awareness with duties I did not choose, owed to people whom I have never met.

This brings us to the nub of the argument. What is the significance of my having a duty to Washington and not to More? How does this impact the formation of my moral imagination? The answer, simply put, is participation. What I mean is this: the duties I incur as a member of the American political community require participation in that community and thus involve me as an active member in a community that is itself ennobled by the virtues and sacrifices of previous generations. This is more, it is important to see, than my being inflated by a superficial or passing identification with Washington. It is, rather, that I am drawn by the bonds of community to active membership in a society ennobled by the greatness of its purpose, the dignity of its heroes, the nobility of its triumphs and glories, and so forth. This, I take it, is the point Burke is essentially making when he says, "This idea of a liberal descent inspires us with a sense of habitual native dignity."[125]

This may seem like a relatively insignificant benefit. It is not hard to imagine my being much more challenged and inspired by the example of Sir Thomas More than George Washington—despite the bonds of community. However, what if this effect is multiplied by a "gallery of portraits" that includes James Madison, Abraham Lincoln, Harriet Tubman, Alvin York, Martin Luther King Jr., and Navy SEAL Team Six Operator Adam Brown? What if its force is compounded in the Battles of Lexington and Concord, Appomattox, the D-Day Invasion, the Marshall Plan, Apollo 11, and endlessly on? What if the beauty and greatness of one's country is expressed in a storehouse of national treasures of all sorts: "The Star-Spangled Banner," Yosemite National Park, the Gettysburg Address, the Smithsonian Institution? If we multiply the ennobling force of icons like George Washington a thousandfold throughout the history of one's country and across the breadth of its cultural treasures and achievements, the impact on the moral imagination—when appropriately cultivated—can be uniquely and profoundly ennobling.

Objections

I have made a case that to some may seem implausible, to others, ingenuous, and to still others, even dangerous. By way of conclusion, I will offer some responses to what I take to be the most salient and important objections.

IGNOBILITY AND AUGUSTINIAN REALISM

The most immediate objection has already been raised implicitly in the argument thus far. It is that the view of the political common good I recommend requires a patriotism with blinders on, so to speak. It is perhaps a commendable desire to be ennobled by the past glories of one's country, but this assumes that the past, and indeed the present, was and is glorious. Yet, for every George Washington there is a Benedict Arnold standing in the shadows of history. For every Yorktown there is a Wounded Knee. Or as Fredrick Douglass put the question in his magnificent address, "What to a Slave is the Fourth of July?": "And am I . . . called upon to bring our humble offering to the national alter, and to confess the benefits and express devout gratitude for the blessings resulting from your independence to us?"[126] Does not the patriotism I commend here depend upon papering over national sins and ignobility?

To push the point further, one may well ask if my argument sufficiently accounts for the reality of self-interest, vice, and abuse of power in political life. Saint Augustine most famously expressed this objection in his monumental indictment of Rome's political pretentions, *The City of God against the Pagans*. Although he concedes the practical utility of politics in the City of Man, Augustine argues that we deceive ourselves if we think that *real* virtue, and thus *real* justice, are possible apart from God. For Augustine, the root of political authority is not Genesis 1:26, "Let us make man in our image," but Genesis 3:6, "She also gave some to her husband who was with her, and he ate."[127] Politics is not a product of natural human goodness but rather a desperate response to the sin of the Fall. As such, it is riddled with every human frailty: ignorance, greed, pride, and the lust for dominance.[128] Even in the best circumstances, what we call "justice" often miscarries against the innocent—and we don't even know it. Politics is not the field of human greatness; it is a tragic necessity that highlights the sin and wretchedness of the human condition. The best we can hope for is enough civic tranquility to allow the City of God (i.e., the Church) to thrive.[129] Therefore, one may object that from an Augustinian perspective a realistic view of history will not elevate, but breed discouragement and pessimism about political life—or at the very least, puncture the pretentions of Burke's "generous sense of glory and emulation."[130] If this is the case, isn't the argument for the possibility of an ennobling engagement with political culture deeply undermined?

One must begin by acknowledging that there is important truth in this objection. Politics "under the sun"[131] will always be subject to human frailty. It is an enterprise fraught with vice and imperfection, and this fact, at the most basic level, should discipline both our aspirations for the future and our understanding of the past. As surely as we cannot create a utopia, we did not come from one. We exist within a realm of incomplete goods, fragile compromises, and partial victories. This is why Burke combines his principles of conservation and transmission with a principle of improvement.[132] Respect for tradition, even veneration of past exemplars, does not entail a smug or unreflective satisfaction with the status quo. Nor does it involve a simple lionization of the past.

Clear-sighted Augustinianism also rightly suggests that we should be vigilant against the abuse of power that authority frequently makes possible. Just as political authority is a response to vice,[133] the vice of those in authority must likewise be constrained. James Madison famously makes this argument in *Federalist* No. 51:

> But what is government itself, but the greatest of all reflections on human nature? If men were angels, no government would be necessary. If angels were to govern men, neither external nor internal controls on government would be necessary. In framing a government which is to be administered by men over men, the great difficulty lies in this: you must first enable the government to control the governed; and in the next place oblige it to control itself. A dependence on the people is, no doubt, the primary control on the government; but experience has taught mankind the necessity of auxiliary precautions.[134]

A politics of prudence—informed by the truth that all humankind is far removed from angelic virtue—will be a politics of divided and balanced power.

I should also reiterate that a concern with restraining political power is at the heart of what Burke takes to be the great genius of the Western chivalric ideal. "Without force, or opposition," he argues, "it *subdued the fierceness of pride and power*; it obliged sovereigns to submit to the soft collar of social esteem, compelled stern authority to submit to elegance, and gave a domination vanquisher of laws, to be subdued by manners."[135] For Burke, politics is not a realm of pure, noble sublimity; rather, it is ennobled as fierce and prideful power is turned toward benevolent care for the common good. It is precisely the difficulty of this task, and the fragility of its accomplishment, that raises his ire so much against the French revolutionaries. It was they who —thinking ordered liberty was an easy thing—were naïve about politics and the danger of unrestrained power. Burke was a political realist and thus predicted the Reign of Terror three years before it occurred.[136]

Finally, we must acknowledge that many political communities will simply fail—often massively—to achieve the goods of which they are capable. The bonds of political community depend upon a shared commitment to a just pursuit of the common good and an extension of legal rights, as well as duties, to everyone. As Roger Scruton argues, government is not only a search for order but an expression of accountability among citizens.[137] Therefore, to the extent that a political order reneges on its fundamental responsibilities, it is a defective form, or often a travesty, of the thing it purports to be. In such cases, the political goods I have argued for in the previous two chapters are severely diminished, even nonexistent.

As important as these Augustinian qualifications are, I do not think they ultimately tell against my argument. In the first place, we should remember that sin and vice affect *all* social relationships and all kinds of human virtue—not just political ones.[138] Our ability to identify and practice virtue, to elevate and strive for ideals, is plagued by imperfection in every human endeavor. Still, this does not prevent us from meaningfully identifying real human goods and achieving them to greater or lesser degrees. The fact that we fail to hit the mark, often spectacularly, does not negate its meaningful existence. It is no disproof of the goods of friendship to point to bad or sham friends. It is no indictment of family life to adduce the plight of abandoned children. It is the same with politics. The potential goods of any association whatsoever depend upon it achieving its purpose to some degree.

Moreover, I think we are compelled to admit, as does Augustine himself, that political communities are capable of achieving very great goods—despite their significant flaws. Although Augustine insists that perfect justice is unattainable in human affairs, he also argues that all people are drawn toward peace by virtue of a common human nature. Even animals desire as much peace as they can manage. "How much more strongly, then, is a man drawn by the laws of his nature, so to speak, to enter into a similarly peaceful association with his fellow men, so far as it lies within his power to do so?" The sin of pride undermines this natural inclination, tempting us to unjust domination of others. Yet, "He who has learnt to prefer right to wrong and the rightly ordered to the perverse, sees that, in comparison with the peace of the just, the peace of the unjust is not worthy to be called peace at all."[139] Thus, our natures incline us toward the good of peace, and *to the degree* that they are well-ordered, we desire to live justly with our neighbors.

Augustine seems to think that these well-ordered inclinations can come to characterize communities as a whole. He famously redefines a "people" as "an assembled multitude of rational creatures bound together by a common agreement as to the objects of their love." The Roman definition had assumed that the earthly city was *actually* just, so Augustine rejects it. A unity of common loves, in comparison, is value neutral; it does not lay claim to justice. Nevertheless, Augustine qualifies his refutation of temporal justice. "Clearly," he acknowledges, "the better the objects of this agreement, the better the people; and the worse the objects, the worse the people."[140] A Christian community has the greatest potential to maximize earthly justice,[141] but Augustine also seems to have gradations of natural goodness in mind. Thus, to the degree that a community comes to love and promote real human goods, and to the degree that it distinguishes between right and wrong and prefers good order to chaos and domination, it will become capable of higher *justice-like* and *peace-like* states. The better they are, the more their temporal peace can serve and promote the complete justice of the City of God.[142]

I think it is undeniable that the Augustinian analysis is confirmed by common experience. If we judge any political community by the standard of a perfectly just pursuit of the common good, it is bound to fail. There is no exception. In fact, against the standard of perfection, the failures are enormous. Even so, it is clear that there are vast differences between the degrees of justice and peace realized in political and national communities throughout human history. On the one hand, many, if not most, have subjected the common good to the interests of the few, and this has often produced political systems riddled with corruption, graft, disorder, and caprice. The political turmoil is corrosive to the institutions of civil society. Some governments are responsible for the deaths of millions of their own people. In such cases, the beauty, nobility, and goodness that emerge from the culture are in spite of its politics, not because of it. On the other hand, there have been other countries where genuine political goods and institutions have come to mark the culture: an aspiration to ordered liberty, inalienable human rights, care for the common good, limited and accountable authority, habits of lawfulness, due process, public service, and so on. Imperfect but healthy political communities like these are the soil in which the goods I have described can grow.[143]

One final question remains: Does my argument require that citizens embrace the kind of pietistic and one-sided reconstruction of history that Parson Weems made infamous? Answering this question, I think, is helpfully illuminated by thinking about the way that we deal with our own personal struggles and faults. Each of us is confronted by what Robert Louis Stevenson's Dr. Jekyll calls "the thorough and primitive duality of man."[144] Or in Alexandyr Solzhenitsyn's words, "The line dividing good and evil cuts through the heart of every human being."[145] Real progress toward the good must begin with an acknowledgment of this fact, because apart from it we are defenseless against our own self-deception and moral rationalizations— fish trapped in the barrels of our own corruption. Once vice is frankly acknowledged and a will toward the good embraced, however, we must "set [our faces] to go to Jerusalem."[146] That is, we must focus intently on the good to be achieved and set about cultivating the virtues necessary to it. To direct our thoughts, intentions, and imaginations toward the good is not a casual dismissal of our vice; rather, it is necessary to its eradication.

Of course, applied to the political community, this picture of moral progress becomes much more complicated. Most of the political disagreement we face in contemporary American politics is stymied at the initial point of recognition: where precisely does the line between good and evil run? Even when there is agreement about this, we conflict about the right response. Who is responsible? How should grievances be redressed? Is "moving on" appropriate or dismissive? These are the perennial questions of politics, and I do not pretend to address them. My point is simply this: there is nothing exploitative or dishonest or Pollyannaish about intentionally directing our focus toward things that are good and admirable. It is dishonest not to frankly acknowledge faults, but it is also unwise not to emphasize and illuminate virtue. We should do this in our personal lives, and it should likewise be our approach to public life and national history. Thus, a healthy political culture will intentionally and unapologetically memorialize the best exemplars of its constitutional aspiration; it will attach national identity to its greatest triumphs. While not whitewashing the past and being careful to correct errors going forward, a healthy citizenry will embrace the best of what a country is as its definitive identity.

DEFINING THE POLITICAL

A second objection might express concern about the definition of the political my argument employs. In talking about a tradition of the moral imagination, I began to incorporate ideas associated with organic forms of attachment, such as, nation, homeland, and country. One might reasonably understand these to exceed the bounds of what might be properly thought of as politics. Indeed, Roger Scruton argues that the nation is a form of *prepolitical membership* presupposed by and necessary to free political societies.[147] Love of a homeland seems to be based primarily on the familiarities and joys of private life, not on abstract legal bonds of citizenship. As Scruton puts it, a nation is comprised of neighbors.[148] It is in large part defined by its culture, its shared traditions, history, language, territory, beliefs, and customs. Yet clearly these extend well beyond the strictly political. One might wonder, for example, if there is any reason to include national treasures like Yosemite National Park in a discussion of the political good. Citizens find their country beautiful "for heroes proved in liberating strife," yes, but "amber waves of grain" and "purple mountains majesty" seem to tap into other, nonpolitical loves.[149] To employ a distinction often used by sociologists and political theorists, politics seems to belong to the domain of "Creed," and not that of "Culture."[150] So then, have I cast my net too broadly, filling out my account of the political common good with things that are not, strictly speaking, political?

This is a helpful distinction, one that demonstrates the deep ambiguity and slipperiness of concepts like political culture and national identity. However, I do not think that it undermines the argument I have made. Any full assessment of the political common good simply has to include cultural dimensions that overlap and are intertwined with—but are not reducible to—the political identity, institutions, and history of a country. The reason for this is that politics is not a discrete activity in which citizens engage when they want to take care of something touching government or the public square. No, politics is a kind of practice according to which neighbors, those who share a common life together, commit to order that life. It is a way of being in community that transforms and in key respects defines the association.

The political bond is a kind of commitment among the members of a community to order the common life according to law, for the sake of the common good. As such, it changes the nature of the prepolitical "we." "We" are now a community bound by bonds of a shared life together, a common territory, and so on—*but also by a shared commitment to a just and lawful way of ordering that common life.* The national "we" is not distinct from the political "we," though Scruton (rightly, I think) argues that the latter presupposes the former. But to celebrate our country, our homeland, our history, our triumphs, our greatness, and so forth, is part of the political common good precisely because our common good is a political one. Love of the homeland, grounded in attachment to and love for one's community and place, is a political love—though not in a way that subsumes natural attachments. Rather, the political bond completes and perfects the preexisting bonds of love and attachment insofar as it represents a shared commitment to order *that very common life* according to principles of justice, the common good, and the rule of law. The prepolitical "we" attached to the homeland, and the political "we" united by bonds of citizenship, are a unified complete identity. Martin Luther King Jr. very naturally expressed this unified identity in his immortal words:

> So let freedom ring from the prodigious hilltops of New Hampshire. Let freedom ring from the mighty mountains of New York. Let freedom ring from the heightening Alleghenies of Pennsylvania. Let freedom ring from the snow-capped Rockies of Colorado. Let freedom ring from the curvaceous slopes of California. But not only that; let freedom ring from the Stone Mountain of Georgia. Let freedom ring from Lookout Mountain of Tennessee. Let freedom ring from every hill and molehill of Mississippi. From every mountainside, let freedom ring.[151]

As King understood, one's love of the shared homeland—from the snow-capped Rockies to the molehills of Mississippi—is expressed precisely in seeking a life there among one's neighbors ordered according to political principles of fairness, justice, and the common good.

Think of it this way. To say that a celebration of one's homeland is non-political is like celebrating the friendship of a married couple, but not their marriage. It simply misunderstands that the marriage is a particular form of friendship that transforms the relationship. There will be, of course, wonderful elements of their friendship that preexisted the marriage and will continue unchanged throughout the relationship, such as a shared love of English literature. And there are elements of the new friendship peculiar to marriage, such as sexual fidelity and procreation. However, the goods that they share as friends are caught up in a larger, more extensive, and permanent network of relational commitments called *marriage* that transform, and for them, complete the friendship that they shared before. To celebrate the friendship of a married couple is to celebrate their marriage.

At the same time, to say that the "we" is political is *not* to say that it is governmental. Government is *not* the only thing we all belong to. It is, rather, an instrument created by a people bound together by their common commitment to order their common life according to political principles. Government is the expression and instrument of that commitment, but it does not embody the common life. The people embody and live out that common life as citizens joined together by bonds of political friendship. As such, *citizens* act for the common good. Citizens see and solve problems in their communities. Citizens actively engage the common life, history, and heritage of their communities, not because of their shared connection to the government but because of their shared bond with each other—and with past and future generations who have shared and will share the same bond. Although the institutions of government vitally express that bond—and in the best cases become ennobling icons of it—government itself is always a product of the deeper political reality grounded in the citizenry itself.

NATIONALISM

The last objection I will briefly consider also springs from my argument's reliance on nobility, sublimity, and greatness—as well as the patriotism that is, at least in part, animated by those things. To speak of the completeness and perfection of the political community invokes Aristotle; speaking of its extension of the common good to all invokes Aquinas; but extolling the greatness and glory of one's country conjures the specters of Periclean Athens, Augustan Rome, or Nazi Germany. Isn't there a danger that a patriotic devotion to the greatness of one's country is the natural seed of an aggressive nationalism? While this is not a concern that can be dismissed lightly, I would argue that there is no essential connection between a robust patriotism and nationalism.

John Stuart Mill indicates the basic reason for this in his distinction between "vulgar" nationalism and a refined sense of national feeling and connection:

> [An] essential condition of stability in political society, is a strong and active principle of cohesion among the members of the same community or state. We need scarcely say that we do not mean nationality, in the vulgar sense of that a term; a senseless antipathy to foreigners; indifference to the general welfare of the human race, or an unjust preference for the supposed interests of our own country; a cherishing of bad particularities because they are national or a refusal to adopt what has been found good by other countries. We mean a principle of sympathy, not of hostility; of union, not of separation. We mean a feeling of common interest among those who live under the same government, and are contained within the same natural or historical boundaries. We mean, that one part of the community do not consider themselves as foreigners with regard to another part; that they have set a value on their connexion—feel that they are one people, that their lot is cast in together, that evil to any of their fellow-countrymen is

evil to themselves, and do not desire selfishly too free themselves from their share of any common inconvenience by severing the connexion. How strong this feeling was in those ancient commonwealths which attained any durable greatness, every one knows.[152]

Mill's distinctions highlight that we need not see patriotism as an expression of national *superiority* over other peoples. It is not even a preference for one's own that disregards the rights and interests of rival communities. It is, rather, an extension of our love of home—an appreciation of one's people because "[our] lot is cast in together." As such, it has no necessary connection—indeed, not even a natural one—to an aggressive nationalism that seeks to subsume other peoples and homelands.

Furthermore, the Burkean kind of patriotism I have been arguing for here is rooted in attachment to the local that does not flag in its vitality even as love moves outward from the little platoons to one's country. Burke's political thought is suffused with an interplay between the beautiful and sublime, the domains of homely warmth and august greatness, which precludes a simple outward trajectory of political aspiration. In this he is in keeping with the Roman republican tradition embodied in Cincinnatus's return to private life after exercising dictatorial power to save the state. Moreover, the Burkean principle of particular attachment applies at the political level as well as the domestic and personal. For Burke, political goods are *cultural*, developed within the shared life of particular communities. They are goods developed through membership and a common patrimony that cannot be simply extended beyond the bounds of one's own political tradition. As G. K. Chesterton observed, "A man is a citizen of that Commonwealth the nature of which he can conceive, and no other."[153] Thus, the imperial impulse is not a function of healthy patriotism but a corruption and misunderstanding of its essential goods. "To put it another way," Roger Scruton writes, "patriotism is an extension of the natural love of home; nationalism is a belief that my home is inherently superior to yours."[154]

Of course, it is often the case that human vice inclines us to claim superiority over others, so perhaps robust patriotism fans the flames of pride that lead to nationalism. The lack of a logical connection between the two is cold comfort in the face of political passions. Here Chesterton's response—and it is important to note that the driving thesis of his argument is a critique of British imperialism—is persuasive, I think: the best way to fight the impulse to universal dominance is to experience and extol the virtues of particular loves. Imperialism is not patriotism run amok, he argues; in reality, it is an "opportunistic cosmopolitanism" unmoored by deep attachment to a particular way of life. Cosmopolitanism is the real danger because it removes from the affections an inherent limitation to political ambition and expansion. Real patriotism grounds the human heart and thus is a positive force restraining its passions.[155]

CONCLUSION

A central tenet of the argument I have advanced throughout this work is what I have called the *inclusivist* claim, that is, if the authoritative position of the political community is to be morally persuasive, the common good of the community must substantively include the good of individual human persons and the distinct goods of each form of association within its purview that is essential to the human good—friendships, families, religious associations, and so forth. This necessitated, following Finnis, a dual way of conceiving the common good. On the one hand, the common good of political society is the good of the community as a whole, including the unique goods of its distinct and irreplaceable parts. So the common good of the United States, in this sense, includes the personal goods of Harry Wright and Mary Clement Wright, the friendship of Jackson Wright and Robby Denham, the flourishing of the Wingard family, the good of institutions like Biola University, and so on. This is what it means for the political community to be an ordered whole. Individual persons and basic associations such as the family are not, in the first instance, directed or subordinated to the good of the political community. They possess unique forms of flourishing—like the educative energy of the family elaborated in Chapter 2—that must be honored, protected, and served by political society. This is the philosophical foundation of the political doctrines of limited government, subsidiarity, and natural human rights.

On the other hand, insofar as a political society is itself a distinct whole, a particular form of association, we must also recognize a specifically political common good. I take the Burkean argument I made in Chapter 5 to bolster my claim that this political common good is (at least in part) *distinctive*, that is, representing the good of the community per se. The Burkean emphasis on the goods of tradition—community extended through time—necessitates the maintenance of political *institutions*, and these call our attention to the fact that *the community itself* has certain requirements of flourishing that are discrete from any aggregated sum of its constitutive parts.

In the previous two chapters I constructed accounts of two key substantive dimensions of the political common good. First, civic friendship represents a partnership for the common good of a whole community, in unique ways embodying the virtue of justice and expressing distinctive facets of the virtues of love and generosity. Political association expresses an *extensive benevolence* that seeks to secure the human good—by means of just governance and the rule of law—not merely for oneself and closest kin, but for a whole community. This would seem to imply a universal trajectory of the political good: if it is better to secure the good for a whole people than merely that of one's own family, wouldn't it be best to secure the good for *all peoples*? Yet, a universalist trajectory is curbed first by the intractable limitations of human nature. *Beneficence* cannot keep pace with the desires of *benevolence*. If we are to provide for and achieve the *intensive goods* of personal relationships and particular associations, our *beneficent actions* must be focused on proximate relationships and the common good of our own political community. Moreover, the substantial goods realized within distinct political cultures limits the universalist aspirations of justice, love, and generosity. Although the actions of a political society on the international stage must be guided and constrained by universal justice and goodwill toward all people, the unique goods of particular political cultures preclude universal extension of a political common good realized in world government.

These particular goods are embodied in what I, drawing on Edmund Burke's thought, have called a tradition of reason and a tradition of the moral imagination. In the first case, our knowledge of the human good is cultivated in the *lived experience, customs, and traditions* of communities extended through time. Our appreciation of that wisdom is based upon our embeddedness in and attachment to the life of that community. In the second case, a tradition of the moral imagination elevates and ennobles members of a political community as they embrace the history, achievements, and icons definitive of their political culture. Thus, political culture is *not only* a "repository of goodwill" that informs the actions of citizens in civic friendship; it becomes a vital source of a deeper, richer "wardrobe of the moral imagination" that shapes the moral sentiments of the community and draws citizens into ennobling participation in the greatness of their country.

In conclusion, I want to consider a question that elaborates the practical implications of the theory I have developed. What kind of political action does this theory entail? If politics is a domain of intrinsic social good, does this mean that a fully flourishing life will involve a high level of involvement in politics, if not as an elected official at least as an active citizen regularly engaged in public affairs? Is the less-involved citizen—more preoccupied with private life—missing out on a core dimension of his or her flourishing?

Insofar as a rejection of the Aristotelian primacy of politics has been an essential piece of this argument, it clearly follows that human flourishing does not require a dominant concern with politics. Many citizens, in fact, such as young parents who are often heavily taxed by the demands of small children and developing careers, might run afoul of their primary responsibilities with a very active involvement in political life. On the other hand, if political life really holds out a unique and intrinsic good, *no* concern with the life of one's political community would necessarily be a loss of real good, a diminished cultivation of human sociability. Now, it goes without saying that, aside from extenuating circumstances, every citizen has a duty of responsible citizenship: informed voting, payment of taxes, jury duty, and so forth. These activities do not so much enter the realm of human flourishing as they simply discharge the obligations one has to one's community—past, present, and future. There is, of course, a wide spectrum of political participation that runs from the many citizens who cannot name the three branches of government established in the US Constitution to the citizen who volunteers with political campaigns or runs for office. If politics is an intrinsic good, where on this spectrum should the average citizen fall?

A key consequence of my argument is that it changes the way we tend to think about involvement in the political community. As I have argued, we are apt to reduce political activity only to things specifically required or organized by law and government. This is a fundamental misstep of the instrumental view of the political common good, and because this account of politics is reductive, its analysis of the political common good is incomplete. In contrast, the perspective of civic friendship views politics *primarily* as the free association and initiative of citizens on behalf of the common good, and the Burkean picture of political culture presses us to think of goods embodied in traditions.

The first consequence of this expanded notion of political community is that meaningful political involvement is not only *action in the present* but also *engagement with the past*. If political life is embodied in a community extended through time, participation in its goods requires knowledge and appreciation of a community's political history, institutions, customs, and icons. If much of the good that political society has to offer is embodied in its past, then participating in those goods requires a deep concern with historically oriented civic education—not so much with the doing of political things. Citizens engaging the intrinsic goods political life has to offer will be actively occupied with understanding and appreciating their country's political past.

This point recalls the question left unresolved at the end of Chapter 2: How should we balance parental guidance of education with the state's interest in civic education? My argument in Chapter 2 rebutted any principled reason for the state to regard parents with suspicion; likewise, Chapters 4 and 5 tie civic education to human flourishing, not merely the utilitarian interests of the state. Thus, parents themselves should take an active interest in civic education as an essential part of raising children. But who has authority over content? The need for a coherent and enduring articulation of the community's history, institutions, and ideals weighs in favor of the state perhaps. On the other hand, parents' natural primacy as educators unites, in a free society, with their (corporate) authority as self-governing citizens to whom the government is ultimately accountable. This supports, I think, extending the curricular authority of local school boards into the realm of civic education. At the same time, the government can and should play an auxiliary role in cultivating the political understanding of its citizens by, among other things, supporting and promoting the development of engaging and informative civic curricula.

Placing an emphasis on political culture has implications for how we think about political action, too. It suggests that our primary concerns with present political issues and debates should be those that involve long-arc political questions, for example, the purpose of government, the meaning of personal liberty, and the nature of political institutions like religious liberty. Of course, these fundamental issues are implicated in day-to-day political questions. Debates over welfare reform, public health care, or the legalization of cannabis turn on one's notion of the role of government and its relationship to civil society. Engaging the quotidian issues of politics is important because over time they add up to real changes in customs and institutions. Tocqueville describes the incremental way that an administrative state chips away at a robust notion of political liberty through the piecemeal provision of one small material benefit after another, until citizens have been entirely relieved of "the trouble of thinking and the pain of living." Still, the daily news cycle can easily obscure the deeper currents of intellectual and institutional change unfolding in a political culture. A primary reason the "soft despotism" Tocqueville predicts is not resisted is that the inverse relationship between expanding bureaucracy and individual liberty is little understood.[1] Thus, becoming immersed in one's political history and culture is necessary even to be able to take a long-arc view of politics. As sociologist James Davison Hunter has observed, "Culture takes form as the slow accretions of meaning in society over long periods of time. In this sense, culture is much less an invention of will than it is a slow product of history." For the historically ignorant citizen, every debate can *only* involve a present conflict of interests. This kind of shallow political consciousness, to use Hunter's apt metaphor, is always distracted with the weather while ignoring the climate.[2] Thus, in a profound way, from a Burkean standpoint the citizen who engages the most essential goods of political community is not the *active* citizen, but the *culturally embedded* citizen. Not the citizen who can tell you name of the White House chief of staff or the details of the Joint Comprehensive Plan of Action, but the one who knows the Anti-Federalists' arguments against the Constitution or the rare achievement of Mary Edwards Walker. In key ways, the active citizen's very ability to engage current politics as a dialogue about the just and the good depends upon his or her understanding how that conversation has unfolded throughout the country's history. The goods of the moral imagination, too, are available in the "gallery of portraits" populated by the icons of history.

At the same time, we must be careful not to push this point too far. Embracing the goods of political society cannot be solely realized in historical knowledge without giving rise to some kind of present action. As I argued in Chapter 5, the ennobling force of political culture is that it invites citizens into meaningful *participation* in a community extended through time. Moreover, that community invests its members with duties to act for the preservation and improvement of what they have received. What kind of political action, then, is necessary to achieving the goods that political life has to offer us?

This brings us to the second way that my argument changes how we tend to think about involvement in political community. Political action, as understood from the vantage point of the civic friendship I defend, is deliberation and action undertaken for the sake of the common good of one's community. In contrast, a narrow view of politics limits the political to whatever is directly related to the official capacities of citizenship, that is, exercising political rights or fulfilling civic duties as they are established under a duly constituted government. This description is political action *post-founding*; it is activity defined by and associated with government. For the following reasons, however, we should bring more into the scope of what counts as political action.

Consider Aristotle's account of political origins in the opening chapters of the *Politics*. As community moves from the household, to the village, to the association of villages, he argues that a particular kind of ordering activity characterizes the community's transformation into uniquely *political society*. Humans differ from other gregarious animals in that language—the faculty of reasoned speech—enables them to communicate more than pleasure and pain. It enables discussion and debate about good and evil, the just and the unjust. Association in these things makes a family and a city.[3] This, then, is the core of political activity as it emerges in the Aristotelian account: deliberation about the good and the just ordered to the common good of a complete community.[4]

Notice that distinctly political activity occurs *before* a political founding. It is, in fact, political activity oriented toward the common good of a complete community that *leads to* the establishment of governmental authority. Of course, establishing government is necessary to the full sufficiency of the polis. Apart from authority, the only way to move from *deliberation about* the common good to *action for* the common good is unanimity.[5] Since unanimity in extended associations is a practical impossibility, political authority is necessary to a fully sufficient common life. Institutions must be created, laws promulgated, and allegiance to these required in order to achieve—not merely debate—a real common good.

Thus, government is necessary to the full completion of the political community, but it does not define political activity. It is itself a *product* of political action. A community is not political that has not established governmental authority because it is not yet complete. Yet it is political action within the community that leads to a political founding—and thus the full sufficiency of the community. This distinction is critical because apart from it we are apt to exclusively identify the political good with the wrong thing. For example, in an argument for the instrumentality of the political common good, Robert P. George contends that "if we all regularly reached consensus we could avoid coordination problems without any serious privation or harm to the human good."[6] In other words, George has identified the political good, the reason we would have for entering into political community, with the function of governmental authority in coordinating society in the absence of consensus. He argues that *if* consensus could be reached, coordination problems would be avoided, and we could dispense with politics without harm to the human good. Thus, the political common good is instrumental. However, in my view George has asked the wrong question. He has asked, per impossible, could we dispense with *government* without harm? The right question—*the political question*—is, could we dispense with *coordination* without harm to the human good?[7] Put differently, could families, churches, civic clubs, reading groups, and so on *not order their lives together* toward a common end without harm to the human good? This, of course, is a very different question. The question George asks essentially retains the *political function* of coordinating life together while removing government from the picture. If we take away government but preserve coordination to the community's common good (again, only a theoretical possibility), it is plausible that no harm results. However, if we really take away *politics*, the act of deliberating and agreeing on a just common good, the harm to the human good is readily apparent.

Government is necessary to achieve the purpose of politics, but it does not define the limits of political action or describe the good attained therein. Because of its necessity, no political society is complete without the authority of government, but George's counterfactual effectively demonstrates that it is merely an instrument to the political good. Political community—insofar as it is *complete*—can never be without it, yet our reasons for entering political community, and the actions we take on its behalf, extend far beyond it.

On this account, therefore, all deliberation and action motivated by a desire to promote the common good of one's political community counts as meaningful political activity. Citizens who volunteer at a soup kitchen or join Habitat for Humanity to build houses for the impoverished in their city are acting politically. A family that debates the value of easily accessed organized sports for the youth of its community at the dinner table is acting politically. A university that makes outreach efforts in its community for the purpose of extending educational opportunities to those who might not otherwise have them or be inclined to seek them is acting politically. A church that tries to contribute to the vitality of families in its area by broadly advertising a marriage seminar or making counseling services easily available to the poor is acting politically.

Now, I do not want to conflate political activity with a general goodwill toward one's neighbor, or confuse it, in the case of the church, with other nonpolitical motivations. It is essential to all of my examples that the actors take the needs and goods of their particular political community (whether local, state, or national) into consideration. In many cases there will be an easy and complete convergence of multiple motivations. The Habitat for Humanity volunteer may be motivated by a general benevolence (such that she volunteers internationally in the summer) *and* by a desire to address needs within her own community. The church may be motivated by a simultaneous desire to share its spiritual message and contribute to the good of its community by building healthy families. Citizens and associations who have learned, in Hugh Heclo's phrase, to "think institutionally" will do both. As Heclo explains, thinking institutionally involves acting within one's community from an "internal point of view"—habitually adopting the purposes, ideals, goods, and customs of the institution into one's own deliberative action. The institutional thinker acts from a sense of duty and a commitment to the common good of the whole.[8] This does not mean that political aims become dominant. A religious association will always consider its spiritual aims and allegiances to be paramount. Given the particular needs and interests of its members, a family may decide to devote its energies to a private chess club rather than to the Boy Scouts of America (an organization with conscious political aims). However, citizens who are mindful of their responsibilities to the larger communities whose political life, institutions, and traditions they participate in (and benefit from) will "think institutionally" about how they can contribute to the political common good. For most people in most day-to-day activities, this will be pursued through the voluntary associations of civil society—the "little platoons" that Burke and Tocqueville emphasized—who orient their activities (sometimes exclusively, often only in part) for the benefit of the community as a whole.

Therefore, the practical upshot of my argument for the intrinsic value of political association is an affirmation of three basic things. Minimally, it underscores a duty to fulfill the basic functions of citizenship reliably and knowledgably. This entails more than simply a knowledge of current political issues; it involves at least a basic knowledge of a country's political culture. Second, it suggests that political virtues of justice, love, and generosity should be cultivated by "thinking institutionally" and acting in accord with the good of one's political community. Often this will be expressed through the many and diverse institutions of civil society, which are the backbone of a strong polity, rather than in direct involvement in legal and governmental concerns. Finally, my argument affirms the connection between patriotism and human flourishing. The goods of politics—in particular, powerful sources of a vibrant moral imagination—emerge in the history, institutions, customs, and icons of a particular people. Embracing those goods requires an embrace of the community from which they emerge. Preserving those goods requires a devotion to that community and the generational partnership it embodies.

NOTES

Abbreviations Used in Notes

CNE   Thomas Aquinas, *Commentary on Aristotle's Nicomachean Ethics*, trans. C. I. Litzinger (Notre Dame, IN: Dumb Ox Books, 1993).

NE   Aristotle, *Nicomachean Ethics*, trans. Martin Ostwald (Upper Saddle River, NJ: Prentice Hall, 1999).

Politics   Aristotle, *Politics*, trans. Ernest Barker and R. F. Stalley (Oxford: Oxford University Press, 1995).

ST   Thomas Aquinas, *Summa Theologica*, trans. Fathers of the English Dominican Province (Notre Dame, IN: Ave Maria Press, 1981).

Introduction

1. Alexander Hamilton, John Jay, and James Madison, *The Federalist Papers: The Gideon Edition*. 2nd ed., eds. George W. Carey and James McClellan (Indianapolis, IN: Liberty Fund, 2001), 43.

2. Ibid., 44.

3. Ibid., 46.

4. *Palko v. Connecticut*, 302 U.S. 319 (1937), 325.

5. For a helpful analysis of the different meanings of these terms in political theory, see Bruce Douglass, "The Common Good and the Public Interest," *Political Theory* 8, no. 1 (1980): 103–117.

6. See, for example, Michael J. Sandel, *Liberalism and the Limits of Justice*, 2nd ed. (Cambridge: Cambridge University Press, 1998); Alasdair C MacIntyre, *After Virtue: A Study in Moral Theory*, 3rd ed. (Notre Dame, IN: University of Notre Dame Press, 2007); Mary Ann Glendon, *Rights Talk: The Impoverishment of Political Discourse* (New York: Free Press, 1993), esp. 109–170; John Rawls, *A Theory of Justice* (Cambridge, MA: Belknap Press of Harvard University Press, 1971); and John Rawls, *Political Liberalism*, John Dewey Essays in Philosophy, no. 4 (New York: Columbia University Press, 1993).

7. For a helpful discussion of this trend in contemporary theory see Will Kymlicka and Wayne Norman, "Return of the Citizen: A Survey of Recent Work on Citizenship Theory," *Ethics* 104, no. 2 (January 1994): 352–381.

8. See, for example, Amy Gutmann, *Democratic Education* (Princeton, NJ: Princeton University Press, 1987), 19–47; and Stephen Macedo, "Liberal Civic Education and Religious Fundamentalism: The Case of God v. John Rawls?," *Ethics* 105, no. 3 (April 1995): 468–496. These theorists are best described as liberal virtue theorists. Russell Hittinger provides a helpful discussion of this general tendency among civil society theorists, including Alexis de Tocqueville, in *The First Grace: Re-*

discovering the Natural Law in a Post-Christian World (Wilmington, DE: ISI Books, 2003), 265–283.

9. Gutmann, for example, is insistent that her view of the political association eschews a "family state" model that subsumes the institutions of civil society under the state. However, her only model of such a monolithic regime is Socratic communism in Plato's *Republic*, so her rejection of such an extreme view is cold comfort to one concerned that her repudiation of the more pluralistic "state of families" model risks overwhelming distinct subpolitical goods in favor of alleged public interests (*Democratic Education*, 19–47). I will take up these issues further in Chapter 2.

10. See, for example, William Galston, "Defending Liberty: Liberal Democracy and the Limits of Public Power," in Robert Faulkner and Susan Shell., eds., *America at Risk: Threats to Liberal Self-Government in an Age of Uncertainty* (Ann Arbor: University of Michigan Press, 2009), 57–74.

11. Moreover, as recent commentators on Catholic social thought have observed, the task of relating and prioritizing goods within the political community is also still a largely unfinished work of subsidiarity theory. Kenneth Grasso makes such an argument in "The Subsidiary State: Society, the State and the Principle of Subsidiarity in Catholic Social Thought," in Jeanne Heffernan Schindler, ed., *Christianity and Civil Society: Catholic and Neo-Calvinist Perspectives* (Lanham, MD: Lexington Books, 2008), 31–65.

12. See especially Michael Pakaluk, "Natural Law and Civil Society," in S. Chambers and W. Kymlicka, eds., *Alternative Conceptions of Civil Society* (Princeton, NJ: Princeton University Press, 2002), 131–148. For a very helpful explication of Thomas Aquinas's views on the basically plural structure of society, both subpolitically and politically, see Nicholas Aroney, "Subsidiarity, Federalism and the Best Constitution: Thomas Aquinas on City, Province and Empire," *Law and Philosophy* 26 (2007) 161–228, esp. 173–184. See also the respective contributions of Jeanne Heffernan Schindler and Russell Hittinger in Schindler, *Christianity and Civil Society*.

13. *NE*, 1098a16.

14. Ibid., 1177b30.

15. *ST*, I–II, q. 3, 2 ad 4.

16. *NE*, 1099b.

17. Thomas Aquinas's position on this is unambiguous. See, for example, *CNE*, I, Lec. 1, n5. While I think Aristotle's fundamental grounding of moral and political goodness is likewise the human person, his views are more obscure than are Aquinas's. Some scholars take his presentation of the natural genesis of the city in the first chapters of his *Politics* to indicate an associational organicity that subsumes the individual as well as subpolitical associations. I think such an interpretation of Aristotle is mistaken, however, and I will take the issue up in Chapter 3.

18. *ST*, I, q. 29, a. 3.

19. See Thomas Aquinas, *De Regno*, 115–118. Citation to paragraphs as marked in St. Thomas Aquinas, *On Kingship, to the King of Cyprus*, trans. G. B. Phelan (Toronto: Pontifical Institute for Medieval Studies, 1982). The editor of this volume, I. Eschmann, introduced the paragraphs.

20. *NE*, VIII.3, 1156b25.

21. *Politics*, I, 2.

22. See helpful discussions in John Finnis, *Aquinas: Moral, Political, and Legal Theory* (Oxford: Oxford University Press, 1998), 242–245; and Mary M. Keys, *Aquinas, Aristotle, and the Promise of the Common Good* (Cambridge: Cambridge University Press, 2006), 79–81.

23. *Politics*, I.2, 1253a18ff.

24. Thomas Aquinas, *Commentary on Aristotle's Politics*, trans. Richard J. Reagan (Indianapolis, IN: Hackett, 2007), I, 1 n22.

25. *Politics*, I, 2, 1253a25.

26. *ST*, I–II, q. 90, a. 2. What exactly "perfect community" means is the subject of some ambiguity and disagreement. In a formal sense, it denotes the ways in which the polis comprises a whole of which individuals, families, clans, and villages are parts. Substantively, Aristotle first arrives at the idea of a perfect or complete community by attending to the material deficiencies of other human associations (*Politics* I.1-2). The political community is perfect because it attains self-sufficiency in meeting human needs. But at precisely this point, Aristotle makes a crucial transition from speaking of "mere life" to the city's existence for the sake of the good life (1252b27–29). Thus, a fulfillment of the good life has to be understood as the fullest meaning of "perfect community." Yet there is still a tremendous amount of content to be supplied in light of the fact that political society is a *composite whole*, comprised of parts that possess their own proper functions. What must be answered, therefore, is in what particular ways political society serves as a whole by fulfilling, completing, and perfecting human experience of the good life.

27. *ST*, I–II, q. 96, a. 4; II–II, q. 65, a. 1. The context of both of these passages indicates a *material* belonging to the community. In the first passage, Aquinas refers to the responsibility of individuals to share in bearing the burdens of the community. In the latter passage, Aquinas argues that to maim an individual is to harm the community, "to whom the man and all his parts belong."

28. *NE*, 1.2, 1094a27.

29. *Politics*, I.1, 1252a5. Although it is not at all clear that Aristotle intends this to be his final word on the subject, it is not far removed from the position affirmed much later in the work at III.9, 1280b29ff. Here Aristotle seems to argue that the various institutions of social life, including marriage, extended family groups, religious gatherings, and communal pastimes, are *means* to a good life primarily instantiated in the city.

30. *Commentary on Aristotle's* Politics, I, 1, n. 2; *De Regno*, 70.

31. *ST*, I–II, q. 94, a. 4.

32. Ibid., q. 21, a. 4, ad 3. For a helpful juxtaposition of texts in the Thomistic corpus indicating both the primacy of the human person and the primacy of the political community, see Jacques Maritain, *Man and the State* (Chicago: University of Chicago Press, 1951), 70–71.

33. For a helpful discussion and evaluation of this debate, see Mary M. Keys, "Personal Dignity and the Common Good: A Twentieth-Century Thomistic Dialogue," in Kenneth L. Grasso et al., eds., *Catholicism, Liberalism, and Communitarianism* (Lanham, MD: Rowan and Littlefield, 1995), 173–195. Although the instrumentality of political community is implicated to some degree in this debate, it has not been useful for my purposes here inasmuch as the dispute concerns the primacy of the person or the community in the transcendent final end, *beatituda per-*

fecta. As my concern is with the relative significance of political community, directed (at best) to the temporal end of human flourishing, its status is fundamentally different than that of the heavenly community. So even if we were to conclude that for Aquinas the eschatological vision of God is fundamentally communal, it is hard to see how that would dispose of the question of the temporal political community's status. The two communities are fundamentally different.

34. Jacques Maritain, *The Person and the Common Good* (Notre Dame, IN: University of Notre Dame Press, 1947).

35. Ibid., 62–65. Maritain does not make the precise meanings of these terms altogether clear. They turn on the distinction he draws between man as a person and as an individual. Individuality describes the material, dependent aspects of man (34–38). As to his individuality, man is subject to the political community. Personhood, on the other hand, refers to the spiritual, deepest essence of man (38–42). In this respect, society is directed to, and subordinate in some sense, to the good of the person. I am in agreement with Ralph McInerny that whereas Maritain's individual person distinction is broadly suggestive, it simply cannot do the work of explaining the priority relationships between the human person and the community that Maritain intends. The distinction ultimately seems to pit an isolated spirituality against a communal materiality. "The Primacy of the Common Good," in Ralph McInerny, *Art and Prudence: Studies in the Thought of Jacques Maritain* (Notre Dame, IN: University of Notre Dame Press, 1988), 77–91. I would add that Maritain's distinction fails to account for the ways in which our *personal dimensions* are social and, moreover, are tied in important ways to our materiality.

36. Maritain, *Man and the State*, 13.

37. "Is Natural Law Theory Compatible with Limited Government?," in Robert P. George, ed., *Natural Law, Liberalism, and Morality: Contemporary Essays* (Oxford: Clarendon Press, 1996), 5.

38. John Finnis, *Natural Law and Natural Rights* (Oxford: Oxford University Press, 1980), 155. It is important to note that Finnis's view differs substantially from all forms of social contractarian "public interest" characteristic of liberalism. Although the political common good is conditional for Finnis, the conditions of society are very important to the ability of its members to make reasonable moral choices. Thus, the public sphere is not a "neutral" territory, for Finnis, but one that should conduce to human goodness. See Finnis, *Aquinas*, 232–234.

39. Because of what traditional Thomists argue are thoroughgoing divergences from the positions of Thomas Aquinas, the brand of Thomism pioneered by Germain Grisez, John Finnis, and Joseph Boyle has been labeled the "new natural law." In addition to the works of Finnis cited here, see Germain Grisez, Joseph Boyle, and John Finnis, "Practical Principles, Moral Truth, and Ultimate Ends," *American Journal of Jurisprudence* 32 (1987): 99–151; and Germain G Grisez, "The First Principle of Practical Reason: A Commentary on the Summa Theologiae, 1–2, Question 94, Article 2," *Natural Law Forum* 10 (1965): 168–201.

40. Some discussions of Finnis's position make this mistake, such as Mary M. Keys, "Personal Dignity and the Common Good," 194.

41. Finnis, *Aquinas*, 246.

42. Ibid., 246. This is my paraphrase of Finnis's distinction at this point. I have put it in terms of "human flourishing" in order to maintain terminological consis-

tency throughout this project. Finnis speaks in the "basic goods" language of the new natural law. There are, of course, substantive differences denoted by the two different terminologies, but for the present no harm is done in eliding them. This dual way of speaking about what is "natural" is evident also in Aristotle's transition from speaking of the city as an organic entity to a rationally directed instantiation of the good life (*Politics*, 1252b27ff).

43. Paul Sigmund, *Philosophical Review* 110, no. 1 (January 2001): 129, 131.

44. John Finnis, *Natural Law and Natural Rights* (Oxford: Oxford University Press, 1980).

45. See, for example, Russell Hittinger, *A Critique of the New Natural Law Theory* (Notre Dame, IN: University of Notre Dame Press, 1987), and the twenty-fifth-anniversary symposium on *Natural Law and Natural Rights* published in the *American Journal of Jurisprudence* 50 (2005).

46. Finnis, *Aquinas*, 228. There have been a few treatments of Finnis's argument on limited government and the political common good: see Michael Pakaluk, "Is the Common Good of Political Society Limited and Instrumental?," *Review of Metaphysics* 55, no. 1 (September 2001): 57–94. Pakaluk's critique is the best I have come across, yet (as I will argue) it is not persuasive on significant points. See also Lawrence Dewan, O.P., "St. Thomas, John Finnis, and the Political Common Good," *The Thomist* 64 (2000): 337–374; and Steven A. Long, "St. Thomas Aquinas through the Analytic Looking Glass," *The Thomist* 65 (2001): 259–300, 291–299. These latter treatments are helpful at several points, but at key junctures they fail to adequately address the nuance of Finnis's arguments.

47. Robert P. George, "The Concept of Public Morality," *American Journal of Jurisprudence* 45 (2000): 30.

48. Prominent examples include George, "The Concept of Public Morality"; Mary M. Keys, *Aquinas, Aristotle, and the Promise of the Common Good* (Cambridge: Cambridge University Press, 2006); Mark C. Murphy, *Natural Law in Jurisprudence and Politics* (Cambridge: Cambridge University Press, 2006); and Christopher Wolfe, *Natural Law Liberalism* (Cambridge: Cambridge University Press, 2006). Keys and Murphy do not directly rely upon Finnis's instrumentality thesis, but their positions, I argue, fundamentally assume it. Murphy, in fact, directly argues *against* Finnis's position, but as I demonstrate in Chapter 3, his final argument against the *distinctiveness* of the common good imports a tacit reliance on the instrumentality thesis.

49. Keys, *Promise of the Common Good*, 96. Emphasis original.

50. Ibid., 190–196, 101. It should be noted that Keys does not appear to be self-consciously building on Finnis's common good thesis. She also is not as careful as Finnis to differentiate between the social and the political. Thus, throughout her study she refers to the "social and civic" nature or inclinations of man (e.g., 131). This ambiguity has the virtue of consistency with ambiguities in Aquinas's thought, but it also has significant drawbacks when particular arguments are being made concerning the relative importance of the social, as specifically differentiated from the political, in Aquinas's thought.

51. *ST*, I–II, q. 95.2: "Every human law has just so much of the nature of law as it is derived from the law of nature."

52. Murphy, *Natural Law in Jurisprudence and Politics*, 169.

53. Ibid., 170.

54. Finnis, *Natural Law and Natural Rights*, 150.

55. Aquinas's formulation is particularly famous: "Law is an ordinance of reason *for the common good* made by him who has care of the community, and promulgated." *ST*, I–II, q. 90, a. 4. Emphasis mine.

56. The point here relates specifically to the subpolitical challenge, so I will not discuss how the argument must be filled out if it is to successfully address the super-political challenge.

57. Aquinas, *De Regno*, 70. See also *De Regno*, 24; Aristotle, *NE*, VIII, 9, 1160a10; and Aristotle, *Politics* I, 1, 1252a3.

58. Finnis, *Aquinas*, 249.

59. *Politics* I, 1, 1252a18–23.

60. *CNE*, Book I, Lec. 1, nn4–6. As is often the case, this first point is much clearer in Aquinas's thought than in Aristotle's. Aristotle emphasizes the second point. Still, I agree with Aquinas that they are both faithful to the Aristotelian methodology.

61. Aristotle is in many places concerned with articulating how the parts relate and fit into the whole. See, for example, *NE* X.9 and *Politics* III.9.

Chapter 1. Critical Assessment of Finnis's Instrumentality Thesis

1. John Finnis, "Is Natural Law Theory Compatible with Limited Government?," in Robert P. George, ed., *Natural Law, Liberalism, and Morality* (Oxford: Clarendon Press, 1996), 8. I should note at the outset that Finnis does not directly attribute this formulation of the distinction between public and private to Aquinas. However, I believe it is clear that the careful reconstruction of the Thomistic position that Finnis argues for in *Aquinas* closely entails the formulation he later specifies. Therefore, I have decided to treat Finnis's writings on this as a single cohesive articulation of the genuine Thomistic position.

2. Finnis allows one possible exception to the instrumentality of the political common good: insofar as restorative justice is integral to the basic good of human sociability, it may be said to be more than merely instrumental. Finnis, *Aquinas*, 245.

3. For an overview of the main themes of this Aristotelian/Thomistic political tradition, see Robert P. George, *Making Men Moral: Civil Liberties and Public Morality* (Oxford: Clarendon Press, 1993), 19–47.

4. Aristotle, *Politics*, III.9 1280a25–1281a10.

5. *ST*, I–II, q. 94, a. 4.

6. *ST*, I–II, q. 90, a. 2.

7. Gregory Froelich, "The Equivocal Status of *Bonum Commune*," *New Scholasticism* 63 (Winter 1989): 38–57.

8. By "state," Finnis means the whole of the political community. He distinguishes this from government, which is the ruling part of the political whole. Finnis, *Aquinas*, 219–220.

9. Ibid., 221–222. Emphasis original.

10. Ibid., 221.

11. *CNE*, Lec. 2, n912.

12. Finnis, *Aquinas*, 235.

13. Ibid., 238.

14. Ibid., 223.

15. *ST*, q. 100, a. 2.

16. Finnis, *Aquinas*, 226.

17. *ST* II–II, q. 29, a. 1.

18. Finnis, *Aquinas*, 227–228. "It is a peace compatible even with tyranny," Finnis says (footnote 48, citing *De Regno*).

19. Per impossible. Aquinas notes that not even divine law requires the fullest mode of virtue. *ST* I–II, q. 100, a. 9c.

20. Finnis, *Aquinas*, 233 n64. The parent's educational role concerns the child "as such."

21. John Finnis, "Is Natural Law Theory Compatible with Limited Government?," in *Natural Law, Liberalism, and Morality: Contemporary Essays*, ed. Robert P. George (Oxford: Oxford University Press, 1998), 1–26, 8, 17.

22. *ST*, I–II, q. 96, a. 3.

23. *ST*, q. 18, a. 6. In any voluntary action, a twofold act can be differentiated, with two different objects of action: (1) an interior act (will), (2) an external act. The object of an interior act is the end of the action; the object of the exterior act is the "that on which the object is brought to bear." The first is the form of the second. Although Aquinas does not specify which kind of object must be referable to the common good, it seems clear that it must be the object of the external act since human law only properly directs external matters. Ordination of the internal act to the common good belongs to the individual.

24. Ibid., a. 6 ad 4; I–II, q. 90, a. 3 ad 3.

25. For example, *ST*, II–II, q. 58, a. 7; *CNE*, V, Lec. 2, n909.

26. *ST*, II–II, q. 80. "Justice alone, of all the virtues," Aquinas says, "implies the notion of duty." *ST*, I–II q. 99, a. 5 ad 1.

27. *ST*, I–II, q. 100, a. 11 ad 3. The law is, however, involved in supporting this domestic good. As the passage Aquinas quotes in Deuteronomy 21 continues, the gluttonous son who would not submit to his parents' discipline was consequently stoned by the community. However, Aquinas indicates elsewhere that it was not for the gluttony that the son was punished by the law, but for his stubborn rebellion. *ST*, I–II, q. 105, Art. 2, ad 10.

28. Thomas Aquinas, *Summa contra Gentiles*, III, c. 123, n6.

29. Ibid., "*ad totius domesticae conversationis consortium.*"

30. *ST*, Supp., q. 41, a. 1; q. 44, a.1; q. 49, a. 2 ad 1.

31. This is implied in Aquinas, *De Regno*, 108. See also Finnis, *Aquinas*, 226.

32. *ST*, I–II, q. 96, a. 3.

33. "Is the Common Good Limited and Instrumental?," 69–72. This is Pakaluk's description of the highest form of peace, which he concludes comes within the legislator's aim as much as is practically possible.

34. Ibid., 87.

35. *Politics* VII.17 1336a30-32. For helpful commentary, see Richard Kraut's comments on this passage in Aristotle, *Politics: Books VII and VIII*, trans. Richard Kraut (New York: Oxford University Press, 1997), 158–159.

36. See *NE* 10.9 (1180a14–1181b14) for Aristotle's account for the importance of the parents in the process of moral formation.

37. Finnis, "Limited Government," in George, *Natural Law, Liberalism, and Morality*, 8.

38. Ibid., 17.

39. Finnis, *Aquinas*, 232.

40. Ibid.

41. Finnis argues that Thomistic texts "suggest" maintenance of a public morality, while "falling short of proving it." Ibid., 233 n62.

42. The exclusivity of Finnis's rationale here is implicit, though still clear. He sets out to consider why Aquinas thinks the law aims at virtue and carefully specifies that it does so in order to secure the public good. He does not explicitly reject the possibility that the law aims at virtue simpliciter in the sense that I argue, but the structure of his argument makes it clear that he takes his stated justification to be exclusive. Moreover, nothing in Finnis's argument in the next chapter, that is, that citizens ideally adopt the law's directives as their own, becoming "partners in public reason," amends this initial position (ibid., 255–258). Incidentally, Michael Pakaluk's reading of Finnis on this point concurs with my own ("Is the Common Good Limited and Instrumental?," 58).

43. See, for example, *ST*, I–II, q. 100, a. 9 ad 2.

44. Finnis, *Aquinas*, 220.

45. Ibid., 235.

46. Ibid., 237–238.

47. Aquinas's word is *inducere*. See, for example, *ST* I–II q. 100, a. 9c.

48. Finnis, *Aquinas*, 231.

49. Ibid., 238.

50. Ibid., 234.

51. *ST*, I–II, q. 100, a. 9 ad 2.

52. See Finnis's discussion of the goods inherent in family life in *Aquinas*, 242–245 and *Natural Law and Natural Rights*, 134–139, 144–150.

53. Finnis, *Aquinas*, 233 n64.

54. I have some reservation in saying that the law only aims at the virtue of justice (as opposed to all virtue). Given that they are, as Aristotle says, "the same in substance" (*NE* V.1.1130a10–13), the conceptual distinction simply may not matter. I am inclined, though, to think that it does. However, parsing this point is not pertinent to my present argument, so I will leave it for another time.

55. Aquinas draws a distinction between a unity of composition and a unity of order. The civitas, as a unity of order, is comprised of parts that themselves exist as wholes distinct from the larger whole. Qua distinct wholes, the parts of the larger whole have functions, virtues, and goods particular to themselves. *CNE*, I, Lec. 1, n5.

56. *ST*, I–II, q. 100, a. 9 ad 2.

57. Finnis, *Aquinas*, 222–229, 232–234. I should make a couple of further minor points for clarification. First, there is a great deal of ambiguity in what Finnis takes to be the substance of the "peace" that falls within governmental jurisdiction. It may be possible for Finnis to contend that insofar as the public good is limited to that "peaceful condition needed to get the benefit [*utilitas*] of social life and avoid the burdens of contention" (227), there is no reason to think that the virtues appurtenant to such a condition would be inherently perfective of the individual. Thus they would be instrumental and therefore not sought for the good of the individual per

se. At the same time, he allows that the public peace necessarily includes a "love of neighbor as oneself," that is, "being willing to do one's neighbor's will as one's own." Still, he concludes that this peace "falls short of the complete justice which true virtue requires of us" (227n46). The problem here is that there is a great deal of conceptual space between mere noncontentiousness and the full unity of virtue and desire that Aquinas attributes to the "thickest" form of peace (see *ST* II–II, q. 29, a. 1). Finnis emphasizes the former, plausibly shows that the public good cannot directly include the latter, and suggests that the substance of political life falls somewhere in between. Given that this "in between" is only gestured toward (for reasons I will subsequently argue), Finnis's brief comments about peace do not warrant the inference that law does not aim at virtue simpliciter. There is, moreover, no reason to assume that virtues pertaining to even a fully instrumental end would not be sought in part for the sake of the individuals themselves.

Second, space does not allow me to include an analysis of Finnis's discussion of the public good in *De Regno*. Those interested will find a detailed critique in Michael Pakaluk's "Is the Common Good of Political Society Limited and Instrumental?," 77–86. Suffice it here to say that Finnis's consideration of *De Regno* adds nothing to the substance of his argument that is not contained elsewhere. The whole point of that discussion is to demonstrate that his interpretation can be squared with the most explicitly Aristotelian of Aquinas's political texts.

58. Finnis, *Aquinas*, 237, 239.

59. Ibid., 235.

60. Ibid., 245, 252.

61. Ibid., 239–245, 239.

62. Ibid., 245.

63. Ibid.

64. Ibid., 221. Although Finnis first says that the two questions "seem" to be equivalent, he immediately states that "Aquinas treats the questions as substantially equivalent" and proceeds as though they are.

65. *Politics*, I.1-2.

Chapter 2. The Familial Good

1. John Rawls, *The Law of Peoples: With "The Idea of Public Reason Revisited"* (Cambridge, MA: Harvard University Press, 2001), 157.

2. Ecclesial association poses difficulties for political community that are equally important and intractable. They arise from a different source, however, and will not concern us here. For an intentionally provocative, though importantly influential, account from the Anabaptist tradition of this ecclesial tension or conflict with political community, see Stanley Hauerwas and William H. Willimon, *Resident Aliens: Life in the Christian Colony* (Nashville, TN: Abingdon Press, 1989).

3. It is worth noting that, given my primary concern with the parent-child relationship, there is some authority for giving particular consideration to Aristotle and Aquinas. In his comprehensive philosophical exploration of the topic, Jeffrey Blustein maintains that in the history of Western philosophy, Aristotle and Aquinas are most sensitive to the moral significance of the relationship between parents and children. See Jeffrey Blustein, *Parents and Children: The Ethics of the Family* (New York: Oxford University Press, 1982), 46.

4. Susan Moller Okin, *Justice, Gender, and the Family* (New York: Basic Books, 1989), 5.

5. Plato, *Republic* 423e6–424a2.

6. *Politics* II.2-4, 1261a10–1262b35. For a concise and helpful restatement of this argument, see Michael Pakaluk, "Natural Law and Civil Society," in S. Chambers and W. Kymlicka, eds., *Alternative Conceptions of Civil Society* (Princeton, NJ: Princeton University Press: 2002), 131–148, 140–141.

7. See Blustein, *Parents and Children*, 35–46, for a helpful discussion of Aristotle's critique of Plato and analysis of filial relationships.

8. *NE* X.9, 1179a33–1181b25.

9. Ibid.

10. Ibid., 1180a30–35, b20–25; *Politics* I.2, 1253a7–17.

11. Earnest Barker, *Political Thought of Plato and Aristotle* (New York: Dover Publications, 1959), 399-400.

12. *The Family in Political Thought* (Amherst, MA: University of Massachusetts Press, 1982), 12, 51–65. Cf. Arlene W. Saxonhouse, "Family, Polity & Unity: Aristotle on Socrates' Community of Wives," *Polity* 15, no. 2 (December 1982): 202–219; Harry V Jaffa, *Thomism and Aristotelianism* (Chicago: University of Chicago Press, 1952), 184; Aristotle, *Politics: Books VII and VIII*, trans. Richard Kraut (New York: Oxford University Press, 1997). Saxonhouse presents a unique defense of the integral importance of the family to political life: the family mitigates core political problems of justice by providing a model of unity despite fundamental inequalities. This is an interesting suggestion insofar as the family's ability to better solve basic associational difficulties suggests that Aristotle may not view it as merely instrumental to political life. However, for reasons discussed in Chapter 4, I think it is very hard to escape an instrumentalist view. Jaffa references *Politics* 1337a10, the beginning of Book VIII, on the necessity of educating *to the regime*. It's a strong statement that perhaps undermines my characterization of Aristotle's treatment as a "dilemma." However, Aristotle *does* say that the common education should be for common things, which raises the question, what should be taken to be common? Perhaps not everything. Yet, he also criticizes everyone privately teaching what they think is best.

13. X.9, 1180b5–20.

14. See Richard Kraut's commentary in *Politics: Books VII and VIII*, 160. Despite Blustein's praise for Aristotle's treatment of the parent-child relationship, most scholars seem to be frustrated by its thinness. As I have noted, he says a number of things that are very suggestive and then fails to deliver a more robust account. This lacuna has been noted, for example, by Mary P. Nichols, *Citizens and Statesmen: A Study of Aristotle's Politics* (Lanham, MD: Rowman and Littlefield, 1992), 34.

15. Rawls, *The Law of Peoples*, 156–164.

16. Okin, *Justice, Gender, and the Family*, 135.

17. See Robert Reich, for an example of this, as well as James Dwyer's argument for a "child's rights" paradigm for education in their respective contributions to Stephen Macedo and Yael Tamir, eds., *Moral and Political Education* (New York: New York University Press, 2002); see also Martha Minow and Mary Lyndon Shanley, "Relational Rights and Responsibilities: Revisioning the Family in Liberal Political Theory and Law," *Hypatia* 11, no. 1 (January 1996): 4–29. Minow and Shanley

provide a helpful categorization of the ways in which the parent-child relationship tends to be discussed: social-contractarian, communitarian, and rights-based. They offer a helpful defense of a *relational model*, although they argue that it should be taken combined with a rights-orientation focused on the interests of children. This is fair enough as a formal matter, though as Reich points out, the rub is: Who has authority to determine what those interests are? (285).

18. Stanley Hauerwas, "The Moral Meaning of the Family," *Commonweal*, August 1, 1980, 433. I merely employ Hauerwas's descriptive phrase, without attributing to him the view I'm outlining.

19. Okin, *Justice, Gender, and the Family*, 17–23.

20. Amy Gutmann, *Democratic Education* (Princeton, NJ: Princeton University Press, 1987), 30–31, 51. William Galston rejoins very sensibly in part that both civic tolerance and deliberation are "perfectly compatible with unswerving belief in the correctness of one's own way of life." William A. Galston, *Liberal Purposes: Goods, Virtues, and Diversity in the Liberal State* (New York: Cambridge University Press, 1991), 253.

21. Amy Gutmann, "Civic Education and Social Diversity," *Ethics* 105, no. 3 (1995): 557–579.

22. Alasdair MacIntyre, *Dependent Rational Animals: Why Human Beings Need the Virtues* (Chicago: Open Court, 2001), 83–90.

23. Ibid., 83.

24. Aristotle, *NE* I.4, 1095a30–b12; *Whose Justice? Which Rationality?* (Notre Dame, IN: University of Notre Dame Press, 1988), 6–10.

25. MacIntyre, *Dependent Rational Animals*, 89. What MacIntyre's "ordinary good mother" provides generally are: (1) security in setting; (2) responsive recognition, not retaliation and insistence upon the child's adaptation to her; and (3) unconditionally preferential stance toward *this* child in which the needs of the child are paramount. These characteristics provide MacIntyre's baseline; further aims and characteristics of parental education will be discussed in what follows.

26. Robin West, "The Harms of Homeschooling," *Philosophy and Public Policy Quarterly* 29, no. 3/4 (2009): 9. I will have more to say about West's provocative argument below.

27. Stanley Hauerwas, *A Community of Character: Toward a Constructive Christian Social Ethic* (Notre Dame, IN: University of Notre Dame Press, 1981), 81.

28. VIII.12, 1161b15–35.

29. Lorraine Smith Pangle, *Aristotle and the Philosophy of Friendship* (Cambridge: Cambridge University Press, 2003), 87.

30. *CNE*, nn1705–1706. Cf. Michael Pakaluk's commentary in Aristotle, *Nicomachean Ethics: Books VIII and IX*, trans. Michael Pakaluk (Oxford: Clarendon Press, 1999), 128–129. Pakaluk considers a number of interpretations for Aristotle's comment here, and Aquinas's is not among them. Without negating the validity of Aquinas's general point, it does perhaps indicate that he was interested in more directly tying parental love into a broader context of friendship than was Aristotle.

31. This latter point supports Aristotle's observation that maternal affection tends to be greater than is paternal. It is worth noting, therefore, that I do not wish to make any distinction between paternal and maternal love in my analysis. Whereas it is certainly the case that a mother has a greater physical connection to a child by virtue of

his/her gestation and early dependence, the paternal physical bond is equally real, if initially more abstract. And at any rate, the argument does not *depend* on an actual genetic relationship inasmuch as a full parental love may characterize adoptive parents.

32. *NE*, 1161b20.

33. *ST*, II–II, q. 26, a. 9; *CNE*, VIII, Lec. 12, n1708.

34. For an additional example, see James G. Dwyer, "Changing the Conversation about Children's Education," in Macedo and Tamir, eds., *Moral and Political Education*, 325.

35. Aquinas notes that bonds of affection (in general) may be either friendly or selfishly desiring. In the former case, the lover stands to the beloved "as to himself" (*ad seipsum*), in the latter, "as to something belonging to himself" (*ad aliquid sui*). *ST* I–II, q. 28 a. 1 ad 2.

36. *ST*, I, q. 60, a. 2.

37. See John Finnis, *Natural Law and Natural Rights* (Oxford: Clarendon Press, 1980), 141–144.

38. A general dyadic distinction like this is helpful insofar as it maintains the difference between friendship and a simple conflation of personalities. However, it is likely that close relationships fall along a continuum running between these poles with a strong conflation of selves (for adults) being as unlikely as it would be psychologically unhealthy. Yet insofar as friendship involves an appreciation of likeness between parties, close friends are likely to share a more personal identification, such that, for example, an insult to one is taken as a personal affront by the other as well. Nevertheless, the distinction demonstrates that there is a solid conceptual basis for friendship without having to posit an either unhealthy or impossible enmeshment of persons.

39. *CNE* n1708.

40. *NE*, 1168a5–10.

41. MacIntyre, *Dependent Rational Animals*, 81–98.

42. *NE*, 1161b20.

43. *CNE*, nn1706, 1708.

44. *NE*, IX.4, 1166a1–10. Michael Pakaluk helpfully labels these "Assistance," "Joy," "Association," and "Sympathy," respectively (combining 4 and 5 in the idea of sympathy). Michael Pakaluk, *Aristotle's Nicomachean Ethics: An Introduction* (Cambridge: Cambridge University Press, 2005), 277.

45. *NE*, VIII.8, 1159a27–30.

46. *ST*, I–II, q. 26, a. 2: Aquinas describes love (*amor*) as taking pleasure in or one's affections being captured by an object (*complacentia*), resulting in a movement toward the object (*desiderium*), resulting finally in rest (*quies*) in the object of love, which is joy (*gaudium*).

47. Blustein, *Parents and Children*, 129. Blustein writes from a modern liberal perspective, intending to contribute to Rawlsian theory by strengthening the liberal account of the family as a basic social institution.

48. For example, *NE*, 1162a5–10.

49. *NE*, VIII.12, 1161b30. This simple fact of a child's immediately perceivable distinct existence highlights the fact that what is under discussion here is not a sequential process according to which a parent first sees or understands a child to be "of himself" and then perceives him or her to be "other." It is a relational dy-

namic grounded and expressed in numerous factors that parents (and children) become more and less aware of throughout the relationship. For example, the physical connection a mother feels with a child immediately upon birth is very strong, while it may not be so for a father. On the other hand, the physical and personal resemblances between a father and child may develop over time (while the mother's fades, perhaps) so that the reminders and awareness of the connection between father and child predominates. So this relational dynamic of identity and separation is characterized by ebb and flow. At the same time, the process of personal and moral formation that we have discussed, that is, moving from a significant conflation of desires to the ability to independently distinguish temporary desires from long-term rational goods, is a process of development moving from extreme dependence through stages of increasing capacity for independent reasoning.

50. Robert P. George, *The Clash of Orthodoxies: Law, Religion, and Morality in Crisis* (Wilmington, DE: ISI Books, 2001), 320.

51. See, for example, Aristotle's discussion of self-love as the basis of friendship; *NE* IX.8, 1168a27–1169b.

52. The salience of this fact was no doubt obscured for Aristotle and Aquinas by the mistakes of Aristotle's theory of human reproduction (which Aquinas accepted). In commenting on this discussion, Aquinas cites *On the Generation of Animals*, in which Aristotle hypothesizes that the male provides a child's principal part, that is, the form, which informs the material part provided by the mother (*CNE*, n1710, citing *De Generatione Animalium*, II.1, 731b13ff). Aquinas takes this to mean that the discussion of belonging (one of the three reasons Aristotle gives for the primacy of parental love) relates *only* to fathers as principle parts. Thus, in the generation of a child, a father's role and relationship of belonging is primary. However, in the very next comment (n1711) Aquinas takes Aristotle to clarify his point about belonging, affirming that *both* parents love their children "as it were the parents themselves, differing from them only in the fact of their distinct existence" (*quasi ipsi parentes, alteri ab eis existentes in hoc solum quod ab eis separantur*). The incongruence of these comments appears to follow directly from the ambiguity in the relationship between the physical and personal or affective elements of familial belonging. Clearly, Aquinas takes his "part/whole" language to correspond to the specifics of biological procreation, and thus to relate to a primacy of *paternal* love (and thus, it would seem, to claims of paternal authority). Insofar as a father contributes the *form* of the child, he is the principal source of a child in the way that a mother is not given that she simply supplies the material subsistence of the child. On the other hand, insofar as this physical connection affects one's self-conception, relational phenomena, and affective attachment, Aquinas understands *belonging* to describe both the relationship of mothers and fathers to their children. (And some of these aspects should be more strongly attributed to mothers over fathers.) Thus, it would seem that the *experiential* or *phenomenological* aspects of belonging were not entirely obscured by Aristotle's misbegotten biology. At the same time, we can see that the basic *asymmetry* entailed in Aristotelian biology would tend to affect one's conception of an *other self* in profound ways. It is not difficult to see that positing a fundamental asymmetry in the procreative relationship would tend to undermine these relationships of mutual belonging. To adopt such an outlook, that is, there is not equal unity in procreation insofar as paternal *form* unites with maternal *matter*, is to affect the relationship

of oneself to the *other*. Inasmuch as parents are related vis-à-vis a child, the priority of the father's role bestows a relational priority between parents. The nature and degree of *mutual* belonging and responsibility derogates according to a father's superior donation and greater claim on the child. Likewise in the parent-child relationship, insofar as the connection here is balanced by the child's equal connection to *another parent*, a new kind of relational priority is entailed. If a child is to a greater degree or in a more important way *of* the father, the father himself is consequently less of the child, drawn out of himself to a lesser degree. He stands to the child as a bestower of form, uniquely the principle source of the child in a way that procreative equality does not allow. Insofar as form precedes matter, a child's *belonging* to a father is greater, the independent identity of the child is lessened, and a relational subordination of the mother is entailed. Whereas it is important to note that for both Aristotle and Aquinas children constitute a powerful *common good* in spousal relationships (*NE*, VIII.12, 1162a28; *CNE*, Lec. 12, n1724), this does not undermine the point being made here. Positing asymmetry in the relationship may well allow children to function as a bond between parents, and perhaps even the greatest common good between them. Nevertheless, it would seem to profoundly affect the basic orientation of their friendship and thus the degree to which it might be characterized by mutual belonging. Obviously this account comports well with patriarchal accounts of the traditional family. However, it seems likely that the significance of this biological theory is overwhelmed by the cultural and political dimensions of patriarchy. These ideas, it would seem, would be more likely to affect an asymmetry of parent-child belonging than a particular theory of generation.

53. *NE*, IX.7, 1168a5–10; *CNE*, n1846.

54. *ST*, I–II, q. 90, a. 4 (The one charged to exercise care [*cura*] for the community is the one with authority to propound binding law); *Politics* 1254a17–b1.

55. MacIntyre, *Dependent Rational Animals*, 84. Emphasis original.

56. Gutmann, *Democratic Education*, 31.

57. MacIntyre, *Dependent Rational Animals*, 84.

58. *NE*, VIII.12, 1161b20–25.

59. Kyle D. Pruett, clinical professor of child psychiatry at the Yale School of Medicine, indicates that there is a rapidly growing body of research demonstrating the profound effects that father engagement has on the long-term development and mental health of children (personal correspondence). See, for example, Glen Palm and Jay Fagan, "Father Involvement in Early Childhood Programs: Review of the Literature," *Early Child Development & Care* 178, no. 7/8 (2008): 745–759; Anna Sarkadi et al., "Fathers' Involvement and Children's Developmental Outcomes: A Systematic Review of Longitudinal Studies," *Acta Paediatrica* 97, no. 2 (February 2008): 153–158.

60. Hauerwas, *The Moral Meaning of the Family*, 435.

61. Jean Bethke Elshtain, *Public Man, Private Woman: Women in Social and Political Thought* (Princeton, NJ: Princeton University Press, 1981), 328–329.

62. Blustein, *Parents and Children*, 129.

63. This point is one among several ways that Aristotelian-Thomistic moral psychology differs from Kantian-based approaches. For further helpful discussion of this issue, see Vincent A. Punzo, "After Kohlberg: Virtue Ethics and the Recovery of the Moral Self," *Philosophical Psychology* 9, no. 1 (March 1996): 7; Gilbert Meilaender,

The Theory and Practice of Virtue (Notre Dame, IN: University of Notre Dame Press, 1988), 84–99.

64. West, "The Harms of Homeschooling," 9. Emphasis original. I do not wish to conflate Blustein's and West's positions. Whereas Blustein credits parental love with establishing a child's sense of self, West seems to think that it militates against a real sense of self. The positions are of a piece, however, in their orientation toward Kantian autonomy. West exaggerates an element present in Blustein's account.

65. MacIntyre, *Dependent Rational Animals*, 84–86.

66. *ST*, I–II, q. 26, a. 4. Aquinas builds on Aristotle's idea that "To love is to wish good to someone" (*Rhetoric* ii, 4).

67. In the weakest sense, the goodwill evident in the conversation one strikes up with a fellow passenger on the train makes one inclined to take his directive assistance concerning an upcoming transfer as well-intentioned and (all things being equal) trustworthy. Even friendships of utility and pleasure, John Cooper convincingly demonstrates, should not be taken to be devoid of this basic fellow feeling, in which one is wished good for one's own sake, and not merely treated by a utility or pleasure friend as a means to an end. The force of Cooper's point seems to be relatively limited, however, insofar as such friends want good things for a friend "in that respect in which they are friends . . . that is, qua persons pleasant or advantageous to themselves." John Cooper, "Aristotle on Friendship," in Amélie Rorty, ed., *Essays on Aristotle's Ethics* (Berkeley: University of California Press, 1980), 314. Cf. *ST*, I–II, q. 26, a. 4 ad 3.

68. *ST* II–II, q. 26, a. 7. In discussing the proper order of charity, Aquinas distinguishes the object of love from the agent of love. The *intensity* of love's affection inheres in the agent, and the proper order of charity importantly turns on this personal reality, for Aquinas, not simply the objective lovableness or worthiness of the object loved.

69. M.F. Burnyeat, "Aristotle on Learning to Be Good," in Rorty, ed., *Essays on Aristotle's Ethics*, 73.

70. *NE* I.4, 1095b.

71. Jacques Maritain, *Natural Law: Reflections on Theory & Practice*, 1st ed. (South Bend, IN: St. Augustine's Press, 2001), 15. See also Yves R. Simon, *The Tradition of Natural Law: A Philosopher's Reflections*, ed. Vukan Kuic (New York: Fordham University Press, 1999), 125–136; and J. Budziszewski, *The Line through the Heart: Natural Law as Fact, Theory, and Sign of Contradiction* (Wilmington, DE: ISI Books, 2009), 61–77.

72. "Testing the Boundaries of Paternal Authority," in Macedo and Tamir, eds., *Moral and Political Education*, 275–313.

73. Galston, *Liberal Purposes*, 251–256.

74. "A Philosophy of Childhood," Monograph (The Poynter Center for the Study of Ethics and American Institutions, Indiana University, January 2006), http:// poynter.indiana.edu/publications/m-matthews.pdf. See also Gareth B. Matthews, *The Philosophy of Childhood* (Cambridge, MA: Harvard University Press, 1994), 54–67; and Gilbert Meilaender, *Neither Beast Nor God: The Dignity of the Human Person* (New York: Encounter Books, 2009), 37–51.

75. *NE* VIII.12, 1161b18.

Chapter 3. Formal Characteristics of Political Association

1. *Politics*, I.1, 1252a1–5.

2. *NE*, I.2, 1094a25–1094b10.

3. *Politics*, I.1, 1252a7–20.

4. Gregory Froelich, "The Equivocal Status of *Bonum Commune*," *New Scholasticism* 63 (1989): 38–57; Mark Murphy, *Natural Law and Practical Rationality* (Cambridge: Cambridge University Press, 2001), 126–131. Calling the third category "commonness by distribution" is Murphy's innovation, which is helpful since it maintains a syntactical parallelism that Froelich's term, "common goods," does not. Murphy's more important conceptual elaboration will be discussed shortly.

5. For example, *ST*, I–II, a. 90, a. 2 ad 2.

6. *NE*, VIII.7, 1159a5–12.

7. Thomas Hobbes, *Leviathan*, chapters 13–14, 17. Or, as Leo Strauss makes this general point: "Justice is the common good *par excellence*; if there are to be things which are by nature just, there must be things which are by nature common." Leo Strauss, *The City and Man* (Chicago: University of Chicago Press, 1964), 16.

8. *Politics* I.1, 1252b13.

9. Murphy, *Natural Law and Practical Rationality*, 126–131.

10. *NE*, VIII.3, 1156a10–30.

11. Ibid., 1156a15–20.

12. John Finnis, *Natural Law and Natural Rights* (Oxford: Clarendon Press, 1980), 140.

13. See John M. Cooper's very helpful discussion of this dynamic in utility and pleasure friendships in "Aristotle on Friendship," in Amélie Rorty, ed., *Essays on Aristotle's Ethics* (Berkeley: University of California Press, 1980), 301–340, esp. 308–315. Cooper argues that all forms of friendship are, for Aristotle, directed in an important sense to the good of the other for his own sake. In no case of friendship does a crass instrumentalization of the other person obtain, but only in the case of virtue friendship is one's "intention in maintaining the friendship . . . fixed on the goodness of the other person, not on his pleasantness or profitability" (315). Aquinas, too, makes the point thus: "When friendship is based on usefulness or pleasure, a man does indeed wish his friend some good: and in this respect the character of friendship is preserved. But since he refers this good further to his own pleasure or use, the result is that friendship of the useful or pleasant, in so far as it is connected with love of concupiscence, loses the character to true friendship." *ST*, I–II, q. 26, a. 4 ad 3.

14. Aristotle, of course, provides the classic rejection of the common good as a mere alliance (*Politics*, III.9). We should note that truly shared descriptions of the common good are possible even in the frequent event that common resources are scarce. A Lockean optimism that "enough, and as good" will be generally available is not required in order for members to intend and act for a shared good (John Locke, *Second Treatise on Civil Government*, chapter 5, section 27). Murphy is right in arguing that the "common good can serve as a *regulative ideal*, perhaps unrealizable in practice, but the basis on which realizable objectives and binding common norms can be justified." Mark C. Murphy, *Natural Law in Jurisprudence and Politics* (Cambridge: Cambridge University Press, 2006), 64.

15. Murphy, *Jurisprudence and Politics*, 128.

16. Finnis, *Natural Law and Natural Rights*, 155.

17. *NE* VIII.3, 5; IX.4.

18. Finnis, *Natural Law and Natural Rights*, 143.

19. *NE* VIII.1, 5; IX.4.

20. Ibid., VIII.3.

21. *Politics*, II.4.

22. As will become clear, this is not necessarily to say that the "unity of the group" is the most important or controlling element of the common good, only that the fullest expression of commonness requires that the group itself instantiate part of the good sought by its members.

23. *Politics* I.2, 1253a7–17; III.9, 1280b30; see also *CNE*, Book I, Lec. 1, n4. It is statements like the one included here—"but these other things are for the sake of the end"—that often make discerning Aristotle's meaning difficult. Does he take subpolitical associations to be for the sake of the political end? I will address this problem in what follows.

24. *CNE*, Lec. 2, n30.

25. *Politics* I.2, See, for example, David Keyt, "Three Fundamental Theorems in Aristotle's 'Politics,'" *Phronesis* 32, no. 1 (1987): 54–79, esp. 57–59, 63–65. Wayne Ambler suggests that "the city is seen at first . . . as a natural creature with a life of its own." See W. H. Ambler, "Aristotle's Understanding of the Naturalness of the City," *Review of Politics* 47, no. 2 (1985): 163–185, at 169. Richard Kraut provides a helpful correction to Keyt and Ambler's respective readings, but he also reads Aristotle as holding that the city has a priority of *substance* to subpolitical associations, so that it makes sense to say that these smaller associations *are* a city in inchoate form (as boy is to man). See Richard Kraut, *Aristotle* (Oxford: Oxford University Press, 2002), 244, 259–261.

26. "We may now proceed to add that the city is prior in the order of nature to the family and the individual. The reason for this is that the whole is necessarily prior to the part. If the whole body is destroyed, there will not be a foot or a hand, except in that ambiguous sense in which one uses the same word to indicate a different thing, as when one speaks of a 'hand' made of stone; for a hand, when destroyed [by the destruction of the whole body], will be no better than a stone 'hand.'" *Politics* I.2, 1253a18–24.

27. *NE* I.2, 1094b5.

28. See Aquinas's famous differentiation of the kinds of unity found in unitary beings and associations in *CNE*, Book I, Lec. 1, nn4–6.

29. On these issues, see respectively, for example, Strauss, *The City and Man*, 26–28; and John Finnis, *Aquinas: Moral, Political, and Legal Theory* (Oxford: Oxford University Press, 1998), 170–180, 239–245, citing among other texts, Aquinas, *ST*, I, q. 113, a. 2 ad 3; I–II, q. 91, a. 4; q. 100, a. 9; II–II, q. 104, a. 5.

30. For a very helpful discussion of constitutive parts and final ends, see J. L. Ackrill, "Aristotle on Eudaimonia," in Rorty, *Essays*, 15–34, esp. 18–20.

31. *NE* VIII.1, 1155a23.

32. *Politics: Books I and II*, 68.

33. *NE*, 1.2 1094b6.

34. Aquinas's reading of Aristotle follows this line. See *CNE*, Book I, Lec. 2, nn24–31.

35. See Robert C. Bartlett, "Aristotle's Introduction to the Problem of Happiness: On Book One of the 'Nicomachean Ethics,'" *American Journal of Political Science* 52, no. 3 (2008): 677–687, especially 678. "The political community regards and wishes to have regarded as settled not only the specific character of the good life for its citizens—be it the life of commerce, piety, or martial courage, for example—but also the superiority of the good of the community to that of any private good." For a somewhat different interpretation of this argument than the two offered here, see Michael Pakaluk, *Aristotle's Nicomachean Ethics: An Introduction* (Cambridge: Cambridge University Press, 2005), 48–53.

36. For both Aristotle and Aquinas, quantitative extension of the human good grounds the primacy of politics in this argument. The best reading is not, I think, to contrast the good of one man with the good of the state per se, but to juxtapose the good of one person with the good of many people.

37. It is worth noting that the position I am attributing to Aristotle is consistent with his thinking—as Barlett and others want to maintain—that there is ultimately no real common good. The principle I am advancing does not say that the claims of political community are justified. It simply specifies what conditions must be met for them *to be* justified. So if it is the case, for example, that the political community cannot facilitate and sustain the philosophic life (granting that Aristotle takes it to be essential to human flourishing), its claims to primacy are vitiated.

38. Murphy, *Jurisprudence and Politics*, 61–90. As I have given my own assessment of Finnis's instrumental account in Chapter 1, I will not discuss Murphy's engagement with Finnis here but will instead focus on his engagement with the distinctive view of the common good.

39. Ibid., 63–65.

40. Ibid., 73, citing *ST*, I–II 96.3: "Nevertheless human law does not prescribe concerning all the acts of every virtue: but only in regard to those that are ordainable to the common good—either immediately, as when certain things are done directly for the common good—or mediately, as when a lawgiver prescribes certain things pertaining to good order, whereby the citizens are directed in the upholding of the common good of justice and peace."

41. Murphy, *Jurisprudence and Politics*, 75.

42. Charles Taylor, "Irreducible Social Goods," in *Philosophical Arguments* (Cambridge, MA: Harvard University Press, 1995), 127–145. Defining the common good as the aggregated good of each member of the community saves Murphy from a Hobbesian ethical egoism, but it is this recognition of irreducible social goods that distinguishes his position from methodological individualism, that is, "The events and states which are the subject of study in society are ultimately made up of the events and states of component individuals" (Taylor, 129). Classical philosophy described this distinction as a formal difference between wholes and their parts. See *ST* II–II, q. 58, a. 7 ad 2, citing *Politics* I.1. For further discussion see, M. S. Kempshall, *The Common Good in Late Medieval Political Thought* (Oxford: Clarendon Press, 1999), 118.

43. Murphy, *Jurisprudence and Politics*, 77.

44. Murphy repeatedly raises the issue of content in addition to that of allegiance in ibid., 76–77.

45. By "parasitic" Murphy means that one conception of the common good ultimately derives what force it has by appealing to another. The distinctive common

good is parasitic on the aggregative, Murphy contends, because a fully reasonable account of allegiance to a particular community requires some explanation of contribution to the (individual) human good. Ibid., 63, 69, 76–80.

46. Charles Taylor, for example, gives a helpful account of the intellectual and cultural possibilities enabled by the "background of available meaning" developed within communities in "Irreducible Social Goods," 131–140. For another very helpful description of social entities and their characteristics, particularly as the idea developed in the jurisprudential doctrines of legal personhood, see Russell Hittinger, "The Coherence of the Four Basic Principles of Catholic Social Doctrine: An Interpretation," in Pontificia Accademia delle Scienze Sociali, *Pursuing the Common Good: How Solidarity and Subsidiarity Can Work Together: The Proceedings of the 14th Plenary Session, 2–6 May 2008, Casina Pio IV* (Vatican City: Pontifical Academy of Social Sciences, 2008), 75–123.

47. Murphy, *Jurisprudence and Politics*, 77–79.

48. Ibid.

49. *NE* VIII.3, 5.

50. Finnis, *Natural Law and Natural Rights*, 129.

51. This raises the further issues of how one's various social roles are to factor into an overall assessment and ordering of the human good and how the goods are to be ordered and balanced in particular circumstances. Adjudicating these questions goes beyond the scope of the present inquiry. For now it is enough to conclude that in the process of practically ordering a life according to a range of available goods and responsibilities, the distinctive goods of basic associations should be included in fundamental deliberation.

52. Alasdair MacIntyre, "Politics, Philosophy, and the Common Good," in Kelvin Knight, ed., *The MacIntyre Reader* (South Bend, IN: University of Notre Dame Press, 1998), 241. The whole thought is this: "Such a form of community is by its nature political, that is to say, it is constituted by a type of practice through which other types of practice are ordered, so that individuals may direct themselves towards what is best for them and for their community." My main objection is that it does not seem to me that political community is unique in ordering types of social practice. While it may be the topmost association that so orders, other associations, such as the family, perform a similar function. Thomas Hibbs has criticized MacIntyre for essentially the same reason, that is, an insufficient distinction between politics and other ordering associations, but his criticism comes from the opposite direction. He contends that MacIntyre's account of politics does not, in fact, rise to the level of political association due to its lack of a regime theory that is necessary to ground political sovereignty. I will have more to say about this in Chapter 5. See Thomas Hibbs, "MacIntyre, Aquinas, and Politics," *Review of Politics* 66, no. 3 (2004): 357–383.

53. Hittinger, "The Coherence of the Four Basic Principles of Catholic Social Doctrine: An Interpretation," 78–94.

54. Finnis, *Aquinas*, 231.

55. Ibid.

56. Jacques Maritain, *Man and the State* (Chicago: University of Chicago Press, 1951).

Chapter 4. Civic Friendship: Paradox and Possibility

1. Alasdair MacIntyre, "Politics, Philosophy, and the Common Good," in Kelvin Knight, ed., *The MacIntyre Reader* (Cambridge: Polity Press, 1998), 235–252, 241.

2. "What the Enlightenment made us for the most part blind to and what we now need to recover is . . . a conception of rational enquiry as embodied in a tradition, a conception according to which the standards of rational justification themselves emerge from and are part of a history in which they are vindicated by the way in which they transcend the limitations of and provide remedies for the defects of their predecessors with the history of that same tradition." Alasdair C. MacIntyre, *Whose Justice? Which Rationality?* (Notre Dame, IN: University of Notre Dame Press, 1989), 7.

3. *NE* IX.10, 1171a1. "Just as cities are friends to one another, so in the like way are citizens. 'The Athenians no longer know the Megarians'; nor do citizens one another, when they are no longer useful to one another." *Eudemian Ethics*, trans. J. Solomon, in Jonathan Barnes, ed., *The Complete Works of Aristotle: The Revised Oxford Translation*, vol. 2 (Princeton, NJ: Princeton University Press, 1984), 1242b22.

4. *CNE*, nn1923–1924.

5. Gilbert Meilaender, *Friendship: A Study in Theological Ethics: Philosophy*, 1st ed. (Notre Dame, IN: University of Notre Dame Press, 1985), 74–75.

6. *NE* VIII.1, 1155a25. A lawmaker's attention to friendship must concern giving room for its growth in nonpolitical contexts, of course. Aristotle's rebuff of Socratic communism demonstrates this point. But he is also clearly concerned here with friendship at the level of the political community.

7. *Politics* III.9, 1280b29–1281a2.

8. Although I take John Cooper's point that no form of friendship for Aristotle treats the other simply as a *means* to one's own end, I agree with Aquinas that insofar as friendships of utility and pleasure refer the other's good to one's own use or enjoyment, they lose the essential nature of true friendship. See Cooper's argument in "Aristotle on Friendship," in Amélie Rorty, ed., *Essays on Aristotle's Ethics* (Berkeley: University of California Press, 1980),301–340, esp. 308–315. Aquinas's point is made at *ST*, I–II, q. 26, a. 4 ad 3.

9. *NE* VIII.9. See Michael Pakaluk's translation of Aristotle, *Nicomachean Ethics: Books VIII and IX* (Oxford: Clarendon Press, 1999), 111–114, for a helpful explanation of the structure of Aristotle's thinking here.

10. *NE* VIII.2, 1155b31, 56a3–5.

11. Cf. *NE* IX.5, 1166b30–67a20.

12. *Eudemian Ethics*, 1242a5–8.

13. *NE* IX.6, 1167a25–30.

14. Pakaluk, *Nicomachean Ethics: Books VIII and IX*, 180–181.

15. *Politics* I.1, 1252b27–1253a18.

16. Lorraine Pangle, "Civic Friendship and Reciprocity in Aristotle's Political Thought," 6 (forthcoming). See also John Cooper, "Aristotle on Friendship," in Rorty, *Essays on Aristotle's Ethics*, on the cultivation of friendliness in utility and pleasure friendships.

17. Cf. Alexis de Tocqueville's discussion of "self-interest well understood," *De-*

mocracy in America, trans. Harvey C. Mansfield and Delba Winthrop (Chicago: University of Chicago Press, 2000), 500–506.

18. *NE* IX.10.

19. "Political Animals and Civic Friendship," in Symposium Aristotelicum, *Aristoteles "Politik": Akten Des XI, Symposium Aristotelicum, Friedrichshafen/Bodensee, 25.8.–3.9.1987*, ed. Günther Patzig (Göttingen: Vandenhoeck & Ruprecht, 1990), 220–241.

20. Ibid., 230.

21. Ibid., 232. Julia Annas objects to Cooper's account primarily by noting that diffused political relationships simply cannot plausibly sustain the personal regard and intimacy that Aristotle attributes to *philia*. See "Comments on J. Cooper," in Symposium Aristotelicum, *Aristoteles "Politik,"* 242–248, 243. Given that Aristotle clearly recognizes the attenuation of political relationships, the question is whether he still thinks that some version of *philia* is still attributable to civic relations. As Lorraine Pangle points out, Annas fails to observe that Aristotle both equates political friendship with concord (at 1155a22–25 and 1167b2–3) and explicitly attributes concord to cities (at 1167a26–28). "Civic Friendship and Reciprocity," n8. Pangle, however, is critical of the extent to which Cooper wants to take civic friendship, noting that he fails to acknowledge "the essentially competitive nature of the goods on which political friendship turns" Ibid., n16.

22. *Politics* III.9, 1280b35–40.

23. Concern for a fellow citizen's virtue for his or her own sake should not be equated with the love of the other self that characterizes the truest friendship between persons. It is, however, as Aristotle seems keen to show, much more than utilitarian interest. Whereas the concern is not rooted in close personal identity, it springs from a broader political identity that does seem substantial enough to ground real concern for fellow citizens.

24. "Comments on T. Irwin," Symposium Aristotelicum, *Aristoteles "Politik,"* 100. Striker's observations were made in response to Terence Irwin's view of Aristotelian civic friendship, but they are applicable here, even though I have focused on Cooper's account rather than Irwin's.

25. Note, for example, that Aquinas's theoretical defense of kingship does not turn on the superior knowledge, virtue, and merit of the king as it does for Aristotle. Aquinas, rather, relies upon an argument derived from Avicenna that points to the need for a unified executive in directing a group toward a common end.

26. See John Finnis, *Aquinas: Moral, Political, and Legal Theory* (Oxford: Oxford University Press, 1998), 219–254.

27. See Mary M. Keys, *Aquinas, Aristotle, and the Promise of the Common Good* (Cambridge: Cambridge University Press, 2008), 64.

28. Michael Pakaluk, "Is the Common Good of Political Society Limited and Instrumental?," *Review of Metaphysics* 55, no. 1 (2001): 57–94.

29. I do not take this observation to support Mary Keys's claim that Aquinas does not have an idea of the best regime analogous to Aristotle's. Keys argues that nowhere in Aquinas's writings do we find an account parallel to Books VII–VIII of the *Politics*. This seems to me a dubious assertion given that Book II of *De Regno* seems to be headed toward just such an account of the best regime. It appears to be

only an accident of history that we do not have Aquinas's thoughts on the matter. Keys, *Promise of the Common Good,* 64.

30. Gregory Froelich, "The Equivocal Status of *Bonum Commune,*" 39–40.

31. *NE* 1.2 1094b6.

32. *CNE,* I, Lec. 2, nn24–31.

33. See especially Finnis, *Aquinas,* 219–254.

34. Note that the differences between Aristotle and Aquinas on the nature of the family have direct implications for their differing views on political life. This corroborates Aristotle's method of studying the city by first considering its origin and constituent parts (*Politics,* Book I). Whatever your understanding of the political common good, it will either consciously or implicitly rely on ideas about the human person, friendships, the family, religious groups, and so forth.

35. Charles Taylor, *Sources of the Self: The Making of the Modern Identity* (Cambridge, MA: Harvard University Press, 1992), 211–233.

36. M. S. Kempshall, *The Common Good in Late Medieval Political Thought* (Oxford: Clarendon Press, 1999), 85–88.

37. *ST* II–II, q. 58, a. 1.

38. See, for example, *ST* I–II, a. 96, a. 3.

39. *ST* II–II, a. 58, a. 5.

40. *ST* II–II, q. 58. a. 6.

41. *ST* II–II, q. 58, a. 5 ad 2. Aquinas is explaining how it is that justice functions as a general virtue—directing virtues to a common good. Thus, we should not take this response to a universal good to denote "goodness as such" as the object of human action, abstracted from its character as a good for human beings. The point is that the intellect is able to distinguish between the particularity of "this is good for me" and the universality of "this is a human good." Justice requires response to the latter insofar as it substantiates the claims of each person in the community.

42. For a helpful discussion of these issues see Finnis, *Aquinas,* 111–131, and Keys, *Promise of the Common Good,* 118–124.

43. Aquinas, *CNE,* n30.

44. Jacques Maritain, *The Person and the Common Good* (Notre Dame, IN: University of Notre Dame Press, 1973), 47; Yves R. Simon, *The Tradition of Natural Law: A Philosopher's Reflections,* edited by Vukan Kuic (New York: Fordham University Press, 1999), 90. Although I agree with Maritain that there is a dimension of generosity of spirit expressed in the commitment to political justice, as will become clear, I do not follow him in extending this to an endorsement of universal world government. See Jacques Maritain, *Man and the State* (Chicago: University of Chicago Press, 1951), 188–216.

45. Keys, *Promise of the Common Good,* 81.

46. For a helpful restatement of this view, see Martha Nussbaum, "Patriotism and Cosmopolitanism," in Martha Nussbaum and Joshua Cohen, *For Love of Country?* (Boston, MA: Beacon Press, 2002).

47. See, for example, Thomas Aquinas, *ST* I–II, q. 91, a. 3 ad 2.

48. For a very helpful expansion of this theme in Catholic natural law theory, see W. A Barbieri and A. William Jr., "Beyond the Nations: The Expansion of the Common Good in Catholic Social Thought," *Review of Politics* 63, no. 4 (2001): 723–754.

49. For a succinct articulation of this problem, see Mark C. Murphy, *Natural*

Law in Jurisprudence and Politics (Cambridge: Cambridge University Press, 2006), 168–176.

50. *ST*, II–II, q. 26, a. 6.

51. *ST*, II–II, q. 31, a. 3.

52. *ST*, I–II, q. 95, a. 4.

53. Simon, *The Tradition of Natural Law*, 95–96. Simon's analysis of "immanent social actions" could be characterized as a subset of what Charles Taylor refers to as "irreducible social goods." Taylor's category is much broader insofar as it includes not only the basic good of community (i.e., intrinsically desirable common activity) but also the very creation of intellectual and social meaning *through* the practices of a community. See Charles Taylor, "Irreducible Social Goods," in *Philosophical Arguments* (Cambridge, MA: Harvard University Press, 1995), 127–145.

54. *Politics* II.2, 1261a10–b15.

55. *NE* VIII.1, 1155a20–30.

56. Gilbert Meilaender, *Friendship: A Study in Theological Ethics Philosophy* (Notre Dame, IN: University of Notre Dame Press, 1985), 74. Emphasis original.

57. Ibid., 73–74.

58. Recall the distinction Aquinas draws between benevolence, affection, and beneficence, mentioned earlier. Although a rational standard informs an equality of *benevolence* and may require *beneficence* contrary to our subjective wishes, it is unreasonable to think that our affections will be anything other than unequal. *ST* II–II, q. 26, a. 6. See also *ST* II–II, a. 26, a. 7 treating whether we ought to love those who are better more than those who are more closely united to us.

59. *ST* I–II, q. 19, a. 10.

60. I do not mean to imply by my argument here that direct, material intention toward the common good can be dispensed with entirely. I am critical, in fact, of accounts such as Simon's that in my view go too far in deemphasizing the need for direct and conscious orientation to act for the common good. See Yves R. Simon, *Philosophy of Democratic Government* (Chicago: University of Chicago Press, 1951), 36–71.

61. S. A. Schwarzenbach, "On Civic Friendship," *Ethics* 107, no. 1 (1996): 97–128. See Schwarzenbach's response to criticism that a universalized "ethic of care" ill defines civic friendship at 120–121.

62. This worry is, of course, along the same lines as the concern with attenuation. However, the two are importantly different. Attenuation concerns the compatibility of friendship with the *any sort* of association beyond the intimate associations of private life. Now we address whether it makes sense to speak of civic friendship beyond small, highly participatory polities.

63. Alexis de Tocqueville, *Democracy in America* (Chicago: University of Chicago Press, 2000), 225–227.

64. *CNE*, I, Lec. 1, nn5–6.

65. John Finnis, *Natural Law and Natural Rights* (Oxford: Clarendon Press, 1980), 135.

Chapter 5. Political Culture as an Intrinsic Good

1. *Politics*, I.2, 1252b27–1253a25; III.4, 1277b7–1277b16.

2. For accounts of political culture focused on its intellectual dimensions, see

Richard J. Ellis, *American Political Cultures* (Oxford: Oxford University Press, 1993); James Ceaser, "Alexis de Tocqueville on Political Science, Political Culture, and the Role of the Intellectual," *American Political Science Review* 79, no. 3 (1985): 656–672. David Hackett Fischer, *Liberty and Freedom: A Visual History of America's Founding Ideas* (Oxford: Oxford University Press, 2005), gives a stunning presentation of the expression of political ideas in cultural artifacts. Samuel Huntington unpacks the dimensions of political culture under the rubric of American identity in *Who Are We?: The Challenges to America's National Identity* (New York: Simon and Schuster, 2004); James Ceasar's review of that work demonstrates the protean character of the concepts involved; Ceasar, "O, My America," *Weekly Standard*, Washington, May 3, 2004; see also Bradley C. S. Watson, "Creed & Culture in the American Founding," *Intercollegiate Review* 41, no. 2 (Fall 2006): 32–39.

3. Alasdair MacIntyre, *Whose Justice? Which Rationality?* (Notre Dame, IN: University of Notre Dame Press, 1989), 353.

4. For a review of the utilitarian view, see Peter J. Stanlis, *Edmund Burke and the Natural Law* (Lafayette, LA: Huntington House, 1986), 29–34; Gertrude Himmelfarb's description of her own evolution on Burke is a helpful microcosm of this larger scholarly dispute. See Gertrude Himmelfarb, "Reflections on Burke's 'Reflections,'" *New Criterion* 27, no. 6 (February 2009): 4–10.

5. See also Yuval Levin, *The Great Debate: Edmund Burke, Thomas Paine, and the Birth of Right and Left* (New York: Basic Books, 2014), 71–78.

6. There is, of course, difference of opinion in how closely to associate Burke with the natural law tradition. Some are inclined to read Burke's political thought as "a conservative version of the natural law" (Wilkins, 252). See Stanlis, *Edmund Burke and the Natural Law*; Burleigh Taylor Wilkins, *The Problem of Burke's Political Philosophy* (Oxford: Clarendon Press, 1967); Joseph Pappin, *The Metaphysics of Edmund Burke* (New York: Fordham University Press, 1993); and Russell Kirk, *Edmund Burke: A Genius Reconsidered* (New York: Arlington House, 1967). Others do not go so far, but they nevertheless recognize Burke's reliance on natural law concepts. For example, Jesse Norman, *Edmund Burke: The First Conservative* (New York: Basic Books, 2013); and Richard Bourke, *Empire and Revolution: The Political Life of Edmund Burke* (Princeton, NJ: Princeton University Press, 2015).

7. Norman, *Edmund Burke*, 3–4.

8. Edmund Burke, *Reflections on the Revolution in France*, ed. L. G. Mitchell (New York: Oxford University Press, 2009).

9. Ibid., 33.

10. Ibid., 35.

11. Ibid., 33.

12. H. C. Black, *Black's Law Dictionary*, 6th ed. (St. Paul, MN: West Publishing, 1994), defines *entailment* in part as "An interference with and curtailment of the ordinary rules pertaining to the devolution by inheritance."

13. Burke, *Reflections*, 34–35.

14. Ibid., 64–65.

15. I do not take Burke's argument here to be inconsistent with my discussion of the relationship between the personal good and associations constitutive of human flourishing on 5–6.

16. Burke, *Reflections*, 58.

17. Ibid.

18. Ibid., 62.

19. Jesse Norman helpfully points out that we must not overstate Burke's resistance to abstract thought, however. Burke does, in fact, "effectively mak[e] a series of rather sophisticated and challenging philosophical points: that absolute consistency, however desirable in mathematics and logic, is neither available nor desirable in the conduct of human affairs; that universal principles are never sufficient in themselves to guide practical deliberation; and that it is a deep error to seek to apply concepts from the exact sciences willy-nilly to the messy business of life." Norman, *Edmund Burke*, 195.

20. Stanlis, *Edmund Burke and the Natural Law*, 40–46, 58–66. See also Bourke, *Empire and Revolution*, 627–675, esp. 644–646.

21. Compare Aquinas's discussion of how specific applications are derived from the general principles of the natural law. In some cases human law must follow the natural law by deduction—logical conclusions that necessarily follow from premises, for example, the injunction against murder logically follows from the moral imperative not to harm others. In other (and most) cases, however, the human law reflects the natural law by way of *determinatio*—specifications of general principles that may have any number of appropriate dispositions. For example, Aquinas argues, the general principle that an evildoer must be punished does not specify *what* that punishment must be. Here the natural law has a good deal of openness that allows for variation according to culture and custom. *ST*, I–II, 95.2. A narrow misidentification of the natural law only with the deductive application of general principles leads interpreters such as Yuval Levin to dismiss any connection between Burke and the natural law, even while acknowledging that Burke relies on a "real standard beyond mere convention" (Levin, *The Great Debate*, 77). The problem is, however, that once you are committed to the irrelevance of the natural law, there is no way to define that "real standard" in a way that does not itself ultimately reduce to another form of mere cultural convention.

22. Burke, *Reflections*, 58.

23. Ibid., 96.

24. Ibid., 61.

25. Ibid., 152–153. See Aquinas's views on the potential legal authority of custom. *ST*, I–II, 97.2–3. Commenting on Aquinas, J. Budziszewski says the following: "The argument is that since the people can express their reasonable will not only by words, but even more clearly by repeated deeds, it follows that if they have the authority to make law at all, then they have the authority to make law by custom." J. Budziszewski, *Companion to the Commentary* [on Aquinas's Treatise on Law], http://undergroundthomist.org/sites/default/files/related-documents/Companion-to-the-Commentary-FINAL.pdf, 441.

26. Burke, *Reflections*, 33.

27. Ibid., 33.

28. Ibid., 127.

29. Ibid., 157.

30. Ibid., 64.

31. Ibid., 34.

32. See, for example, Plato, *Republic*, 435b–442.

33. Norman, *Edmund Burke*, 29.
34. Burke, *Reflections*, 34.
35. Ibid., 33.
36. Ibid., 77.
37. Ibid.
38. Ibid.
39. David Bromwich, "Moral Imagination," *Raritan* 27, no. 4 (Spring 2008): 6.
40. Burke, *Reflections*, 79.
41. "The Moral Imagination," 206–218, 207, in Russell Kirk, *The Essential Russell Kirk: Selected Essays*, ed. George A. Panichas (Wilmington, DE: Intercollegiate Studies Institute, 2006). My agreement with Kirk on this point is at variance with Richard Bourke's more limited notion of the moral imagination. Bourke seems to identify the concept as more narrowly focused on "the beauty and sublimity of manners" (Bourke, *Empire and Revolution*, 705; see also 159). I certainly agree that the moral imagination includes manners. Right moral sentiment underwrites a refined sensibility that imaginatively creates customs and manners appropriate to the underlying sentiment. But the underlying sentiment may be suitably expressed in any number of ways. One may express awe toward a ruler, for example, by bowing to a monarch or kowtowing to an emperor. Burke expects a wide divergence among cultures, reflecting the breadth of human imagination. At the same time, I think it is clear that he takes the underlying moral sentiments—the awe due a king, respect for the dignity of humanity—to be objective and rooted in nature. Thus, I think the moral imagination is a weightier idea in Burke's thought than Bourke allows. My view is also at odds with that of David Bromwich, who takes the moral imagination to be entirely a function of convention, albeit a helpful one. He writes, "We need the coverings that enlightenment and reason want to strip away" (Bromwich, "Moral Imagination," 7, emphasis original). However, if, as Burke says, the understanding ratifies the ideas of the moral imagination, Bromwich would have more aptly said that we need the coverings "Enlightenment reason" wants to strip away.
42. Burke, *Reflections*, 77.
43. Ibid., 86–87.
44. This specific justification is my own, but it makes good Burkean sense in light of the majesty he accords the state as a partnership "in all perfection" (Burke, *Reflections*, 96), and his indication, right after the mention of regicide, that English constitutionalism embodies institutions in persons (ibid., 77).
45. Edmund Burke, *A Philosophical Enquiry into the Sublime and Beautiful* (New York: Routledge, 2008), 17.
46. Ibid., 17–18.
47. Although I think the connection between Burke's aesthetics and his political theory is important, I generally agree with Richard Bourke's insistence that the two not be conflated. It was not the intention of the *Enquiry*, Bourke notes, to "resolve our duties into the empire of taste" (Bourke, *Empire and Revolution*, 159). The content of our duties is not determined by aesthetical criticism. My analysis of the connection between Burke's aesthetics and political theory is also in general agreement with Neal Wood, although I do have significant disagreement with him about the purpose, in Burke's view, of the dignity and majesty of the state. Wood takes these features to support the coercive power of the state. Neal Wood, "The Aesthetic Di-

mension of Burke's Political Thought," *Journal of British Studies* 4, no. 1 (1964): 62–63. Coercion is, of course, necessary to control the impulses of the bad man, but for Burke, dignity and majesty serve the higher function of elevating and ennobling the good citizen. See, for example, Burke, *Reflections*, 98–99.

48. Bourke, *Empire and Revolution*, 120.

49. Burke, *Enquiry*, 57.

50. Bourke, *Empire and Revolution*, 145.

51. Burke, *Enquiry*, 36, 91.

52. Ibid., 110.

53. Ibid., 17–18.

54. Burke, *Reflections*, 79.

55. Bourke, *Empire and Revolution*, 704.

56. Burke, *Reflections*, 76. Emphasis mine.

57. Ibid., 77.

58. This does not entail, however, a general leveling. Burke takes fierce aim at the unmitigated and doctrinaire egalitarianism of the revolutionaries. See, for example, Burke, *Reflections*, 49–51.

59. Burke, *Enquiry*, 18.

60. Ibid., 40.

61. Burke, *Reflections*, 87.

62. Ibid., 78.

63. Ibid., 34, 77.

64. Sir Roger Scruton criticizes Burke for describing society as a "partnership" because, he argues, the term denotes choice. Yet, we do not choose our political communities, at least not in the first instance. "In Defence of the Nation," in Roger Scruton, *The Philosopher on Dover Beach: Essays* (New York: St. Martin's Press, 1990), 319. This is a valid point as far as it goes. Burke, however, consistently underscores that we must indeed choose to embrace our political patrimony as an active member of a generational community. Although we naturally find ourselves with duties we did not choose—to family, country, and so forth—we do make a choice to discharge those duties as an active participant in a multigenerational enterprise—"acting as if in the presence of canonized forefathers." Thus, Burke's use of the term *partnership* does helpfully convey an important, and I think correct, dimension of his view.

65. Burke, *Reflections*, 34.

66. Fischer, *Liberty and Freedom*, 14.

67. Burke, *Reflections*, 92. Note, however, that this fame is subordinate to one's concern with eternal fame before God.

68. Burke, *Enquiry*, 110; Burke, *Reflections*, 96.

69. *Second nature* refers to things that become thoroughly engrained in us by habit or custom. In the *Enquiry* Burke notes that "use" and "custom" are "very justly . . . called . . . second nature" (103). The meaning and significance of second nature is well-developed in the Thomistic tradition, often under the name *connaturality*. See J. Budziszewski's very helpful discussion in *The Line through the Heart*, 61–78.

70. Burke, *Reflections*, 198, 36.

71. Ibid., 34.

72. Jacques Maritain called this kind of resonance "the inner melody that the vibrating strings of abiding tendencies make present in the subject," *Man and the State*

(Chicago: University of Chicago Press, 1951), 92. Joseph Pappin uses Maritian's work to very good effect in demonstrating the compatibility of Burke's philosophy and Thomistic natural law in "Edmund Burke and the Thomistic Foundations of Natural Law," in Ian Crowe, ed., *An Imaginative Whig: Reassessing the Life and Thought of Edmund Burke* (Columbia: University of Missouri, 2005), 203–227.

73. Burke, *Reflections*, 48.

74. "To be attached to the subdivision, to love the little platoon we belong to in society, is the first principle (the germ as it were) of public affections. It is the first link in the series by which we proceed towards a love to our country and to mankind." Ibid., 47.

75. Ibid., 198. Emphasis mine.

76. Burke is particularly attuned to the intrinsic good of religious associations— and their necessity to the health of the state. See especially Burke, *Reflections*, 90–93, 157, 168, 276.

77. Alasdair C. MacIntyre, *Dependent Rational Animals: Why Human Beings Need the Virtues* (Chicago: Open Court, 2001), 90.

78. Jonathan Mummolo, "Father Who Saved Son Is Remembered for Generosity," *Washington Post*, September 16, 2008, sec. B.

79. Burke, *Reflections*, 32, 34, 95.

80. Fischer, *Liberty and Freedom*, 14.

81. Burke, *Reflections*, 93.

82. Ibid., 276. On this point, I take Yuval Levin's reduction of Burke's view of religion to "a necessary prop for peace" to be badly mistaken. Levin, *The Great Debate*, 75.

83. Burke, *Reflections*, 96–97.

84. See Thomas Aquinas, *De Regno*, Book I, chaps. 4–7. J. Budziszewski comments, "If the tyranny is of the everyday sort . . . St. Thomas thinks it is better to tolerate it than resist it, because still worse evils threaten no matter how the resistance turns out. . . . What if the tyranny is of the extreme sort? For that case, St. Thomas does propose resistance, but constitutionally, by public authority, not by private presumption." Budziszewski, *Companion to the Commentary*, 196.

85. Alexis de Tocqueville, *Democracy in America* (Chicago: University of Chicago Press, 2000), 479–482.

86. Ibid., 252–256.

87. No doubt the reasons for this are complex, but it seems in large part to be the fallout of an almost complete collapse of the distinction between law and politics in America's law schools. Forms and tradition gave way to politics and policy, and now the legal class considers itself at the forefront of social change and emerging equalities. For an account of this transformation by a sympathetic legal historian, see Laura Kalman, *The Strange Career of Legal Liberalism* (New Haven, CT: Yale University Press, 1998), esp. 13–59.

88. In *Whose Justice? Which Rationality?*, MacIntyre identifies four such traditions, that is, Aristotelianism, Augustinianism, the Scottish Enlightenment, and Liberalism. I do not wish to too closely identify Burke's concept of a tradition of reason, rightly understood, with MacIntyre's. There are important similarities—most centrally an emphasis on working out conceptions of duty and obligation within the lived experience of communities over time. Nevertheless, there are also important

differences, the most notable of which is the centrality of conflict to MacIntyre's understanding of traditions of reason. See Kelvin Knight, *Aristotelian Philosophy: Ethics and Politics from Aristotle to MacIntyre* (Malden, MA: Polity, 2013), 132–133.

89. Burke, *Reflections*, 79.

90. *ST*, II–II, q. 58, a. 5 ad 2.

91. MacIntyre, "Politics, Philosophy, and the Common Good," in Kelvin Knight, ed., *The MacIntyre Reader* (Notre Dame, IN: University of Notre Dame Press, 1998), 241.

92. Thomas S. Hibbs, "'MacIntyre, Aquinas, and Politics,'" *Review of Politics* 66, no. 3 (Summer 2004): 357–383. Hibbs argues: "But what is absent [in MacIntyre's thought] is any reference to legislation, the key mark of politics for Aristotle and Aquinas. Indeed, in the *Summa Theologiae* Aquinas treats politics under the topic of human law. The only way that the natural law of Aquinas can become political is by becoming human law. Within the confines of the nation-state with its invasive and seemingly omnipresent legal apparatus, what sort of legislative self-determination can a local community have?" (366). Cf. Mark C. Murphy, "MacIntyre's Political Philosophy," in Mark C. Murphy, ed., *Alasdair MacIntyre* (New York: Cambridge University Press, 2003), 152–175. Murphy points out that MacIntyre takes institutions to be necessary to sustain practices (164). Yet, Murphy also ultimately worries, in a manner similar to Hibbs, that MacIntyre's immediate, practice-oriented view of politics renders his commitment to institutions insufficient. Murphy suggests that some institutional structure closer to the modern state than MacIntyre will allow is necessary to sustain the kind of politics he envisions (170–172).

93. In this criticism, I do not mean to imply disagreement with MacIntyre's main line of criticism of the modern nation-state, that is, its conceit of liberal neutrality on matters of the human good (see, for example, MacIntyre, "Politics, Philosophy, and the Common Good," 236–238). The modern state's commitment to liberalism, however, is a distinct issue from what particular form politics and traditions of reason ought to take. I join my own criticisms of MacIntyre on this latter issue to those of Hibbs and Murphy, and suggest that Burke's view is more truly political.

94. Burke, *Reflections*, 95.

95. Ibid., 14–34; Edmund Burke, "Speech on Moving Resolutions for Conciliation with the Colonies," in *Select Works of Edmund Burke*, vol. 1., ed. Francis Canavan (Indianapolis, IN: Liberty Fund, 1999), 221–289, esp. 279, 287.

96. Fischer, *Liberty and Freedom*, 121–126.

97. Ibid., 125–126.

98. Or as Burke might say, the abstract rights of man expressed in the Declaration's Preamble may have been discernable enough, but *defining* the *real rights of man* would have to be worked out in the life of the American people.

99. Prentice Hall submitted a "Petition for Freedom" by "A Great Number of Blackes" to the Massachusetts legislature on January 13, 1777; see Justin Buckley Dyer, *American Soul: The Contested Legacy of the Declaration of Independence* (Lanham, MD: Rowman and Littlefield, 2015), 44.

100. "Speech on the Kansas-Nebraska Act at Peoria, Illinois," in Don E. Fehrenbacher, ed., *Lincoln: Speeches and Writings 1832–1858* (New York: Library of America, 1989), 338.

101. "'House Divided' Speech at Springfield, Illinois," in Fehrenbacher, *Lincoln*, 426; Matthew 12:25.

102. "To Henry L. Pierce and Others," in ed. Don E. Fehrenbacher, ed., *Lincoln: Speeches and Writings: 1859–1865* (New York: Library of America, 1989), 19.

103. "Speech at Peoria," in Fehrenbacher, *Lincoln: Speeches and Writings 1832–1858*, 339.

104. Richard Brookhiser, *Founders' Son: A Life of Abraham Lincoln* (New York: Basic Books, 2014), 164–165.

105. "Speech at Peoria," in Fehrenbacher, *Lincoln 1832–1858*, 328.

106. Ibid., 340.

107. Burke, *Reflections*, 77.

108. Thus, the abolitionist Frederick Douglass offered not argument but denunciation: "But, I submit, where all is plain there is nothing to be argued. What point in the anti-slavery creed would you have me argue? On what branch of the subject do the people of this country need light? . . . For it is not light that is needed, but fire; it is not the gentle shower, but thunder." "What to a Slave Is the Fourth of July?," in Dyer, *American Soul*, 63–67, 64, 66.

109. "Speech at Peoria," in Fehrenbacher, *Lincoln 1832–1858*, 338.

110. Justin Buckley Dyer, *Natural Law and the Antislavery Constitutional Tradition* (Cambridge: Cambridge University Press, 2012), 99.

111. Ibid., 146–147.

112. "Speech at Peoria," in Fehrenbacher, *Lincoln 1832–1858*, 315.

113. My claim, of course, is not that the Declaration itself is a Burkean document. Rather, it is that general features of Burke's political understanding account for the role of the Declaration in the American political experience—even though he would not have written the document himself.

114. Fehrenbacher, *Lincoln 1832–1858*, 31.

115. Fischer, *Liberty and Freedom*, 14.

116. C. S. Lewis, *The Abolition of Man* (New York: HarperCollins, 2009), 24.

117. Homer, *The Odyssey*, trans. Robert Fagles (New York: Penguin Classics, 1996), Book 9, Ln. 240.

118. Burke, *Reflections*, 33.

119. Patrick M. Gardner, "Thomas and Dante on the *Duo Ultima Hominis*," *The Thomist* 75 (2011): 415–459, esp. 425–435.

120. "Why We Respect the Dignity of Politics," in James R. Stoner and Harold James, eds., *The Thriving Society: On the Social Conditions of Human Flourishing* (Princeton, NJ: Witherspoon Institute, 2015), 92.

121. Burke, *Reflections*, 97.

122. Lord Byron, "Ode to Napoleon Buonaparte," ln. 168.

123. Burke, *Reflections*, 34, 59.

124. It is an interesting question whether a duty to forbears or posterity *corporately* can be disaggregated to create personal duties to specific people. Do I owe a *personal duty* to George Washington? I do not dispose of that question here because I do not think my argument requires it. It makes sense to say that I owe a duty to Washington as a member of the historical American community, and moreover, that as an icon of the American moral imagination, Washington particularizes and fo-

cuses my corporate duty. That is enough, I think, to bear the weight of the significance I want to attribute to it.

125. Burke, *Reflections*, 34.

126. In Dyer, *American Soul*, 63.

127. Augustine, *The City of God against the Pagans* (Cambridge, UK: Cambridge University Press, 1998), XIX.14, 942–943. Scriptural quotations are from the English Standard Version.

128. Ibid., XIX.6, 12, 21.

129. Ibid., XIX.26.

130. Burke, *Reflections*, 48.

131. Ecclesiastes 1:9.

132. Burke, *Reflections*, 33.

133. This is true only *in part*. I will say more about this in a moment.

134. Alexander Hamilton, John Jay, and James Madison, *The Federalist Papers: The Gideon Edition*, edited by George Carey and James McClellan (Carmel, IN: Liberty Fund, 2010), 269.

135. Burke, *Reflections*, 76. Emphasis mine.

136. Himmelfarb, "Reflections on Burke's 'Reflections,'" 4.

137. Roger Scruton, "The Good of Government," *First Things*, June 2014, 33–38, 35.

138. Augustine, *City of God*, XIX.5, 25.

139. Ibid., XIX.12, 936. The naturalness of politics in Augustine's thought is a complicated subject. He takes political authority to be a response to the Fall while recognizing a natural inclination to live peacefully in society. See Paul J. Weithman, "Augustine and Aquinas on Original Sin and the Function of Political Authority," *Journal of the History of Philosophy* 30, no. 3 (1992): 353–376, esp. 360.

140. Augustine, *City of God*, 19.24, 960.

141. Ibid., 5.24, 232.

142. Ibid., 19.13, esp. 940; 19.17, esp. 945, 947. As soon as this potential for good is acknowledged, an Augustinian outlook cautions against the corrosive effects of sin, especially pride. This again highlights the importance of balancing and constraining political power.

143. Although I think this point goes a long way to reconcile Augustine's view of politics with my own Thomistic/Burkean account, an underlying tension remains. Paul Weithman explains the foundational difference between Augustine and Aquinas thus: "For Augustine, political subjection improves by humbling and disciplining; other qualities that pursuit of the common good requires are not true virtues. For Aquinas, on the other hand, political authority genuinely improves those subject to it by fostering in them a concern for the common good of political society. The improvement is not merely a remedy for sin; this function of political authority would, Aquinas says, have been exercised even had original sin not been committed. The most profound difference between Augustine and Aquinas is therefore in the value each attaches to a citizen's concern for the common good of political society." Paul J. Weithman, "Augustine and Aquinas on Original Sin and the Function of Political Authority," *Journal of the History of Philosophy* 30, no. 3 (1992): 353–376, 360.

144. Robert Louis Stevenson, *Strange Case of Dr. Jekyll and Mr. Hyde*, ed. Martin

A. Danahay (Tonawanda, NY: Broadview Press, 2015), 76. Cf. Augustine, *City of God*, XIX.13.

145. Aleksandr Solzhenitsyn, *The Gulag Archipelago: An Experiment in Literary Investigation* (New York: Harper Perennial Modern Classics, 2007), 75.

146. Luke 9:51 (English Standard Version).

147. Roger Scruton, *A Political Philosophy: Arguments for Conservatism* (New York: Continuum, 2006), 8.

148. Ibid., 10.

149. Katharine Lee Bates, "America the Beautiful."

150. Samuel P. Huntington, *Who Are We?: The Challenges to America's National Identity* (New York: Simon and Schuster, 2004), 37–58; Watson, "Creed & Culture in the American Founding."

151. "I Have a Dream," in James M. Washington, ed., *A Testament of Hope: The Essential Writings and Speeches of Martin Luther King Jr.* (San Francisco: HarperOne, 2003), 220.

152. J. S. Mill, *A System of Logic: Ratiocinative and Inductive*, 8th ed., vol. 2 (London: Longmans, Green, Reader, and Dyer, 1872), 522–523.

153. "The Patriotic Idea," in *G. K. Chesterton, Collected Works*, vol. 20 (San Francisco: Ignatius Press, 2001), 593–619, 614.

154. "Patriotism," in Roger Scruton, *The Palgrave Macmillan Dictionary of Political Thought*, 3rd ed. (New York: Palgrave Macmillan, 2007), 514.

155. Chesterton, "The Patriotic Idea," 597–601.

Conclusion

1. Alexis de Tocqueville, *Democracy in America* (Chicago: University of Chicago Press, 2000), 661–665, 663.

2. James Davison Hunter, *To Change the World: The Irony, Tragedy, and Possibility of Christianity in the Late Modern World* (New York: Oxford University Press, 2010), 33; James Davison Hunter and Christopher Benson, "Faithful Presence," *Christianity Today* 54, no. 5 (May 2010): 35.

3. *Politics*, I.2, 1253a7–17. Obviously, the rational character of the polis does not make it unique from all other associations. The family too operates according to a rational principle. This defining rational element, however, does distinguish it from other associations that reach a similar level of completeness and self-sufficiency. So Aristotle distinguishes political communities from nations, which move beyond the village on the principle of hereditary authority alone. Unlike the polis, the nation is simply an extension of paternal authority to a wider community (1252b17).

4. Again, what distinguishes the rational activity of the family from that of the political community is that political activity takes place in the context of a community that has reached full sufficiency for life.

5. John Finnis, *Natural Law and Natural Rights* (Oxford: Clarendon Press, 1980), 232.

6. Robert P. George, "The Common Good: Instrumental but Not Just Contractual," *Public Discourse* (blog), May 17, 2013, http://www.thepublicdiscourse.com/2013/05/10166/.

7. Notice George's specific wording: if agreement is reached, "coordination problems" are avoided. Coordination itself is not dispensed with, and thus the hypothetical presupposes political life.

8. Hugh Heclo, *On Thinking Institutionally* (New York: Oxford University Press, 2011), 82–89.

BIBLIOGRAPHY

Ambler, W. H. "Aristotle's Understanding of the Naturalness of the City." *Review of Politics* 47, no. 2 (April 1985): 163–185.

Aquinas, Thomas. *Commentary on Aristotle's Nicomachean Ethics*. Translated by C. I. Litzinger. Aristotelian Commentary Series. Notre Dame, IN: Dumb Ox Books, 1993.

———. *Commentary on Aristotle's Politics*. Translated by Richard J. Reagan. Indianapolis, IN: Hackett Publishing, 2007.

———. *On Kingship to the King of Cyprus*. Rev. Translated by Gerald B. Phelan. Toronto: Pontifical Institute of Mediaeval Studies, 1949.

———. *Summa Contra Gentiles: Volumes 1–4 in Five Books*. Translated by Charles J. O'Neil, Anton C. Pegis, James F. Anderson, and Vernon J. Bourke. Notre Dame, IN: University of Notre Dame Press, 1997.

———. *The Summa Theologica of St. Thomas Aquinas*. Translated by Fathers of the English Dominican Province. Christian Classics. Notre Dame, IN: Ave Maria Press, 1981.

Aristotle. *The Complete Works of Aristotle: The Revised Oxford Translation*. Edited by Jonathan Barnes. Bollingen Series, No. 71, Part 2. Princeton, NJ: Princeton University Press, 1984.

———. *Eudemian Ethics in the Complete Works of Aristotle: The Revised Oxford Translation*, vol. 2. Edited by Jonathan Barnes. Translated by J. Solomon. Bollinger Series, LXXI. Princeton, NJ: Princeton University Press, 1984.

———. *Nicomachean Ethics*. 1st ed. Translated by Martin Ostwald. Upper Saddle River, NJ: Prentice Hall, 1962.

———. *Nicomachean Ethics: Books VIII and IX*. Translated by Michael Pakaluk. Clarendon Aristotle Series. Oxford: Clarendon Press, 1999.

———. *Politics*. Translated by Ernest Barker and R. F. Stalley. New York: Oxford University Press, 1998.

———. *Politics: Books I and II*. Translated by Trevor J. Saunders. Clarendon Aristotle Series. New York: Oxford University Press, 1996.

———. *Politics: Books VII and VIII*. Translated by Richard Kraut. Clarendon Aristotle Series. New York: Oxford University Press, 1998.

Aroney, Nicholas. "Subsidiarity, Federalism and the Best Constitution: Thomas Aquinas on City, Province and Empire." *Law and Philosophy* 26, no. 2 (March 2007): 161–228.

Augustine. *The City of God against the Pagans*. Cambridge: Cambridge University Press. 1998.

Barbieri, W. A., and A. William Jr. "Beyond the Nations: The Expansion of the

Common Good in Catholic Social Thought." *Review of Politics* 63, no. 4 (2001): 723–754.

Barker, Ernest. *The Political Thought of Plato and Aristotle*. New York: Dover Publications, 1959.

Bartlett, Robert C. "Aristotle's Introduction to the Problem of Happiness: On Book I of the 'Nicomachean Ethics.'" *American Journal of Political Science* 52, no. 3 (July 2008): 677–687.

Black, H. C. *Black's Law Dictionary*. 6th ed. St. Paul, MN: West Publishing, 1994.

Blustein, Jeffrey. *Parents and Children: The Ethics of the Family*. New York: Oxford University Press, 1982.

Bourke, Richard. *Empire and Revolution: The Political Life of Edmund Burke*. Princeton, NJ: Princeton University Press, 2015.

Bromwich, David. "Moral Imagination." *Raritan* 27, no. 4 (Spring 2008): 4–33.

Brookhiser, Richard. *Founders' Son: A Life of Abraham Lincoln*. New York: Basic Books, 2014.

Budziszewski, J. "Companion to the Commentary." Accessed January 21, 2017. http://undergroundthomist.org/sites/default/files/related-documents/Companion-to-the-Commentary-FINAL.pdf.

———. *The Line through the Heart: Natural Law as Fact, Theory, and Sign of Contradiction*. Wilmington, DE: ISI Books, 2009.

———. *What We Can't Not Know: A Guide*. Dallas: Spence Publishing, 2003.

Burke, Edmund. *A Philosophical Enquiry into the Sublime and Beautiful*. New York: Routledge, 2008.

———. *Reflections on the Revolution in France*. Reissue ed. Edited by L. G. Mitchell. New York: Oxford University Press, 2009.

———. "Speech on Moving Resolutions for Conciliation with the Colonies." In *Select Works of Edmund Burke, Volume 1*, edited by Francis Canavan. Indianapolis, IN: Liberty Fund, 1999.

Ceaser, James W. "Alexis de Tocqueville on Political Science, Political Culture, and the Role of the Intellectual." *American Political Science Review* 79, no. 3 (1985): 656–672.

———. *Liberal Democracy and Political Science*. Baltimore: Johns Hopkins University Press, 1990.

———. "O, My America." *Weekly Standard* (Washington), May 3, 2004.

Chambers, Simone, and Will Kymlicka. *Alternative Conceptions of Civil Society*. Princeton, NJ: Princeton University Press, 2001.

Chesterton, G. K. "The Patriotic Idea." In *G. K. Chesterton, Collected Works*, vol. 20, 593–619. San Francisco: Ignatius Press, 2001.

Crowe, Ian, ed. *An Imaginative Whig: Reassessing the Life and Thought of Edmund Burke*. Columbia: University of Missouri, 2005.

Douglass, Bruce. "The Common Good and the Public Interest." *Political Theory* 8, no. 1 (February 1980): 103–117.

Dyer, Justin Buckley. *American Soul: The Contested Legacy of the Declaration of Independence*. Lanham, MD: Rowman and Littlefield, 2015.

———. *Natural Law and the Antislavery Constitutional Tradition*. Cambridge: Cambridge University Press, 2012.

Ellis, Richard J. *American Political Cultures*. Oxford: Oxford University Press, 1993.

Elshtain, Jean Bethke. *The Family in Political Thought*. Amherst: University of Massachusetts Press, 1982.

———. *Public Man, Private Woman: Women in Social and Political Thought*. Princeton, NJ: Princeton University Press, 1981.

Faulkner, Robert, and Susan M. Shell. *America at Risk: Threats to Liberal Self-Government in an Age of Uncertainty*. Ann Arbor: University of Michigan Press, 2009.

Fineman, Martha Albertson. "Taking Children's Interests Seriously." Emory University School of Law. Public Law and Legal Theory Research Paper Series. Research Paper No. 69–75. *SSRN eLibrary*. Accessed September 30, 2011. http://papers.ssrn.com/sol3/papers.cfm?abstract_id=1516652.

Finnis, John. *Aquinas: Moral, Political, and Legal Theory*. Founders of Modern Political and Social Thought. Oxford: Oxford University Press, 1998.

———. "Is Natural Law Theory Compatible with Limited Government?" In *Natural Law, Liberalism, and Morality: Contemporary Essays*, edited by Robert P. George. Oxford: Clarendon Press, 1996.

———. *Natural Law and Natural Rights*. Oxford: Clarendon Press, 1980.

Fischer, David Hackett. *Liberty and Freedom: A Visual History of America's Founding Ideas*. New York: Oxford University Press, 2005.

Froelich, Gregory. "The Equivocal Status of *Bonum Commune*." *New Scholasticism* 63 (1989): 38–57.

Galston, William A. *Liberal Purposes: Goods, Virtues, and Diversity in the Liberal State*. Cambridge Studies in Philosophy and Public Policy. New York: Cambridge University Press, 1991.

Gardner, Patrick M. "Thomas and Dante on the Duo Ultima Hominis." *The Thomist* 75 (2011): 415–459.

George, Robert P. *The Clash of Orthodoxies: Law, Religion, and Morality in Crisis*. Wilmington, DE: ISI Books, 2001.

———. "The Common Good: Instrumental But Not Just Contractual." *Public Discourse*, May 17, 2013. http://www.thepublicdiscourse.com/2013/05/10166/.

———. "Concept of Public Morality, The." *American Journal of Jurisprudence* 45 (2000): 17–31.

———. *Making Men Moral: Civil Liberties and Public Morality*. Oxford: Clarendon Press, 1993.

———. "Moral Particularism, Thomism, and Traditions." *Review of Metaphysics* 42, no. 3 (March 1989): 593–605.

Glendon, Mary Ann. *Rights Talk: The Impoverishment of Political Discourse*. New York: Free Press, 1993.

Grasso, Kenneth L., Gerard V. Bradley, and Robert P. Hunt. *Catholicism, Liberalism, and Communitarianism*. Lanham, MD: Rowman and Littlefield, 1995.

Grisez, Germain G. "The First Principle of Practical Reason: A Commentary on the Summa Theologiae, 1–2, Question 94, Article 2." *Natural Law Forum* 10 (1965): 168–201.

Grisez, Germain, Joseph Boyle, and John Finnis. "Practical Principles, Moral Truth, and Ultimate Ends." *American Journal of Jurisprudence* 32 (1987): 99–151.

Gutmann, Amy. "Civic Education and Social Diversity." *Ethics* 105, no. 3 (1995): 557–579.

———. *Democratic Education*. Princeton, NJ: Princeton University Press, 1987.

Hamilton, Alexander, John Jay, and James Madison. *The Federalist Papers: The Gideon Edition*. 2nd ed. Edited by George Carey and James McClellan. Carmel, IN: Liberty Fund, 2010.

Hauerwas, Stanley. *A Community of Character: Toward a Constructive Christian Social Ethic*. Notre Dame, IN: University of Notre Dame Press, 1981.

———. *In Good Company: The Church as Polis*. Notre Dame, IN: University of Notre Dame Press, 1995.

———. "The Moral Meaning of the Family." *Commonweal*, August 1, 1980.

Hauerwas, Stanley, and William H. Willimon. *Resident Aliens: Life in the Christian Colony*. 1st ed. Nashville, TN: Abingdon Press, 1989.

Heclo, Hugh. *On Thinking Institutionally*. New York: Oxford University Press, 2011.

Hibbs, Thomas S. "'MacIntyre, Aquinas, and Politics.'" *Review of Politics* 66, no. 3 (Summer 2004): 357–383.

Himmelfarb, Gertrude. "Reflections on Burke's 'Reflections.'" *New Criterion* 27, no. 6 (February 2009): 4–10.

Hittinger, F. Russell. "The Coherence of the Four Basic Principles of Catholic Social Doctrine: An Interpretation." In Pontificia Accademia delle Scienze Sociali, *Pursuing the Common Good : How Solidarity and Subsidiarity Can Work Together : The Proceedings of the 14th Plenary Session, 2–6 May 2008, Casina Pio IV*. Vatican City: Pontifical Academy of Social Sciences, 2008.

———. *A Critique of the New Natural Law Theory*. Notre Dame, IN: University of Notre Dame Press, 1989.

———. *The First Grace: Rediscovering the Natural Law in a Post-Christian World*. Wilmington, DE: ISI Books, 2003.

Hobbes, Thomas. *Leviathan*. New York: Penguin Classics, 1982.

Homer. *The Odyssey*. Translated by Robert Fagles. New York: Penguin Classics, 1996.

Hunter, James Davison. *To Change the World: The Irony, Tragedy, and Possibility of Christianity in the Late Modern World*. New York: Oxford University Press, 2010.

Hunter, James Davison, and Christopher Benson. "Faithful Presence." *Christianity Today* 54, no. 5 (May 2010): 32–36.

Huntington, Samuel P. *Who Are We?: The Challenges to America's National Identity*. New York: Simon and Schuster, 2004.

Jaffa, Harry V. *Thomism and Aristotelianism*. Chicago: University of Chicago Press, 1952.

Kalman, Laura. *The Strange Career of Legal Liberalism*. New Haven, CT: Yale University Press, 1998.

Kempshall, M. S. *The Common Good in Late Medieval Political Thought*. Oxford: Clarendon Press, 1999.

Keys, Mary M. *Aquinas, Aristotle, and the Promise of the Common Good*. 1st ed. Cambridge: Cambridge University Press, 2008.

Keyt, D. "Three Fundamental Theorems in Aristotle's 'Politics.'" *Phronesis* 32, no. 1 (1987): 54–79.

King, Martin Luther, Jr. *A Testament of Hope: The Essential Writings and Speeches of Martin Luther King, Jr.* Edited by James M. Washington. San Francisco: HarperOne, 2003.

Kirk, Russell. *Edmund Burke: A Genius Reconsidered.* New York: Arlington House, 1967.

———. *The Essential Russell Kirk: Selected Essays.* Edited by George A. Panichas. Wilmington, DE: Intercollegiate Studies Institute, 2006.

Knight, Kelvin. *Aristotelian Philosophy: Ethics and Politics from Aristotle to MacIntyre.* Malden, MA: Polity, 2013.

Kraut, Richard. *Aristotle: Political Philosophy.* Founders of Modern Political and Social Thought. New York: Oxford University Press, 2002.

Kymlicka, Will, and Wayne Norman. "Return of the Citizen: A Survey of Recent Work on Citizenship Theory." *Ethics* 104, no. 2 (January 1994): 352–381.

Lawrence, Dewan. "St. Thomas, John Finnis, and the Political Common Good." *The Thomist* 64 (2000): 337–374.

Levin, Yuval. *The Great Debate: Edmund Burke, Thomas Paine, and the Birth of Right and Left.* New York: Basic Books, 2014.

Lewis, C. S. *The Abolition of Man.* New York: HarperCollins, 2009.

Lincoln, Abraham. *Lincoln: Speeches and Writings 1832–1858.* Edited by Don E. Fehrenbacher. New York: Library of America, 1989.

———. *Lincoln: Speeches and Writings 1859–1865.* Edited by Don E. Fehrenbacher. New York: Library of America, 1989.

Locke, John. *Two Treatises of Government.* 3rd ed. Cambridge: Cambridge University Press, 1988.

Long, Steven A. "St. Thomas Aquinas through the Analytic Looking Glass." *The Thomist* 65 (2001): 259–300.

Macedo, Stephen. "Liberal Civic Education and Religious Fundamentalism: The Case of God v. John Rawls?" *Ethics* 105, no. 3 (April 1995): 468–496.

Macedo, Stephen, and Yael Tamir, eds. *Moral and Political Education.* Nomos 43. New York: New York University Press, 2002.

MacIntyre, Alasdair C. *After Virtue: A Study in Moral Theory.* 3rd ed. Notre Dame, IN: University of Notre Dame Press, 2007.

———. *Dependent Rational Animals: Why Human Beings Need the Virtues.* Chicago: Open Court, 2001.

———. *Ethics and Politics: Selected Essays.* Vol. 2. Cambridge: Cambridge University Press, 2006.

———. "I'm Not a Communitarian." *The Responsive Community,* Summer 1991.

———. "Politics, Philosophy, and the Common Good." In *The MacIntyre Reader,* edited by Kelvin Knight, 235–252. Notre Dame, IN: University of Notre Dame Press, 1998.

———. "The Theses on Feuerbach: A Road Not Taken." In *The MacIntyre Reader,* edited by Kelvin Knight, 223–234. Notre Dame, IN: University of Notre Dame Press, 1998.

———. *Whose Justice? Which Rationality?* Notre Dame, IN: University of Notre Dame Press, 1989.

Maritain, Jacques. *Man and the State.* Chicago: University of Chicago Press, 1951.

———. *Natural Law: Reflections on Theory & Practice.* 1st ed. South Bend, IN: St. Augustine's Press, 2001.

———. *On the Use of Philosophy: Three Essays.* Princeton, NJ: Princeton University Press, 1961.

————. *The Person and the Common Good*. Notre Dame, IN: University of Notre Dame Press, 1973.

Matthews, Gareth B. *The Philosophy of Childhood*. Cambridge, MA: Harvard University Press, 1994.

McInerny, Ralph M. *Art and Prudence: Studies in the Thought of Jacques Maritain*. Notre Dame, IN: University of Notre Dame Press, 1988.

Meilaender, Gilbert. *Friendship: A Study in Theological Ethics Philosophy*. 1st ed. Notre Dame, IN: University of Notre Dame Press, 1985.

————. *Neither Beast nor God: The Dignity of the Human Person*. New York: Encounter Books, 2009.

————. *The Theory and Practice of Virtue*. 1st ed. Notre Dame, IN: University of Notre Dame Press, 1988.

Mill, J. S. *A System of Logic: Ratiocinative and Inductive*. Vol. 2, 8th ed. London: Longmans, Green, Reader, and Dyer, 1872.

Minow, Martha, and Mary Lyndon Shanley. "Relational Rights and Responsibilities: Revisioning the Family in Liberal Political Theory and Law." *Hypatia* 11, no. 1 (January 1996): 4–29.

Mummolo, Jonathan. "Father Who Saved Son Is Remembered for Generosity." *Washington Post*, September 16, 2008, sec. B.

Murphy, Mark C. *Natural Law and Practical Rationality*. Cambridge: Cambridge University Press, 2001.

————. *Natural Law in Jurisprudence and Politics*. Cambridge: Cambridge University Press, 2006.

————, ed. *Alasdair MacIntyre*. New York: Cambridge University Press, 2003.

Nichols, Mary P. *Citizens and Statesmen: A Study of Aristotle's Politics*. Lanham, MD: Rowman and Littlefield, 1992.

Norman, Jesse. *Edmund Burke: The First Conservative*. New York: Basic Books, 2013.

Nussbaum, Martha, and Joshua Cohen. *For Love of Country?* 1st ed. Boston: Beacon Press, 2002.

Okin, Susan Moller. *Justice, Gender, and the Family*. New York: Basic Books, 1989.

Pakaluk, Michael. *Aristotle's Nicomachean Ethics: An Introduction*. Cambridge Introductions to Key Philosophical Texts. Cambridge: Cambridge University Press, 2005.

————. "Is the Common Good of Political Society Limited and Instrumental?" *Review of Metaphysics* 55, no. 1 (2001): 57–94.

Palm, Glen, and Jay Fagan. "Father Involvement in Early Childhood Programs: Review of the Literature." *Early Child Development & Care* 178, no. 7/8 (October 2008): 745–759.

Pangle, Lorraine Smith. *Aristotle and the Philosophy of Friendship*. Cambridge: Cambridge University Press, 2003.

Pappin, Joseph. *The Metaphysics of Edmund Burke*. New York: Fordham University Press, 1993.

Plato. *The Republic Of Plato: Second Edition*. Translated by Allan Bloom. New York: Basic Books, 1991.

Punzo, Vincent A. "After Kohlberg: Virtue Ethics and the Recovery of the Moral Self." *Philosophical Psychology* 9, no. 1 (March 1996): 7.

Rawls, John. *The Law of Peoples: with "The Idea of Public Reason Revisited."* 1st ed. Cambridge, MA: Harvard University Press, 2001.

———. *Political Liberalism.* John Dewey Essays in Philosophy, no. 4. New York: Columbia University Press, 1993.

———. *A Theory of Justice.* Cambridge, MA: Belknap Press of Harvard University Press, 1971.

Rorty, Amélie, ed. *Essays on Aristotle's Ethics.* Major Thinkers Series 2. Berkeley: University of California Press, 1980.

Sandel, Michael J. *Liberalism and the Limits of Justice.* 2nd ed. Cambridge: Cambridge University Press, 1998.

Sarkadi, Anna, Robert Kristiansson, Frank Oberklaid, and Sven Bremberg. "Fathers' Involvement and Children's Developmental Outcomes: A Systematic Review of Longitudinal Studies." *Acta Paediatrica* 97, no. 2 (February 2008): 153–158.

Saxonhouse, Arlene W. "Family, Polity & Unity: Aristotle on Socrates' Community of Wives." *Polity* 15, no. 2 (December 1982): 202–219.

Schindler, Jeanne Heffernan, ed. *Christianity and Civil Society: Catholic and Neo-Calvinist Perspectives.* Lanham, MD: Lexington Books, 2008.

Schwarzenbach, S. A. "On Civic Friendship." *Ethics* 107, no. 1 (1996): 97–128.

Scruton, Roger. "The Good of Government." *First Things,* June 2014, 33–38.

———. *The Palgrave Macmillan Dictionary of Political Thought.* 3rd ed. New York: Palgrave Macmillan, 2007.

———. *The Philosopher on Dover Beach: Essays.* New York: St. Martin's Press, 1990.

———. *A Political Philosophy: Arguments for Conservatism.* New York: Continuum, 2006.

Simon, Yves R. *Philosophy of Democratic Government.* Chicago: University of Chicago Press, 1951.

———. *The Tradition of Natural Law: A Philosopher's Reflections.* Edited by Vukan Kuic. New York: Fordham University Press, 1999.

Solzhenitsyn, Aleksandr. *The Gulag Archipelago: An Experiment in Literary Investigation.* Abridged. New York: Harper Perennial Modern Classics, 2007.

Stanlis, Peter J. *Edmund Burke and the Natural Law.* Lafayette, LA: Huntington House, 1986.

Stevenson, Robert Louis. *Strange Case of Dr. Jekyll and Mr. Hyde.* 3rd ed. Edited by Martin A. Danahay. Tonawanda, NY: Broadview Press, 2015.

Stoner, James R., and Harold James, eds. *The Thriving Society: On the Social Conditions of Human Flourishing.* Princeton, NJ: Witherspoon Institute, 2015.

Strauss, Leo. *The City and Man.* Chicago: University of Chicago Press, 1978.

Symposium Aristotelicum. *Aristoteles "Politik": Akten Des XI, Symposium Aristotelicum, Friedrichshafen/Bodensee, 25.8.–3.9.1987.* Edited by Günther Patzig. Göttingen: Vandenhoeck & Ruprecht, 1990.

Taylor, Charles. *Philosophical Arguments.* Cambridge, MA: Harvard University Press, 1995.

———. *Sources of the Self: The Making of the Modern Identity.* Cambridge, MA: Harvard University Press, 1992.

Tocqueville, Alexis de. *Democracy in America.* Translated by Harvey C. Mansfield and Delba Winthrop. Chicago: University of Chicago Press, 2000.

Watson, Bradley C. S. "Creed & Culture in the American Founding." *Intercollegiate Review* 41, no. 2 (Fall 2006): 32–39.

Weithman, Paul J. "Augustine and Aquinas on Original Sin and the Function of Political Authority." *Journal of the History of Philosophy* 30, no. 3 (July 1992): 353–376.

West, Robin. "The Harms of Homeschooling." *Philosophy and Public Policy* Quarterly 29, no. 3/4 (Summer/Fall 2009): 7–12.

Wilkins, Burleigh Taylor. *The Problem of Burke's Political Philosophy*. Oxford: Clarendon Press, 1967.

Wolfe, Christopher. *Natural Law Liberalism*. 1st ed. Cambridge: Cambridge University Press, 2009.

Wood, Neal. "The Aesthetic Dimension of Burke's Political Thought." *Journal of British Studies* 4, no. 1 (1964): 41–64.

INDEX

Abolition of Man, The (Lewis), 144–145
Adams, John, 140
Adams, John Quincy, 143
affections. *See* human affections
aggregative conception of the common
    good, 82, 83–89
all-round virtue, 14, 22, 23, 24, 34
American constitutional identity, 1–2
American Revolution, 140
Annas, Julia, 189n21
Aquinas (Finnis), 11
*Aquinas, Aristotle, and the Promise of the
    Common Good* (Keys), 11–12
Aquinas, Thomas
    on the appropriate scope of love,
        105–106
    Aristotle's notion of human
        reproduction and, 181–182n52
    on civic friendship, 6–7
    on the common good and pursuit of
        private goods, 112–114
    on extension of the political society,
        13
    on the family and "affirmation of
        ordinary life," 100–101
    Finnis's delineation of private/public
        goods and, 23–27
    Finnis's instrumentality thesis and,
        10–11, 19
    on friendship and family relationships,
        50
    on friendship and the good of the
        other, 184n13
    on the greatness of politics, 146
    Gregory Froelich's analysis of the
        account of common good by,
        72–76
    on human flourishing referring to the
        good of individual humans, 5, 6

in Mary Keys's account of the political
    common good, 11–12
on law and acts of virtue, 24–25
on law and common good, 21
on law and the virtue of individuals,
    32–33
Mark Murphy's account of the
    aggregated good and, 84
modifications of Aristotelian civic
    friendship, 98–104
on natural law and human law, 193n21
on parental and governmental
    authorities, 23–24, 32
on the parent-child relationship, 51
on the perfect community, 9, 25
on political authority, 199n143
on the political common good, 9, 101
on the political community, 8–9, 101,
    103
on political life and human
    flourishing, 3–4
on the social and the political, 8
on species of virtuous action, 22
architectonic arts, political science as, 79,
    81–82
Aristotelian civic friendship
    Aristotle's cautions with respect to,
        108–109
    explication of, 93–98
    intrinsic political good and, 120
    Thomistic modifications, 98–104
Aristotle
    on the affections of justice, 102
    on associations, 71
    on benefaction, 58–59
    on children as distinct "others," 57
    on the conditional means to
        happiness, 4
    on extension of the political society, 13